I wandered lonely as a clo

That floats on high, oer t

When when all at once I saw
~~I came upon~~ ∧ a

A host of golden daffodils,

Beside the lake, beneath the trees,

Fluttering and dancing in the breeze.

AYRTON
Senna

Other books by the same author:

NIGEL MANSELL
The Lion at Bay

MICHAEL SCHUMACHER
Defending the Crown

AYRTON SENNA
The Legend Grows

AYRTON SENNA
The Second Coming

GERHARD BERGER
The Human Face of Formula 1

JAMES HUNT
Portrait of a Champion

GRAND PRIX SHOWDOWN!
The full drama of the races which decided
the World Championship 1950-92

TWO WHEEL SHOWDOWN!
The full drama of the races which decided
the World 500cc Motor Cycle Championship
from 1949

TORVILL AND DEAN
The Full Story

As part of our ongoing market research, we are always pleased to receive comments about our books, suggestions for new titles, or requests for catalogues. Please write to:

The Editorial Director, Patrick Stephens Limited, Sparkford, Nr Yeovil, Somerset BA22 7JJ.

A Y R T O N
Senna
HIS FULL CAR RACING RECORD

CHRISTOPHER HILTON

Christopher Hilton

November 1995

PSL

Patrick Stephens Limited

First published in 1995

British Library Cataloguing-in-Publication Data:
A catalogue record for this book is
available from the British Library

ISBN: 1 85260 543 X

Library of Congress catalog card no. 95 79119

All pictures are from Allsport UK Ltd except where stated.

Patrick Stephens Limited is an imprint of Haynes Publishing
Sparkford, Nr Yeovil, Somerset BA22 7JJ.

Designed and typeset by Camway Autographics
Sparkford, Nr Yeovil, Somerset BA22 7JQ.
Printed in Great Britain by Butler & Tanner Ltd, London and Frome

Contents

Introduction

One late winter's day in 1981 a shoal of little cars fled towards an adverse camber corner called Paddock Hill. The wan, slender, shy young man with the yellow helmet was lost in the shoal; and that was the beginning. Between this corner and another – Tamburello – 13 years later Ayrton Senna became mysterious, with a universal mythology. This book is about his life of movement: the 235 races from Paddock Hill to Tamburello. Some were ordinary, some flawed, some cunning, many magnificent, most turbulent. Ayrton Senna expressed himself profoundly through this medium of movement and quite possibly did it better than any man had ever done before him. Here it is.

✳ ✳ ✳

I have tried to give something from each qualifying session as well as the races, because the endless complexities of racing are revealed there. Whenever possible I have used the words Senna spoke and I have set in italics some of the words he used to demonstrate the logic of his thinking, even at 190mph. It is how he reached the conclusions he did.

I pay tribute to my sources, each invaluable. First, the magazine *Autosport*, and most particularly the reporting of Nigel Roebuck. I thank him and Simon Taylor, Chairman of Haymarket, for permission to quote. *Motoring News* served a similar purpose and thanks to the editor Mark Skewis for permission to quote from that. The TAG-Heuer/Olivetti computerised results gave me virtually every lap Senna ever drove at Grand Prix weekends and I have unashamedly fed on that. Sometimes the simple statistics of a race construct a poignant and precise framework. The *Autocourse* annuals are always concise compendiums. For easy reference I've used *The Guinness Complete Grand Prix Who's Who* by Steve Small; the *Grand Prix Data*

Book by David Hayhoe and David Holland; the *Marlboro Grand Prix Guide*. I've consulted and used brief extracts from *Driven to Win* by Nigel Mansell and Derick Allsop, *Life in the Fast Lane* by Alain Prost with Jean-Louis Moncet, and *To Hell and Back* by Niki Lauda (all Stanley Paul). A video library of the BBC coverage helps too, and so thanks to the Corporation and Murray and Jonathan and the late James for being there and doing it so well.

John Nicol of the British Racing Sports Car Club passed me on into the safe and sympathetic hands of their archivist Martin Hadwen, an amazing man. On the strength of a phone call he ransacked all manner of records to help. I repay his care and kindness now I hope by this: he is trying to assemble a reference point for motor racing records and memorabilia and if you have any, then write to me care of the publishers. I'll make sure he gets your letter. I thank him and David Hayhoe for reading the manuscript. That said, any mistakes are mine, not theirs. Thanks equally to Lyn Patey and Irene Ambrose for helping bring the early years alive; and to Dave Coyne for Formula Ford 1600 insights. I must add a footnote of gratitude to the bookshop Chater and Scott who delved into their backnumbers of *Autosport*, found one I was missing and mailed it overnight, no charge.

Because such a fantastic array of statistics falls to hand, I've rationed them into the manageable. You simply can't be comprehensive about Senna's races prior to Formula 3, but when we reach Formula 1 I've given: the chronological number of the race, where and when it was; his qualifying time and placing in brackets in both sessions; which row of the grid he was on; who had pole if he didn't and their time; the weather on race day; his time in the race morning warm-up and his placing in brackets; his place in the race. Here is a random example:

RACE 201 – South Africa, Kyalami, 1 March 1992. Qualifying: 1:16.815 (3); 1:16.227 (2). Front row. Pole: Mansell 1:15.486. Race weather: warm, overcast.

Warm-up: 1:20.347 (4). Result: Third.

There follows a description of the race; the podium, whether he was on it or not; if he was on it the comparative times; the fastest lap of the race and, if he didn't set it, his time for comparison; the championship points in the seasons when he was in contention. The example from South Africa:

Podium: Mansell 1h 36m 45.320s, Patrese at 24.360, Senna at 34.675. Fastest lap Mansell 1:17.578. Senna 1:18.140. Championship: Mansell 10, Patrese 6, Senna 4.

I'm not sure anything like this has been attempted before and, anyway, few drivers have deserved the effort. Please note that he was born Ayrton Senna da Silva and only later shortened this to Ayrton Senna. To preserve authenticity, wherever I have quoted contemporary sources in the early days – before the name change – I've left it the way it was reported, mis-spellings and all. In other words, da Silva was Senna.

The evolution of a man and his career. This is Senna at the World Karting Championships at Le Mans, 1978.

Chapter 1

Formula Ford 1600

Ayrton Senna raced karts from the age of 13, beginning in his native Sao Paulo, Brazil, and broadening to the national and South American championships. In 1978, 1979 and 1980 he contested the World Championships in Europe, twice finishing second. He'd reached a familiar and decisive point in any racing career. He talked it over with his father Milton and they decided to go for the big option: cars. That meant England, hub of the motor racing community. They contacted Ralph Firmin of Van Diemen, who ran Formula Ford 1600s which is where virtually everybody gets in. The cars are small, nervous and lovingly (or unlovingly) basic.

One day in 1981 Senna and his bride Liliane presented themselves at the factory at Snetterton, Norfolk. Firmin immediately felt there was something about this shy, quiet 21-year-old. The other front-runners were Enrique Mansilla from Argentina, Mexicans Alfonso Toledano and Ricardo Valerio, Britons Rick Morris (who had a Royale car), Andy Ackerley and Dave Coyne. These drivers apart, others come and go like strangers. "It was more friendly then than it is now," Coyne says, "although the racing was hard. A 1600 car was the most difficult of all to drive correctly and FF1600 was never a pleasure! Every corner was an accident waiting to happen." Senna contested three championships, the Townsend-Thoresen, the RAC, and – just once – the P & O Ferries. The Townsend-Thoresen scoring descended 20-15-12-10-8-6-4-3-2-1 with 2 for fastest lap and 11 best finishes counting; the same scoring applies in the RAC but with nothing for fastest lap. As points were awarded for the first 10 places, drivers could increase their championship totals without being anywhere near the podium.

✳ ✳ ✳

RACE 1

P & O Ferries round 1. Brands Hatch, 1 March 1981.
Result: Fifth.

The day is important only in retrospect. At the time it seemed ordinary, the race one of seven on the programme amidst those for saloons and modified sports cars and Formula Ford 2000. In the 1600 Coyne (regarded as the coming man) led into Paddock Hill Bend, the wrench of a corner at the end of the start-finish straight, Senna sixth. *Autosport* reported that "Toledano climbed back to fourth at the expense of former kart sensation de Silva, who will definitely be all the better for the race." It is necessary to see in your mind's eye these sharp, basic little cars fleeing round the club circuit, jousting and jostling and weaving, and perhaps necessary to see in your mind's eye Senna understanding that he could not announce himself instantly; so he ran to the end instead. I find that thought instructive. Across the years to come, when people insisted a consuming rage burned within him to win regardless of consequences, he could also – when he wanted – recognise the art of the possible and be governed by this. It would seem he already had.

• **Podium:** Mansilla, Morris, Coyne.
• **Fastest lap:** Toledano.

Townsend-Thoresen round 1. Thruxton,
8 March 1981.
Result: Third.

The meetings tumbled weekly. In deepest
Hampshire, at a disused airforce base of
rudimentary pretensions, Morris and David
Wheeler contested the lead throughout but "all
eyes were on Ayerton de Silva who engaged and
got the better of the recovering Mansilla in a
thrilling all-angles tussle" *(Autosport)* after
"dicing" with Howard Groos.

- **Podium:** Morris 14 minutes 41.5 seconds,
  Wheeler at 2.1, Senna at 9.4.
- **Fastest lap:** Morris.

Townsend-Thoresen round 2. Brands Hatch,
15 March 1981.
Result: First.

Senna now had the latest Van Diemen and
exploited it. There were two heats and a final.
In the second heat a downpour flooded the
track but he beat Mansilla by a second after
holding off a heavy attack. This is the first
recorded instance of Senna's control in the wet
and it must have been intuitive, sensing the
nuances of the car as you feel changes to your
own body, because he can scarcely have driven
a racing car in the wet before. It was also the
first time he had led; that would become a
familiar experience between here and
Tamburello on 1 May 1994. The final, over 15
laps, began in another downpour and Senna
resisted pressure from Ackerley, who floundered
and vanished. Senna led in a "typically hectic"
race, but on lap 4 Ackerley "bravely" drove
round him at Paddock. They surged abreast up
the incline to the horseshoe of Druids, Ackerley
trying to out-brake Senna on the outside and
going off. As Senna crossed the line for what
Motoring News described as "an untypically
easy win" (in FF1600 context) his wife Liliane

was almost in tears. That must have been partly
the intoxication of the moment and partly that
she knew he needed this so much. This is the
first recorded instance of how calm and clinical
Senna could be when he led a race. Steve
Lincoln, an Englishman, said perceptively "I
was looking forward to a really good year...and
now this bloke arrives!" Coyne says that Senna
"kept himself to himself. He didn't really speak
to many people, although he learnt English
quite quickly. He knew he was good. He
wouldn't give anything away but he was a
pleasant person. He had good equipment, good
everything, and it was unusual to find someone
with the talent to be able to use it all. That's
what he did."

- **Podium:** Senna 15m 07.2s, Toledano at 9.4,
  Lincoln at 10.4.
- **Fastest lap:** Kevin Gillen.
- **Championship:** Senna 32, Morris 26.

Townsend-Thoresen round 3. Mallory Park,
22 March 1981. Pole.
Result: Second.

The very first pole but Mansilla rushed from the
flag, shedding Senna into the embrace of Valerio,
Toledano and Morris. Valerio and Senna
duelled. They took and retook each other twice
in the opening laps before Valerio dropped back
and Toledano thrust up on lap 4 of the 15 to
challenge. By then Senna was moving
methodically on Mansilla and reduced a
comfortable lead to a car's length by lap 11. He
screwed down Mansilla under real pressure.
Motoring News estimated Mansilla must have
felt Senna's "breath down his neck," just a
phrase but you get the meaning. Senna drove so
forcefully that he went onto the grass several
times trying to overtake. Into the final lap he
emerged from the long loop of Gerard's Bend
faster, drew alongside but was "uncere-
moniously edged off onto the grass by the
Argentinian and angrily had to settle for second
place with Toledano right on his tail." This is the

A decade and more further on, this is Senna at Marlboro McLaren, contemplating.

first recorded instance of Senna anger. Others would receive it too, the last of them five races before Tamburello, more than a decade away.

- **Podium:** Mansilla 12m 44.3s, Senna at 1.2, Toledano at 1.6.
- **Fastest lap:** Toledano.
- **Championship:** Senna 47, Morris 34.

RACE 5

Townsend-Thoresen round 4. Mallory Park, 5 April 1981.
Result: Second.

A tight finish behind Morris. Senna went round Toledano at the esses at the back of the circuit to lead but Morris came through and Senna held off Toledano – although Toledano broke the lap record. You see the way it is with the great ones: they compel their opponents to become better.

- **Podium:** Morris 12m 38.1s, Senna at 0.1, Toledano at 1.2.
- **Fastest lap:** Toledano.
- **Championship:** Senna 62, Morris 54.

RACE 6

Townsend-Thoresen round 5. Snetterton, 3 May 1981. Pole.
Result: Second.

Because the overall entry for the meeting was low (54 cars and 4 races) the Townsend-Thoresen stretched over two heats, aggregate to count. England in spring: a damp surface, a keening wind. Toledano led the first heat from Morris but Senna overtook Morris during the opening lap and as they crossed the line to complete it these three hauled themselves from the rest. They moved in tandem for another couple of laps before Senna overtook Toledano and so did Morris. Senna won by 2.3 seconds. In the second heat Morris led from Senna but after both had been on the grass they touched and spun at the esses on lap 3. Senna accepted responsibility. This is the first recorded instance of Senna being prepared to put someone off and the first recorded instance of him saying it was his fault. Meanwhile "Steve Lincoln inherited second place but was caught and passed by the recovering da Silva" *(Autosport)*. Morris beat Senna by 6.2 seconds.

He'd know many different machines. This is the kart at Le Mans.

- **Podium on aggregate:** Morris 28m 45.8s,
  Senna at 3.9, Toledano at 8.3.
- **Fastest lap:** (heat 1) Toledano, (heat 2) Morris.
- **Championship:** Senna 77, Morris 74.

RACE 7

RAC round 1. Oulton Park,
24 May 1981. Pole.
Result: First.

Senna took pole and equalled the two-year-old track record in taking it. Toledano led from Morris, Senna and Mansilla but Senna was through by lap 2. Often he had the car virtually sideways but caught it each time. This is the first recorded instance of what his reflex mechanisms could do. To illustrate the difficulty of control in an FF1600 car, Toledano spun and dropped far back down the field. (Coyne stresses that the cars were intrinsically difficult to control.) *Autosport* reported that "mutterings of 'another Piquet' and 'future World Champion' accompanied the presentation of spoils", while *Motoring News* noted that Senna was visibly and unashamedly "delighted." The reporter cannot have understood the profundity of delight. You only get that in retrospect, with what we know now.

- **Podium:** Senna 16m 48.0s, Morris at 1.7,
  Mansilla at 9.0.
- **Fastest lap:** Senna.
- **Championship:** Senna 20, Morris 15, Mansilla 12.

RACE 8

Townsend-Thoresen round 6. Mallory Park,
25 May 1981.
Result: First.

Senna made a sure start and led into Gerard's from Toledano, who may well have jumped the flag and settled to blocking Morris, third. Senna built a lead. This is the first recorded instance of The Tactic: construct an opening lap so fast that it settled the race before the others had warmed their tyres, sorted themselves out, reached their pace; and it worked, all the way from here to

Formula 1 and nearly to Tamburello. *Motoring News* wrote of him "stamping his authority." Valerio crashed with Toledano. In FF1600 it happens. Senna made no semblance of a mistake and ticked the laps off. In retrospect it's tempting to read great meanings into small events long ago, to wring the future from them, and that can be misleading. Not in this case.

- **Podium:** Senna 12m 43.9s, Morris at 5.8,
  Chris Marsh at 15.7.
- **Fastest lap:** Morris.
- **Championship:** Senna 97, Morris 91.

RACE 9

Townsend-Thoresen round 7. Snetterton,
7 June 1981.
Result: First.

Senna dominant. It had taken only 14 weeks from Paddock Hill that very first time. *Autosport* reported that "the works Van Diemen driver looked very assured throughout and Rick Morris had to drive much less tidily to separate the Brazilian from his team-mate Toledano in third." *Motoring News* set the context. "Morris is the season's yardstick to gauge new talent by. It thus augurs well for Ayerton da Silva, the works Van Diemen driver, that he is the only runner in the T-T series to consistently beat the experienced Englishman."

- **Podium:** Senna 18m 16.5s, Morris at 0.7,
  Toledano at 5.5.
- **Fastest lap:** Senna.
- **Championship:** Senna 119, Morris 106.

RACE 10

RAC round 2. Silverstone,
21 June 1981.
Result: Second.

Morris made a poor start, Senna away clear, but Morris, dogged, pursued and by lap 5 caught him. Morris had five laps to plot an overtaking move. On lap 9 into the tight curve of Stowe he "scrabbled" by on the inside but under braking

And this is the Williams Renault, 1994.

at the Woodcote chicane Senna retook him. Along Hangar Straight on the final lap – at maximum speed, 125mph – Morris tried to weave inside but Senna blocked that, Morris tried to weave outside but Senna blocked that too, and put Morris on the grass. Morris recovered and made a gambler's throw at Woodcote, the chicane before the finishing line. He went outside under braking and that pitched him across the chicane but just inside the yellow penalty line. A contemporary account says that Senna realised and braked as late as he could, Morris braked as late as he could to "bounce his Royale RF29 over the chicane and come out a clear winner, much to Ayrton's obvious disappointment." Ah, the power of understatement. Morris remembers Senna's "unbearable" anger. This is the first recorded instance of how Senna found defeat very, very difficult to accept, and the first recorded instance of his reaction when he perceived something unfair – Morris going over the chicane while he went through it.

Podium: Morris 17m 01.8s, Senna at 0.9, Mansilla at 6.3.
Fastest lap: Morris.
Championship: Senna and Morris 35, Mansilla 24.

RACE 11

Townsend-Thoresen round 8. Oulton Park, 27 June 1981.
Result: First.

In practice Senna went 0.1 of a second inside the track's "long-standing" FF1600 record and so did Morris. However a shower before the race sponged away any chance of beating the official record (only set in races). Senna led from Morris, who spun on lap 2. At that instant any threat to Senna had gone although Toledano bustled late on.

- **Podium:** Senna 16m 49.5s, Toledano at 0.6, Fernando Macedo (a Brazilian) at 45.9.
- **Fastest lap:** Senna.
- **Championship:** Senna 141, Morris 106, Toledano 94.

RACE 12

RAC round 3. Donington Park, 4 July 1981.
Result: First.

Senna and Morris went in sharing the Championship lead, of course, but now Senna moved ahead. He led the race and though Morris moved on him towards the end of the 15 laps he couldn't get close enough to conjure a proper attack.

- **Podium:** Senna 20m 35.6s, Morris at 2.8, Mansilla at 14.3.
- **Fastest lap:** Senna and Morris (1:21.5s).
- **Championship:** Senna 55, Morris 50, Mansilla 36.

RACE 13

RAC round 4. Brands Hatch, 12 July 1981.
Result: Fourth.

Senna suffered problems setting the car up in practice and started from the third row of the grid. He made "a truly sensational" start and reached Paddock level with Mansilla for the lead "having displaced four cars instantly, seemingly without contact!" This is the first recorded instance of what Senna could make a car do from an unfavourable grid position. Mansilla resisted but "had to relent at the hairpin, da Silva forging ahead immediately. The brilliance of the former karter, once free, was a joy to behold. Deft flicks of opposite lock through Paddock – such elegant car control can only be natural talent – took him ever further out of reach until, dramatically, the Van Diemen slewed sideways beyond instantaneous recall at Clearways with three laps remaining, Ayrton resuming fourth with a water hose adrift." This lovely description came from Marcus Pye in *Autosport*.

- **Podium:** Morris, Toledano, Mansilla.
- **Fastest lap:** Senna.
- **Championship:** Morris 70, Senna 65, Mansilla 48.

RACE 14

Townsend-Thoresen round 9. Oulton Park, 25 July 1981.
Result: First.

A potentially explosive front row, Toledano, Senna and Macedo, but it didn't detonate: Toledano faster away than Senna who overtook him on the opening lap. Senna fashioned "an impressive lead" while Morris needed until lap 6 to move into second place.

- **Podium:** Senna 16m 59.7s, Morris at 2.9, Toledano at 8.6.
- **Fastest lap:** Senna.
- **Championship:** Senna 163, Morris 121.

Autosport reported that "a tremendous race eclipsed everything that had gone before" – six other races of various kinds. Senna had pole and the lead but behind him a "monumental second place struggle" between Toledano, Mansilla and Morris lasted the whole 15 laps. Senna "took advantage of the infighting to establish a comfortable cushion." By now, in a caption to an action photograph, *Autosport* were describing Senna as "FF1600's man of the moment" and published a picture of him

He'd know the foamy rituals of the podium.

smiling. It was the same smile which would become globally famous and it never altered.

- **Podium:** Senna 12m 44.4s, Morris at 1.6, Mansilla at 2.2.
- **Fastest lap:** Senna, Mansilla and Morris (50.1s).
- **Championship:** Senna and Morris 85, Mansilla 60.

RACE 16

Townsend-Thoresen round 10. Brands Hatch, 2 August 1981.
Result: First.

Senna stormed the lead and never lost it. He completed the opening lap with at least a six length lead – The Tactic. On that lap Toledano and Morris crashed at Druids but recovered. Their crash removed any distant threat to Senna.

- **Podium:** Senna 12m 58.0s, Morris at 0.1, Toledano at 2.4.
- **Fastest lap:** Toledano.
- **Championship:** Senna 183, Morris 136.

RACE 17

RAC round 6. Snetterton, 9 August 1981.
Result: First.

Drizzle fell during race morning practice but, although heavy cloud covered the circuit, the surface dried for the race. Only Senna, Mansilla, Toledano and Morris remained in contention for the championship and they were the front row. In "treacherous conditions" Toledano led until Senna overtook him on lap 2. By half distance rain drifted over and "the pace slowed dramatically. At the Esses, where the wet track was first encountered, da Silva went wide and tiptoed through. Mansilla was off into the rough but regained the track and then the next bunch imitated a bomb-burst, shooting off in all directions" (*Autosport*). Senna carefully guarded a two second lead over Mansilla. "A measure of Ayrton's talent can be gained by the fact that he equalled the long-standing lap record in the opening laps." A man

Karting stayed close to his heart. He competed – for charity – at Bercy, Paris, in 1993.

The slight, shy, almost wan young man who came to England in 1981 to contest Formula Ford 1600 *Autosport*.

called Dennis Rushen of Rushen Green Racing – running a car in the Pace British Ford 2000 Championship, the next step upwards – witnessed what Senna did and drew an immediate conclusion.

If any youngster can handle such conditions in the way he has just done he must be exceptional. Rushen drew a further conclusion: We must have him in FF2000 in 1982. Rushen introduced himself to Senna and made a generous offer. The history of motorsport changed up a gear at that moment; not to mention that Senna was now RAC champion.

- **Podium:** Senna 19m 19.8s, Mansilla at 1.1, Toledano at 18.9.
- **Fastest lap:** Senna.
- **Championship:** (best five finishes counted) Senna 95, Morris 85, Mansilla 63.

RACE 18

Townsend-Thoresen Euroseries.
Donington Park, 15 August 1981.
Result: First.

Senna was a late entrant but led and only Morris could compete with him. *Autosport* reported that "Brazilian Ayrton da Silva really is in a class of his own in FF1600 this season and his fellow competitors must have been dismayed when his Van Diemen appeared as an additional entry in the Townsend-Thoresen EFDA Euroseries counter. Sure enough Ayrton rushed off as he pleased, troubled only towards the end by Rick Morris."

- **Podium:** Senna 16m 13.7s, Morris at 0.9, John Booth at 8.0.
- **Fastest lap:** Morris.

He was instantly and instinctively quick *Autosport*.

Senna wins round 11 of the Townsend-Thoresen championship at Thruxton in August, 1981 *Autosport.*

Townsend-Thoresen round 11. Thruxton,
31 August 1981. Pole.
Result: First.

Senna took pole by 0.5 and took his second championship. He seized the lead, Morris third and, crossing the line to complete the first lap, led narrowly from Toledano. Morris probed for second place but dropped out with mechanical problems. By lap 3 Senna was in complete command from Toledano. *Autosport* reported that "while the two Brazilians pulled away, the rest of the pack crowded round in a separate race, constantly changing places. On the last lap Macedo pulled across Lincoln, who'd driven back into contention following a spin. Lincoln was catapulted into the air over the Mexican. Chris March had to take avoiding action and Timothy Atkinson came through the mêlée to take third." Marcus Pye was in this race (and had forgotten until I told him!). He finished twelfth "and at least I didn't get in the way. I remember one race at Thruxton – it may not have been this one – where Senna did seven or eight laps to within a hundredth of a second each time. You almost felt you were watching sleight of hand because it did not seem possible in an FF1600 car. The nature of the car wouldn't allow it. OK, you can do it in Formula 1, maybe, with big tyres and so forth – but an FF1600!" Two further witnesses to the phenomenon of this: Morris who once followed Senna and noticed he adopted the same line through a corner to an inch every lap (which Morris had imagined impossible) and Coyne, who says "however difficult the cars were to control, Senna was consistent, that was the thing."

• **Podium:** Senna 14m 25.4s, Toledano at 3.3, Atkinson at 19.7.
• **Fastest lap:** Senna.
• **Championship:** Senna 205, Morris 136.

Many who watched him glimpsed the future and suspected it would look something like this.

RACE 20

Townsend-Thoresen round 12. Brands Hatch,
29 September 1981.
Result: Second.

The contemporary accounts capture it exactly. *Autosport* reported that "two incidents on the first lap put the brilliant Ayrton de Silva way down the field but his drive through to second place was undoubtedly the talk of the race. Morris backed off when he saw a plus 6s board to his pursuers, led by Toledano, until da Silva swept by Toledano a lap from home." *Motoring News* reported that "da Silva's performance in the race was incredible. After a slow practice, he made a good start but clipped Morris and spun down the field and then he was chopped by a back-marker, spinning again. All this didn't prevent him from eventually finishing second and setting fastest lap by nearly two seconds!

Da Silva's antics virtually defied belief. From a third row start, the works Van Diemen made a terrific getaway, chopped its way past several drivers on the acceleration up to Paddock Bend, and then promptly slewed across the track in a lazy spin. By nothing more than exceptional luck, no-one collected the Brazilian. So he collected it all together again and resumed in sixteenth place. In a phenomenal charge he picked off cars by half a dozen a lap – then had another spin! But it didn't seem to matter: by the time the 12 laps had elapsed, Ayrton had clambered boldly up the order to second again!" The exclamation marks capture it exactly, too.

- **Podium:** Morris 23m 20.1s, Senna at 6.4, Toledano at 9.2.
- **Fastest lap:** Senna.
- **Championship:** Senna 222 (210 counting), Morris 156.

Straight line speed, 1982 *Autosport*

Senna in 1982, poised to shake up FF2000 *Autosport*.

Chapter 2

Formula Ford 2000

S enna took up Dennis Rushen's offer for 1982. Liliane did not return to England with him. The received wisdom is that she could not or would not accept motor racing being the main theme of their marriage. They divorced. Formula Ford 2000 did represent the distinct step upwards. The cars had wings, allowing sophisticated permutations. Senna would be in a Van Diemen and his main competitor, Englishman Calvin Fish, initially in a Royale. The other front-runners: Senna's team-mate Kenny Andrews (Van Diemen), Russell Spence (Van Diemen), Frank Bradley (Van Diemen) and Tim Davies (Royale). These drivers apart, others come and go like strangers. Scoring in the Pace British: 20-15-12-10-8-6-4-3-2-1, plus 1 for pole, 1 for fastest lap; scoring in the EFDA Euroseries the same but 2 points for fastest lap. Some confusion remains over the points totals and it may be that these can never be resolved because records were incomplete, not kept or destroyed. Strange but true. As a consequence I give only the totals of Senna and Fish in the Pace British.

✳ ✳ ✳

RACE 21

Pace British FF2000 round 1. Brands Hatch, 7 March 1982. Pole.
Result: First.

Senna arrived in England late and Rushen can't even remember him testing the car to explore its innate differences from FF1600. Rushen explained the differences as best he could – including the possibilities of adjusting wing settings – and settled back to see what happened next. In practice Senna went 1.3 seconds faster than anybody else and at the start of the race "simply rushed off into the distance" while "Fish came back from a slow start to take Spence" (*Motoring News*). Half way round the opening lap Senna held a lead of some 60 yards over Fish. The Tactic transferred effortlessly.

• **Podium:** Senna 11m 57.4s, Fish at 9.8, Spence at 10.7.
• **Fastest lap:** Senna.
• **Championship:** Senna 22, Fish 15.

RACE 22

Pace British FF2000 round 2. Oulton Park, 27 March 1982. Pole.
Result: First.

Senna "rocketed" from the green light so that as the others reached for their rhythm he'd already found his and was a long way in front. The Tactic. He gave a "masterful display of his undoubted ability and headed into the distance. Da Silva polished off the race with a new lap record, his only problem coming when he lapped back-markers" (*Motoring News*). He beat the two-year-old track record by 0.2 of a second.

• **Podium:** Senna 15m 37.6s, Fish at 10.1, Mike Taylor at 14.4.
• **Fastest lap:** Senna.
• **Championship:** Senna 44, Fish 30.

RACE 23

Pace British FF2000 round 3. Silverstone,
28 March 1982. Pole.
Result: First.

Senna was majestic in his manipulation of the car. He bestrode practice and took pole by 0.9. In the race, well, The Tactic then he broke the track record.

- **Podium:** Senna 14m 30.8s, Colin Jack at 17.1, Spence at 18.5.
- **Fastest lap:** Senna.
- **Championship:** Senna 66, Fish 40.

RACE 24

Pace British FF2000 round 4. Donington Park,
4 April 1982. Pole.
Result: First.

A poser from *Motoring News*. "The question hanging over event four [of the race day programme] was 'will Ayrton da Silva walk away with another win?' The answer was 'yes!'"

- **Podium:** Senna 18m 49.1s, Fish at 18.3, Spence at 21.9.
- **Fastest lap:** Senna.
- **Championship:** Senna 88, Fish 55.

RACE 25

Pace British FF2000 round 5. Snetterton,
9 April 1982. Pole.
Result: First.

Senna into the lead unimpeded by a considerable crash behind to give a first lap order of Senna, Andrews, Bradley, Spence, Fish. Moving into lap 2 Senna picked through the debris of the crash and suddenly slowed. Andrews and Spence immediately closed and went by. Senna had lost front brakes but adjusted to that and retook them both. This is the first recorded instance of Senna surmounting a sudden defect in the car by ability alone. Andrews, who briefly thought the unthinkable – I'm going to win! – wondered afterwards where he was going wrong. "You brake too early for the esses," Senna said. "I was braking later than you with only rear brakes." This is the first recorded instance of Senna's actual braking distance, or more accurately the possibilities within his braking distance.

- **Podium:** Senna 17m 07.1s, Andrews at 12.6, Victor Rosso at 17.3.
- **Fastest lap:** Senna.
- **Championship:** Senna 110, Fish 55.

RACE 26

Pace British FF2000 round 6. Silverstone,
12 April 1982. Pole.
Result: First.

Senna equalled the record he'd set on 28 March. *Motoring News* reported that he "romped off into the distance right from the start and lapped within 0.40 of the record from his first flying lap. Over the first four laps he extended his lead by a second a time. Half way through the 15 lap event he equalled the FF2000 record and may have bettered it on the next circuit had he not had to lift whilst lapping a back-marker. Not even a misfire held back the ragged but incredibly quick da Silva." Ragged? Conflicting evidence about that, coming along in just a moment.

- **Podium:** Senna 14m 31.5s, Rosso at 14.2, Spence at 15.0.
- **Fastest lap:** Senna.
- **Championship:** Senna 132, Fish 63.

RACE 27

EFDA FF2000 round 1. Zolder, Belgium,
18 April 1982. Pole.
Result: Retired after 3 laps, engine.

Senna's first car race outside Britain. The anticipation was of a battle between him and Dutchman Cor Euser, the reigning European,

Dutch and Benelux FF1600 champion. It didn't happen. In qualifying Senna went quickest in both sessions and took pole by a clear second. Euser, very much an amateur doing it for fun, had a two-year-old Delta car which he managed to put on the front row. The start was delayed through oil on the track and Senna's engine overheated. He led in spite of that and in a couple of laps built a two second lead over Euser. Then he felt the engine tightening and cruised into the pits. He would always do this rather than risk destruction.

- **Podium:** Euser, Jesper Villumsen, Maarten Henneman.
- **Fastest lap:** Euser.

RACE 28

EFDA FF2000 round 2. Donington Park, 2 May 1982. Pole.
Result: First.

Contemporary reports suggest that Spence looked capable of getting closer to matching Senna. Hmmm. In the race Senna suffered a misfire, which did not prevent him winning or breaking his own lap record by 0.11s.

- **Podium:** Senna 24m 57.5s, Spence at 7.1, Kristian Nissen at 25.8.
- **Fastest lap:** Senna.
- **Championship:** Senna 24, Spence 15, Bradley 10.

RACE 29

Pace British FF2000 round 7. Mallory Park, 3 May 1982.
Result: First.

Victor Rosso (Van Diemen) took pole from Senna, who had an engine which wasn't delivering enough power. It had to be changed at lunchtime. Rosso made a poor start and Senna capitalised, going through and dragging Spence with him. Senna pulled clear while Rosso, recovering, overtook Spence on the third lap. Spence retook him four laps later. These were moves within the race, of course, but with no bearing on the result. Senna displayed what one account describes as his "nimbleness and style." And that's the comparison with ragged.

- **Podium:** Senna 15m 44.3s, Rosso at 8.0, Andrews at 18.6.
- **Fastest lap:** Senna.
- **Championship:** Senna 153, Fish 73.

Senna dominated Formula Ford 2000 in 1982 – in Britain and Europe. Here he wins at Hockenheim *Autosport*.

Somehow he felt or sensed with astonishing accuracy what a car could do in a corner *Autosport*.

EFDA FF2000 round 3. Zolder,
9 May 1982. Pole.
Result: Retired, spin.

The weekend Gilles Villeneuve was killed a few minutes before the end of Saturday second qualifying. What impact this made on Senna is unknown, because I never heard him asked about it or speak about it. Did he harbour doubts about continuing? How did he rationalise such doubts if he experienced them? Did he foresee? An unfair question. The only man who could tell us never will now. We do know that he introduced himself to Nelson Piquet, fellow Brazilian and established in Formula 1, and Piquet snubbed him. Senna never forgot and surely never forgave. Senna took pole but in the race made a "rare error" (*Autosport*) when he was leading by 13 seconds "and spun into the catch fencing, throwing away an almost certain victory."

- **Podium:** Huub Vermeulen, Villumsen, Rob Leeuwenburgh.
- **Fastest lap:** Senna.
- **Championship:** Villumsen 34, Senna 27, Vermeulen 20.

RACE 31

Shell Super Sunbeam for celebrities.
Oulton Park, 30 May 1982.
Result: First.

Nine cars contested this event, run before round 8 of the British FF2000. Evidently the entrants were decided by the fastest qualifiers in selected races but however it was done Senna qualified. He led from an experienced driver, John Brindley, and moved from him at a second a lap setting a class record. Another experienced driver, Chuck Nicholson, guards a vivid semi-memory of the race: he didn't see Senna at all!

- **Podium:** Senna 9m 50.2s, Brindley at 7.1, Nicholson at 9.6.
- **Fastest lap:** Senna.

RACE 32

Pace British FF2000 round 8. Oulton Park,
30 May 1982.
Result: Retired after 11 laps, puncture.

Fish now had a Van Diemen and took pole, Senna on the front row although (again) his engine hadn't been delivering enough power and "even the talented Brazilian could not make up for it" (*Autosport*). Fish led from Senna but Senna was in trouble almost immediately when his right rear tyre exploded in the downhill Cascades left-hander at 125mph. The car snapped sideways. Senna caught it. Andrews could barely believe this was possible. Senna limping beyond Cascades, Andrews naturally overtook him round the outside. Senna retired "after having survived several lurid slides." Fish beat Senna's lap record by 0.1.

- **Podium:** Fish, Andrews, Neil Myers.
- **Fastest lap:** Fish.
- **Championship:** Senna 153, Fish 95.

RACE 33

Pace British FF2000 round 9. Brands Hatch,
31 May 1982.
Result: First.

Fish took pole from Senna but Senna was determined to have the lead and into Paddock he and Fish touched, Fish losing some of his nose-cone. Somehow Fish stayed with Senna for the 20 laps but could do no more.

- **Podium:** Senna 15m 54.8s, Fish at 1.6, Spence at 14.5.
- **Fastest lap:** Senna.
- **Championship:** Senna 174, Fish 111.

RACE 34

Pace British FF2000 round 10. Mallory Park,
6 June 1982.
Result: First.

Tim Davies took pole but *Motoring News* reported that "as expected it was da Silva who shot away to the front from the flag." Andrews attacked Davies and overtook him on lap 3 (of the 15) and Fish overtook Davies too. By half-distance they "were chasing after the Brazilian but it was all in vain."

• **Podium:** Senna 11m 47.2s, Andrews at 9.2, Fish at 10.9.
• **Fastest lap:** Senna.
• **Championship:** Senna 195, Fish 123.

RACE 35

Pace British FF2000 round 11. Brands Hatch,
13 June 1982. Pole.
Result: First.

During qualifying Senna equalled the track record and said "first I think about winning then maybe the record." This is the first recorded instance of Senna being quoted during a race meeting, exploring – however briefly and superficially – his thinking. The race had to be stopped after two laps because Sigurd Krane, a Norwegian, lost control at Paddock and hammered the fencing. At the restart Senna led, Fish matching him and the intensity was such that Senna did break the record and Fish did too. They averaged 93.98mph.

• **Podium:** Senna 11m 44.8s, Fish at 1.0, Andrews at 7.8.
• **Fastest lap:** Senna and Fish (46.4s).
• **Championship:** Senna 217, Fish 139.

RACE 36

EFDA FF2000 round 4. Hockenheim,
20 June 1982. Pole.
Result: Retired on lap 1, accident.

Senna cooked his clutch on the start line and then Euser, in the lead, misjudged the chicane and his Delta was flung into a series of barrel-rolls. Everyone behind darted and dived to avoid him, causing a major crash, Senna in the midst of it. The car was so badly damaged he didn't go to the re-start.

• **Podium:** Rosso, Fish, Bradley.
• **Fastest lap:** Henrik Larsen.
• **Championship:** Villumsen 34, Euser 30, Senna 28.

RACE 37

Pace British FF2000 round 12. Oulton Park,
26 June 1982.
Result: First.

The track was damp, although drying, and Andrews led but on lap 2 Senna overtook him. By lap 4 he commanded the race but on lap 9 (of 15) Fish overtook Andrews and set off in pursuit. Fish pushed himself so hard he set fastest lap then Senna went faster than that.

• **Podium:** Senna 16m 10.4s, Fish at 4.2, Andrews at 8.3.
• **Fastest lap:** Senna.
• **Championship:** Senna 238, Fish 154.

RACE 38

EFDA FF2000 round 5. Zandvoort,
3 July 1982. Pole.
Result: First.

Senna took pole despite missing the opening practice because of a clutch problem and it left him 30 minutes to learn a new circuit. He followed a Dutchman, Ron Kluit, for a couple of laps – seeing and remembering, no doubt, which lines Kluit took and where he braked – then set the time. He made a crisp start but missed second gear which allowed a driver called Jaap van Silfhout in a Lola to "dodge" ahead into the lead. Euser ran third, Fish fourth. On lap 2 at Tarzan, the fabled switchback curve at the end of the start-finish straight, Senna out-braked van Silfhout – a classical move, and a favourite among Formula 1 drivers – and stayed in front for the remaining 10 laps. Euser and Fish fought out second place when they got past van Silfhout. Senna, hampered by gearbox problems, maintained a steady two second lead.

- **Podium:** Senna 20m 08.0s, Fish at 2.3, Euser at 2.7.
- **Fastest lap:** Kluit.
- **Championship:** Senna 49, Euser 42, Villumsen 34.

RACE 39

Pace British FF2000 round 13. Snetterton, 4 July 1982.
Result: Second.

Senna didn't have pole. Heavy rain fell by the second race on the card so that the fourth – the FF2000 – was wet. Bradley gambled on dry tyres and "wallowed in midfield" while Fish led. Senna caught and overtook Fish but Bradley charged. By lap 10 of the 20 he was "clearly the fastest car" and worked a path through to third place with five laps left. Senna "tried hard to conserve his tyres" – wet tyres shred on a dry surface – while Fish caught him and harried, probing, squeezing, but couldn't do more. *Motoring News* reported that "before half distance, with the track drying rapidly, it was obvious that the leaders, particularly da Silva, were intent on conserving their tyres, although Fish, who had closed on the tail of the Brazilian, was not allowing the leader to slow his pace as much as he would have wished." In the background Bradley came on strongly and by the second last lap had reached them. He took Fish at Coram [a curve] and, on the last lap, Senna at Sear [a right-hander onto the back straight]. This was the first race of 1982 when Senna had been beaten when the car was running at the end.

- **Podium:** Bradley 24m 46.4s, Senna at 3.6, Fish at 4.1.
- **Fastest lap:** Bradley.
- **Championship:** Senna 253, Fish 166.

RACE 40

Pace British FF2000 round 14. Castle Combe, 10 July 1982. Pole.
Result: First.

Senna took 0.9 off the record to have pole from Fish by a tenth. Pye wrote that "practice form was repeated in the race, quite the most tedious I've ever seen in this formula, with da Silva just out of Fish's reach throughout and the rest, headed by Spence, following on." Senna and Fish both broke the (official) record.

- **Podium:** Senna 15m 47.2s, Fish at 3.0, Spence at 16.2 .
- **Fastest lap:** Senna and Fish (1m 02.6).
- **Championship:** Senna 275, Fish 182.

Four wins out of four as 1982 unfolds. This is Donington, 4 April *Autosport*.

He always felt homesick for Brazil and returned there whenever he could throughout his career. For an active man, he found relaxing easy and natural.

RACE 41

Pace British FF2000 round 15. Snetterton,
1 August 1982.
Result: First.

RACE 42

EFDA FF2000 round 6. Hockenheim,
8 August 1982. Pole.
Result: First.

Fish pole, Senna alongside and they diced as the race unfolded – Senna leading – but by lap 4 Fish hauled himself to a challenge. Past the pits Senna firmly blocked and "as they sped down the long Revett straight they weaved back and forth" and Fish went to the inside. "Suddenly, Ayrton moved in tighter, leaving Calvin nowhere to go but the grass and he was lucky to survive the long excursion, off course, intact" (*Autosport*). Here is the consuming hunger, the inability to concede, indeed the willingness to push you off rather than concede. Fish's car went 10 feet in the air and the day culminated in a marshal's report condemning Senna, who complained they picked on him because he was Brazilian.

- **Podium:** Senna 16m 52.0s, Andrews at 17.8, Max Busslinger at 18.3.
- **Fastest lap:** Senna.
- **Championship:** Senna 296, Fish 183.

The crowd were evidently astonished by Senna in qualifying. It rained although one practice session was dry and Senna exploited that, taking pole by three seconds. Three cars crashed at the start but at the restart Senna led and didn't lose it. Fish ran evenly in second, no threat to Senna – who broke the lap record – but under no threat himself from anyone behind. There's a curious background tale about this race. Two English women, who did not know each other and did not know Senna, travelled to Hockenheim to watch the Grand Prix. The FF2000 was a supporting event on the same programme. I quote them to show the immediate effect Senna could have on total strangers.

One was called Lyn Patey. "I sat in the start-line grandstand with the colourful panorama of the Stadium section spread in front of my awed eyes. The death of Gilles Villeneuve was the reason I was there. The day after Zolder I woke with the dreadful realisation that I'd never seen

On the race track he was hyper-active. Here he leads at Snetterton *Autosport*.

him race on the race track, only on TV. I made a resolution. This would never happen again [with great drivers]. I decided to give myself a birthday present by booking a trip to Germany. With mild curiosity I watched some funny little cars lining up on the grid. My attention was caught by a pretty yellow helmet in the car on pole. The commentator gave the driver line-up and suddenly a strange, exotic name was ringing round the Stadium. I remember thinking it sounded wonderful and resolved to keep an eye on its owner. He didn't let me down: lights to flag, smooth as silk, miles ahead. Afterwards I fought through the crowd of Brazilians and others to reach him. I held out my hand and he grasped it and had a big smile. We shared a few words and then others demanded his attention. I walked away feeling suddenly sad."

The second stranger was called Irene Ambrose. "Still in shock after Pironi's accident the day before [Didier Pironi crashed his Ferrari and was trapped but survived, crippled] I was huddling in the grandstand by the Stadium entrance overlooking the twisty bit. I remember vaguely seeing the Formula Fords come out and, as the leader pulled away, my lasting impression is of the commentator's triumphant 'Senna da Silva' reverberating around the concrete. Something must have clicked into place then." Patey and Ambrose became dedicated Senna followers. They met on the boat home and are still friends.

- **Podium:** Senna 26m 59.2s, Fish at 4.2,
  Volker Weidler at 20.5.
- **Fastest lap:** Senna.
- **Championship:** Senna 72, Euser 52, Fish 45.

RACE 43

EFDA FF2000 round 7. Osterreichring,
15 August 1982. Pole.
Result: First.

This race supported the Austrian Grand Prix, which Elio de Angelis, a future Senna team-mate, won for Lotus from Keke Rosberg by 0.050 seconds. In the 2000 Senna took pole by a "staggering" 1.561 seconds. *Motoring News*

reported that "da Silva had stamped his authority on the meeting from the first practice session when he set fastest lap with 1m 59.814s (110.946 mph) to take pole position from Fish. The Brazilian made no mistake at the start" and won at a canter.

- **Podium:** Senna 24m 21.3s, Fish at 24.3,
  Nissen at 37.7.
- **Fastest lap:** Senna.
- **Championship:** Senna 95, Fish 60, Euser 53.

RACE 44

EFDA FF2000 round 8. Jyllandsring,
22 August 1982. Pole.
Result: First.

The championship decider. Pole, inevitably, and a smooth, soothed race with the Dane Nissen struggling to stay with him – and failing – early on. Fish, initially third, soon took Nissen but Senna hammered the lap record and finished an age from Fish. Afterwards, Senna, virtually tee-total, got partially drunk...well, drunk enough to ride a bike in the dark with a silly grin on his face.

- **Podium:** Senna 19m 35.0s, Fish at 2.6,
  Nissen at 5.4.
- **Fastest lap:** Senna.
- **Championship:** Senna 118, Fish 75, Euser 57.

RACE 45

Pace British FF2000 round 16. Thruxton,
30 August 1982.
Result: First.

Fish took pole by 0.3 from Senna, and Senna 1.3 from the rest. Spitting rain made conditions dubious for the start. Fish led, Senna harrying him, crowding him at each corner. On lap 4 Senna slowed – the oil pressure gauge giving alarming readings – and Fish eased out to perhaps 50 metres. Fish held the gap at around 0.5 until lap 13 (of the 15) when, baulked by a back-marker, he couldn't prevent Senna going by even with oil smoke billowing from the engine. Fish attacked, Senna defended and broke the lap record in his defence.

- **Podium:** Senna 20m 00.7s, Fish at 1.3, Spence at 16.6.
- **Fastest lap:** Senna.
- **Championship:** Senna 317, Fish 199.

RACE 46

Pace British FF2000 round 17. Oulton Park, 4 September 1982. Pole.
Result: First.

Senna and Fish shared the front row. Fish "scorched" into the lead "frantically pursued by da Silva, these two soon opening a gap. Da Silva couldn't pass Fish but kept up the pressure until Fish made a slight error on the ninth lap and da Silva was through in a flash" *(Autosport)*.

- **Podium:** Senna 20m 40.9s, Fish at 2.9, Spence at 18.4.
- **Fastest lap:** Fish.
- **Championship:** Senna 338, Fish 215.

RACE 47

Pace British FF2000 round 18. Silverstone, 5 September 1982. Pole.
Result: First.

Senna and Fish set identical times in practice. Senna led but Fish hovered and hung for the first five laps. From laps 5 to 10 (of the 15) Senna siphoned a lead of around a second. Fish came back at him – but never close enough to mount an overtaking move.

- **Podium:** Senna 14m 33.6s, Fish at 0.6, Rosso at 13.5.
- **Fastest lap:** Senna and Fish (57.6s).
- **Championship:** Senna 360, Fish 231.

RACE 48

EFDA FF2000 round 9. Mondello Park, 12 September 1982.
Result: First.

"Before the biggest crowd seen at Mondello for years and under the watchful eyes of the TV cameras, the Formula Ford 2000s faced the traffic lights just after 5.30pm and [Joey] Greenan led da Silva away on the green. For two laps the Irish driver led but missed a gear change and the Brazilian swept by on the outside. Once in front da Silva raced away into the distance [and broke the lap record] to win by the huge margin of over 20 secs. Greenan held station behind da Silva, totally out of touch with the leader and equally out of the grips of a furious three-car battle for third." Thus, *Autosport* and with a nice Irish lilt to it.

- **Podium:** Senna 19m 32.7s, Greenan at 18.5, Nissen at 20.5.
- **Fastest lap:** Senna.
- **Championship:** Senna 140, Fish 83, Euser 57.

RACE 49

Pace British FF2000 round 20. Brands Hatch, 26 September 1982.
Result: Second.

Two meetings on consecutive weekends here. Senna did not compete in the first (on 19 September, round 19, which Fish won). He was at Kalmar, Sweden, contesting the World Karting Championships. Next weekend Rosso, Fish and Senna all did 46.5 in qualifying, but Senna on the second row. Fish made a monumental start, overtaking Rosso on the outside at Paddock and led by six lengths. Senna dived inside Rosso at Clearways but Fish continued untroubled until back-markers hampered him. Senna was "quick to pounce" but Fish "clung grimly" to the lead and kept it. This is the first recorded instance of Senna dealing with what they call traffic and doing it as he would always do it: blasting a path through back-markers. *Motoring News* reported that "for a while in mid-race da Silva's second place looked threatened as he grappled with gearbox problems but there were no excuses as he broke the lap record and closed but failed to catch Fish in the closing stages." There's necessary background to this. At Kalmar he finished fourteenth and returned to England in the wrong mood. He and Rushen fell to a niggling discussion over a wing-setting and Rushen sensed that Senna's attitude wasn't right for the race. This is Rushen's first and only instance of such a thing. Then, Rushen remembers, the desire stirred in Senna and he wanted to win: too late. He drove urgently and broke the lap record but...

- **Podium:** Fish 11m 46.7s, Senna at 0.8, Rosso at 3.7.
- **Fastest lap:** Senna.
- **Championship:** Senna 376, Fish 271.

RACE 50

Formula 3, Thruxton, 13 November 1982.
Qualifying: 1:13.34 (1); 1:13.54 (1). Pole.
Result: First.

Senna needed to step upwards again. That would be Formula 3 with a team called West Surrey. "I went home to Brazil in order to enjoy a little bit of the summer, the sunshine, and also to meet my sponsors and talk about this race and about next season. I arrived back in England two weeks ago and did some tests at Thruxton and Snetterton. I went well in the car and I found it very good to work with Dick Bennetts" [of West Surrey]. The race was televised by the BBC, lending it enormous importance for young hopefuls.

"He's a very intelligent driver," Bennetts said, "and he can tell me exactly what the car is doing, which makes my job a lot easier." This is the first recorded instance of Senna's ability to convey the current state of a car exactly. Many of the 1982 Formula 3 front-runners did not go to Thruxton, which possibly diluted what Senna did – who knows what he'd have done to them or they to him? Certainly Senna completed first qualifying 0.75 seconds faster than a Swede, Bengt Tragardh, and 0.85 seconds faster than Tragardh in the second. In Senna's first qualifying in a Formula 3 car, he broke the lap record.

The race was straight Senna. He judged the start exquisitely and led through the first corner, The Tactic now directly applied to Formula 3. "I kept a close watch in my mirrors to see if anybody was going to do anything stupid under braking." They didn't. Into Campbell [a 90 degree right about half way round] he led Tragardh by a length, came out faster and led through the right-left-right Complex; and was already out of reach. Easy? "Well, I don't know about that. I was just making sure that nothing could go wrong and that I didn't make any mistakes." No lap record? "No, it was impossible in the race. The track was very bad, and also I think the wind was a bit stronger against us on the straight."

- **Podium:** Senna 18m 37.4s, Tragardh at 13.1, Fish at 17.4.
- **Fastest lap:** Senna.

The victory at Hockenheim, and Formula 1 team managers were eyeing him now *Autosport.*

The Senna domination extended into Formula 3 with West Surrey Racing *Autosport*.

Chapter 3

Formula 3

This was the final step before Formula 1. In 1983 Senna would drive for West Surrey. Ralts was the car to have – West Surrey had them. Among others Senna would meet Martin Brundle, an ambitious, fresh-faced young man from Norfolk being run by Eddie Jordan. The Senna versus Brundle combat would reach such a pitch that it attracted attention far beyond the motorsport community. The other front-runners: American Davy Jones, Fish, David Leslie and Dumfries. Fewer strangers would come and go now. This season Senna wished to be known simply as Ayrton Senna; and was, and always will be. Points scoring: 9-6-4-3-2-1 plus 1 for fastest lap.

✳ ✳ ✳

RACE 51

Marlboro British F3 round 1. Silverstone, 6 March 1983.
Qualifying: 53.90 (2); 53.77 (1). Front row.
Pole: Leslie (53.54).
Result: First.

Careful observers noticed that Senna seemed more uptight than at the end of 1982. Bennetts explained it was "just because this is the first race. He's been looking forward to it for a long time and there's quite a lot of pressure on him." Senna was swift around Woodcote and said "I think there is a lot more to come just through putting more miles on the car and improving the set-up." This is the first authentic instance of semi-technical Senna-speak and you'll be hearing much, much more of it. Leslie (in a Magnum) had pole, Jones third, Brundle fourth. *Motoring News* reported that "Senna blotted his copybook slightly with a second lap spin on cold tyres in the first session but he avoided contact with anything and finished 0.36 down on Leslie. Later in the day he would better that time despite the second session being slightly slower for rivals Leslie, Brundle and Fish. The handling balance, according to Bennetts, wasn't quite right but it was pretty close. And it looked

it. Out on the circuit the white car flowed round with barely a twitch."

Leslie and Senna ran wheel-to-wheel to Copse where Senna drove round the outside and led – The Tactic – leaving the others to pick up what they could. "I knew I had to try and pass round the outside but I was worried about the grip on coldish tyres. I kept the power on and the car gripped." He meant he and the car gripped.

- **Podium:** Senna 18m 07.14s, Brundle at 6.43, Jones at 7.26.
- **Fastest lap:** Senna.

RACE 52

Marlboro British F3 round 2. Thruxton, 13 March 1983.
Qualifying: 1:13.46 (1); 1:19.22 (2). Pole.
Result: First.

Before this race Senna tested at Donington and on the full Silverstone Grand Prix circuit and beat the records at both. Now in the first session he broke the record here, and against the 1:13.46 Brundle could come no nearer than 1:13.99. Senna judged the car "not very good. I think it would be possible to make it much better with more time." The second session was wet, the first time Senna had driven Formula 3 in such conditions and Brundle did a 1:19.15, quickest.

The rain stopped before the race and although Senna made a lovely, lovely start – everything right – Brundle matched him and stayed with him. "I could see that I was faster through the corners but I also knew that I had to conserve my tyres. Whoever could make their tyres last longer would win." Senna gained in the corners, Brundle regained on the straights. "My engine would not pull more than 5,600 revs," Senna said. He maximised the art of the possible from that.

- **Podium:** Senna 26m 26.31s, Brundle at 0.83, Mario Hytten at 47.94.
- **Fastest lap:** Brundle.
- **Championship:** Senna 19, Brundle 13, Hytten 6.

RACE 53

Marlboro British F3 round 3. Silverstone, 20 March 1983.
Qualifying: 1:34.74 (1); 1:25.14 (1). Pole.
Result: First.

Although Senna had had a heavy mid-week accident testing at Snetterton he took provisional pole on a wet Saturday morning. Brundle held it for most of the session but, with only a few minutes left, Senna did the 1:34.74. This was another fundamental tactic: wait, watch, monitor, gauge, bring everything to a climax when your opponent can't respond to it. He confirmed pole in a dry afternoon session.

Spotting rain forced nearly everyone onto wet tyres for the race. Senna took an immediate lead, Brundle second but into Becketts Senna adopted a cautiously wide line and Brundle went through. They travelled down Hangar Straight close and Senna overtook on the outside at Stowe. Brundle, honest, described the

The sponsors' logos increased ... *Autosport.*

audacity and control of the move as "quite brilliant." The rain fell heavier by six of the 20 laps. A Finn, Jorma Airaksinen, slithered on the start-finish straight and almost collected Senna, who was lapping him. Senna veered from him. The race was halted and restarted for a further six laps, aggregate to count. Brundle led to a great patriotic cheer but at Becketts Senna braked particularly late and went outside. "Incredible," Brundle said. "He had two wheels on the grass but he still kept going." They emerged, Senna holding the inside for Chapel so that he led down the Hangar Straight. The spray his wheels churned made any overtaking by Brundle beyond the art of the possible, or even probable. On the last lap Senna's fire extinguisher bottle exploded ("bloody cold in there"). He kept on, as he would and as he did.

- **Podium:** Senna 19m 36.51s, Brundle at 1.96, Fish at 7.01.
- **Fastest lap:** Senna.
- **Championship:** Senna 29, Brundle 19, Jones and Fish 7.

RACE 54

Marlboro British F3 round 4. Donington Park, 27 March 1983.
Qualifying: 1:19.66 (1); 1:18.06 (1). Pole.
Result: First.

Drizzle for the first session and Senna had new Avon wet tyres, which evidently the Jordan team couldn't afford. In the afternoon, dry, Senna and Brundle traded times in the last 10 minutes but Senna by 0.13. "It was terrible out there, it was like you were driving on oil all the way."

Dry for the race, Senna and Brundle level but Senna inside for the long Redgate horseshoe and ahead. By lap 4 he'd magnified that to a couple of seconds. Brundle's fourth and fifth gears kept jumping out and he had to hold the lever. It gave him no chance.

- **Podium:** Senna 23m 23.35s, Brundle at 5.63, Jones at 6.36.
- **Fastest lap:** Senna and Jones (1m 09.52).
- **Championship:** Senna 39, Brundle 25, Jones 12.

RACE 55

Marlboro British F3 round 5. Thruxton, 4 April 1983.
Qualifying: 1:13.07 (1); 1:13.80 (3). Pole.
Result: First.

Senna had 'flu and Bennetts wondered about letting him race. "I did not feel good but I was not making mistakes in the car so I felt it was OK. I'm not sure whether I was going as well as I should have done." In these early years he measured himself against himself.

He missed second gear at the start. Jones led, Brundle passed Senna too. Senna muscled Brundle outside at Campbell and they crossed the line in a chain, Jones-Senna-Brundle. Into the chicane on lap 2 Brundle tried a move but Senna resisted that and overtook Jones on lap 3. Irene Ambrose was at the race.

"I made my timid way into the West Surrey awning clutching my entrance ticket, the only bit of paper I had. A slight, darkhaired boy [he was 23!] sat on a couple of wheels, smiling at me as I approached. Feeling ludicrously nervous I thrust the ticket at him and asked for his autograph. The smile deepened and as I gazed into those dark brown eyes I thought they looked very old in such a young face. He controlled the race perfectly and, feeling proud, I made my way into the paddock to congratulate him. He was still grinning widely as he shook my hand and thanked me." If you were an opponent, he was the hardest man in the world to beat. If you weren't, he was touchingly normal. Coyne, for example, "joined Ralph Firmin in 1983 to do FF1600. Ayrton, who knew Ralph well, would come across and sit and talk to me, basically trying to help me, and that was nice. The moment you stopped being a threat he was totally different."

- **Podium:** Senna 25m 03.29s, Brundle at 01.24, Fish at 22.04.
- **Fastest lap:** Brundle.
- **Championship:** Senna 48, Brundle 32, Jones and Hytten 12.

Marlboro British F3 round 6. Silverstone,
24 April 1983.
Qualifying: 53.30 (1); 53.38 (1). Pole.
Result: First.

Senna had been back to Brazil to relax and felt
better. It showed. He beat his own lap record in
both sessions and Brundle, trying to mount a
counter-attack, explained that Senna always
seemed to find a little extra when he needed it.

Brundle led towards Copse but, changing
down, missed a gear and floated into midfield.
He struggled to third and challenged Jones in
the closing laps, Senna alone at the front and
breaking the (official) lap record. Jones once
explained to me: "Although I was as quick as
Senna and Brundle, as a race progressed I might
make a mistake, miss a gear change but those
guys wouldn't. Even at Formula 3 it was a very
high level. For example the old Stowe corner
you took flat out in fourth, you arrived in fifth,
changed down, then flat. Well, Senna wasn't
even lifting, he was flat in fifth."

- **Podium:** Senna 22m 33.59s, Jones at 5.14,
  Brundle at 5.41.
- **Fastest lap:** Senna.
- **Championship:** Senna 58, Brundle 36,
  Jones 18.

Marlboro British F3 round 7. Thruxton,
2 May 1983.
Qualifying: 1:33.55 (1); 1:14.08 (1). Pole.
Result: First.

In the first session Senna could only beat the
existing record by 0.01. It's a strange statement
but true among many strange statements in this
book. Everybody, you see, anticipated he'd beat
it by a lot more. "The wind is making it
impossible to make the car perfect at both the
Complex [after the first bend] and the chicane
[feeding onto the start-finish straight]. That is
why we cannot get near the record, but (and
reportedly he shrugged) it is the same for
everyone." Irene Ambrose sat "in the
grandstand to watch qualifying. He seemed to

The duel with Martin Brundle reached rare heights of intensity although on the podium they behaved
impeccably *Autosport*.

be taking a different line through the chicane each time, getting wilder and wilder until the little Ralt twitched ferociously in protest. After that he became smooth and consistent. 'What were you doing out there?' I asked in my innocence. He was sitting on his tyres again, bent over slightly, hands clasped between his knees. 'Just finding my limits' he said, smiling."

Senna led although a "cautious" exit from the Complex let Brundle close enough to slip-stream throughout the opening lap. Out of Church, a right, Brundle urged himself alongside but that left him with the outside line at the chicane still second. Senna drew away at the end of lap 2 and increased the gap.

- **Podium:** Senna 24m 51.88s, Brundle at 3.40, Jones at 4.07.
- **Fastest lap:** Senna.
- **Championship:** Senna 68, Brundle 42, Jones 22.

RACE 58

Marlboro British F3 round 8. Brands Hatch, 8 May 1983.
Qualifying: 43.35 (1); 43.14 (1). Pole.
Result: First.

Senna was sensational, as it seems, through Paddock Hill Bend in qualifying. "It's right on the limit and I can tell you that it feels quite dangerous." Jeremy Shaw wrote in *Autosport*: "Once, during the second session, he missed his down-change, turning into the corner without any positive drive, but even that presented only a minor problem, the Brazilian sliding wide onto the 'old' circuit [a strip of track running alongside] and quickly bringing the car back under his total control." In both sessions he went under the qualifying record, held by Mansilla at 43.64. Mind you, so did Brundle and Jones and Fish. The pace of progress, no doubt.

A deluge delayed the race. Ambrose and Patey watched the grid where Senna sat in the

Ralt surrounded by Brazilian media and an enormous circle of friends. Ambrose recalls: "The pressure is building and so is the awareness that we will soon lose him to celebrity. We sheltered in the grandstand. Umbrellas blossom above each car. The rain is solid. A minor river is squeegeed off the track in the dip before Druids." Senna emerged from Paddock ahead, Brundle reasoning it would be "silly" to try anything there. Senna wasn't to be caught and insisted the win was his best of the season so far: clean, accomplished, assured. Ambrose and Patey remember that. "The lights changed and the white car carrying the yellow helmet was gone. Sure-footed, supremely confident, the gap opens as if there were no rain, as if the water parts for him, closing behind the Ralt. Everyone else looked in slow motion."

- **Podium:** Senna 17m 21.6s, Brundle at 2.4, Jones at 9.5.
- **Fastest lap:** Senna.
- **Championship:** Senna 78, Brundle 48, Jones 26.

RACE 59

Marlboro British F3 round 9. Silverstone, 30 May 1983.
Qualifying: 53.05 (1); 53.39 (2). Pole.
Result: First.

Senna covered a lot of fast laps in first qualifying, dipping below his own record. He'd been to Brazil again but working for his sponsors, not on holiday.

At the green light he moved decisively and by Copse seemed to have the race at his mercy. Leslie followed him through Copse but his clutch failed and Brundle suffered extreme oversteer. On lap 3 Senna led by two seconds and simply (if you can put it like that) increased it over the 30 laps.

- **Podium:** Senna 27m 00.98s, Brundle at 10.10, Berg at 22.49.
- **Fastest lap:** Senna.
- **Championship:** Senna 88, Brundle 54, Jones 28.

Control and concentration *Autosport*.

Marlboro British F3 round 10/ European F3
Championship round 6. Silverstone,
12 June 1983.
Qualifying: 1:32.27 (1); 1:24.08 (2). Front row.
Pole: Brundle 1:23.99 (1).
Result: Retired after 7 laps, accident.

The nature of the race brought some leading Continentals, including John Nielsen (Denmark), Didier Theys (Belgium), Roberto Ravaglia (Italy) and future Formula 1 drivers Pierluigi Martini, Emanuele Pirro and, qualifying twenty-first, Gerhard Berger. A wet first session but Senna seemed to have pole in the second, dry. However with 15 minutes left Brundle put on a new set of Yokohama tyres and stole it. The significance: the British Championship was restricted to Avon tyres so if you ran Yokohamas you'd opted to take the Continentals on. Senna opted for that, too.

Brundle finished lap 1 with Senna directly behind and pressing, and Dumfries pressing him. On lap 3 Dumfries tried to pass at Stowe. Senna reportedly had gambled on three different compound tyres on the car – against the advice of the Yokohama technicians – in an effort to have a set which would last the 20 laps. This is the first recorded instance of Senna making his own decisions whatever experts counselled.

He soon had over-steer. "After two laps the left rear wasn't working at all. There was just no grip." Dumfries says that "I was alongside him down Hangar Straight and he put me on the grass. It was interesting because he was under pressure from me and he was also trying to catch Brundle." On lap 6 Senna lost control at Club and spun off. He rejoined ninth, took Nielsen and Nissen but went off backwards at Woodcote.

- **Podium (European):** Brundle, Tommy Byrne, Theys.
- **Podium (British):** Allen Berg, Jones, Fish.
- **Fastest lap:** Dumfries.
- **Championship:** Senna 88, Brundle 54, Jones 35.

Senna wins a round of the British F3 championship at Silverstone in April. That's former World Champion Alan Jones behind *Autosport*.

Marlboro British F3 round 11. Cadwell Park,
19 June 1983.
Qualifying: 1:22.57 (1); did not take part.
Pole: Brundle 1:22.58.
Result: Did not start race.

In first qualifying Senna and Brundle duelled and were within that fraction of each other – 0.01 – but, lapping a second under Mansilla's year-old record, Senna "strayed slightly wide onto the grass exiting the right-hander at the foot of the hill. He kept the power on in an effort to regain the track but simply ran out of road and smashed virtually headlong into the marshals' post at the top. His car was a sorry mess indeed and both he and the nearby marshals, one of whom was treated for bruises and shock, were most fortunate not to be hurt" (*Autosport*). Here, ultimately and perhaps inevitably, was a single question: could Senna take the heat he himself generated? He'd habitually laid it on others. Eddie Jordan, arch-psychologist, had been exerting his formidable powers of persuasion on Brundle and Brundle was responding.

- **Podium:** Brundle, Fish, Jones.
- **Fastest lap:** Brundle.
- **Championship:** Senna 88, Brundle 64, Jones 39.

Mysterious, because Senna was not on the front row, and that hadn't happened in 1983 before. "I don't know what is wrong. We have changed many things and yet there is no real improvement."

Brundle led at the green light. Dumfries had crashed in qualifying and Senna, lined up on the grid behind where Dumfries would have been, enjoyed a clear run. He was quickly up to Brundle, Jones third. Brundle consolidated but Senna worked nearer and nearer and at lap 12 was within six metres. Brundle held him there. It might have been a major turning point; and was. Out of Sear on the twenty-fourth lap (of the 25) Brundle firmly kept the inside line. They moved along the straight with Senna "oh so slowly creeping up on the inside [to the Esses] with two wheels off the main tarmac throwing dust and stones at Jones" *(Autosport)*. Into the left-hand kink Brundle moved onto the racing line but Senna "still had his foot flat to the floor with two wheels off the track and bouncing in the dirt." Senna's front wheel ran over Brundle's rear which sent Senna "into a high-speed spin across" Jones and backwards into the barrier. A pure racing accident, or the question: could he take the heat?

- **Podium:** Brundle, Jones, Fish.
- **Fastest lap:** Senna.
- **Championship:** Senna 89, Brundle 73, Jones 45.

Senna tested before the meeting and the car was "much more consistent." After the first session the team changed the set-up and he took the pole by 0.04.

Brundle accelerated fractionally ahead but Senna took the inside at Copse and wielded The Tactic. He rattled and rode the kerbs, Brundle hanging on. After two laps the gap stood at a second, Brundle reasoning that because he hadn't taken the lead he'd follow for 10 laps to see if Senna's tyres went off. They drew away from the main bunch but Brundle was briefly baulked by a back-marker and, a lap later, Brundle lost more time when Senna thrust inside two back-markers at the chicane, obliging Brundle to follow them. It created a gap Brundle could not close. You are entitled to wonder if Senna came upon these back-markers and simply despatched them or if he calculated precisely when to overtake them, knowing Brundle must thread through the chicane behind them. Certainly Senna did this in Formula 1, another tactic.

- **Podium:** Senna 28m 59.55s, Brundle at 1.61, Fish at 19.03.
- **Fastest lap:** Senna.
- **Championship:** Senna 99, Brundle 79, Jones 45.

A dry first session proved decisive. "We had been out on old tyres at the beginning and I was just getting the car balanced. Then we put on some new tyres and I went out and set a time. On the second lap I was already in pole position." A dry-wet second session left it undisturbed.

Brundle made an incisive start and commanded Redgate, Jones hard in third. Now Brundle had to handle the heat. On lap 8 he made a supreme effort to shed Senna and squeezed a gap of a second but Senna closed and set fastest lap. Brundle kept his nerve.

- **Podium:** Brundle 35m 09.21s, Senna at 00.40, Jones at 03.17.
- **Fastest lap:** Senna.
- **Championship:** Senna 106, Brundle 88, Jones 49.

Marlboro British F3 round 15. Oulton Park,
6 August 1983.
Qualifying: 57.38 (2); 57.43 (1). Front row.
Pole: Brundle 57.04.
Result: Retired after 28 laps, accident.

Senna crashed heavily in testing on the Thursday – the rear stub axle failed at Druids – and that brought extensive work before Saturday qualifying. After the first session Senna confessed that the car was "very difficult to drive. Very dangerous. I couldn't drive it on the limit." The weather warmed for second qualifying, precluding improvement despite a "heart-stopping" moment when he braked too late.

Brundle and Senna went hard and banged wheels. Maybe that set the tone. Brundle led Senna by a whisker crossing the line to complete the opening lap but Brundle had problems braking. They moved like a concertina. On lap 28 Senna decided to make a move. "I went right up his gearbox into Cascades and I was going much quicker than him. I braked late and went for the inside. I'm sure he didn't see me and he closed in on me when we were already going into the corner." They met, Senna's car riding over Brundle's as they came to rest off the circuit. The heat was burning now.

• **Podium:** Fish, Jones, Berg.
• **Fastest lap:** Senna.
• **Championship:** Senna 107, Brundle 88, Jones 55.

In fact, winning was a familiar feeling *Autosport.*

The shoot-out race at Thruxton. Senna (left) takes an immediate lead from Brundle, Davy Jones (No 1) looking for a way between them *Autosport*

Marlboro British F3 round 16. Silverstone,
29 August 1983.
Qualifying: 53.18 (1); 53.43 (2). Pole.
Result: First.

Senna managed a couple of days testing with the
repaired car. "It is exactly the same as the last
race here." Is it perfect? "No, no but quite close.
I can't see any way to make it much better. The
others are catching up. The cars are very evenly
matched." This is the first recorded instance of
Senna speaking publicly of perfection and how
elusive that might be. His judgement about the
cars being matched was confirmed in first
qualifying with the top six recording laps of 53
seconds and doing it again in the second session.

Senna forced a small lead from Brundle by
Copse before they reached "stalemate," Senna
stretching on the straight (this the Club circuit)
to prevent Brundle trying a move at Woodcote.

- **Podium:** Senna 27m 02.45s, Brundle at 1.44,
  Jones at 2.83.
- **Fastest lap:** Jones.
- **Championship:** Senna 116, Brundle 94, Jones 60.

Marlboro British F3 round 17. Oulton Park,
11 September 1983.
Qualifying: 59.62 (1); 57.24 (1). Pole.
Result: Retired after 7 laps, accident.

Pole turned on the second session, in drying
conditions. Senna explored the track surface and
after 15 minutes pitted for slick tyres. He
couldn't get a clear lap but he did get pole,
Brundle 57.30.

Brundle led, Senna pressing, Jones third. On
lap 8 Senna made his move, outside at Druids. It
took him inevitably off the racing line and he
lost adhesion, slithered into the barrier. That
crumpled the front of the car.

- **Podium:** Brundle, Fish, Leslie.
- **Fastest lap:** Jones.
- **Championship:** Senna 116, Brundle 103, Jones 61.

Marlboro British F3 round 18. Thruxton,
18 September 1983.
Qualifying: 1:17.79 (1); 1:14.01 (1). Pole.
Result: Retired after 2 laps, engine.

Senna had a new car and could have taken the
championship but complained of lack of
balance, a word we shall hear again and again.
The statement, however, was the sort which
always made Senna disconcerting to work with.
He had, after all, just taken pole.

Brundle led but *Motoring News* reported
that "into the Complex he was shadowed very
closely by Senna and promptly locked a wheel in
his eagerness to get round. 'I out-braked myself
and he was alongside.' From a spectator's point
of view, a collision looked more than vaguely
possible as the two went at it hammer and tongs
around the Complex, Brundle deciding to play
safe and settling into second." On this opening
lap, approaching the chicane, Brundle took the
outside line, Berg full on Senna. Because he was
resisting so strongly, Senna went off line through
the chicane and Brundle had him on the exit.
Then Senna's engine let go, a blown head
gasket.

- **Podium:** Brundle, Jones, Fish.
- **Fastest lap:** Brundle.
- **Championship:** Senna 116, Brundle 113,
  Jones 67.

Marlboro British F3 round 19. Silverstone,
2 October 1983.
Qualifying: 1:30.62 (4); 1:35.44 (1). Row 2.
Pole: Jones 1:29.16.
Result: Second.

The real heat now. Drizzle fell at the beginning
of the first session and Jones, emerging from the
pits immediately, set a time. Senna, towards the
back of a line of cars coming out, only reached
the track as Jones completed his lap. The drizzle
hardened and it was already too late. On
Senna's second lap he lost control at Abbey. The

car spun wildly across the track and nudged the barrier backwards. No improvement in the second session in the wet. "There was no point in trying really hard but I kept going. The car was OK but not really good."

Jones crept the start and missed third gear, Brundle into the lead from Senna. At half distance the gap was no more than 1.5 seconds. They lapped back-markers and Senna drew up. On the last lap he made a lunge at Becketts but rather than risk another crash tucked in behind again. Advantage Brundle.

- **Podium:** Brundle 28m 55.23s, Senna at 0.64, Jones at 17.16.
- **Fastest lap:** Brundle.
- **Championship:** Brundle 123, Senna 122, Jones 71.

RACE 70

Marlboro British F3 round 20. Thruxton, 23 October 1983.
Qualifying: 1:13.55 (1); 1:13.36 (1). Pole.
Result: First.

The shootout, all to gain and all to lose. Irene Ambrose "knew he was going to win and I wanted to be there. It involved getting into London at the crack of dawn, getting a train to Andover, switching to a branch line 'somewhere in Hamphire' and the very long slog, dodging traffic down windy country roads to the circuit. The day went quickly..."

The first session lasted no more than 10 minutes because mist hung over the circuit and the session didn't begin until 9.20. It had to end at 9.30 because by convention no cars ran during Sunday service at a local church. Before the church bells rang, Senna pitted, Bennetts adjusted the wings and Senna had time for the "scorching" provisional pole. "I came across a couple of cars stopped at the Complex on the lap and although the car felt good it wasn't perfect for the conditions." The temperature rose for the second session, Senna and Brundle (third overall) improving.

The race proved anti-climactic, Senna making a vast start to lead by two lengths from Jones by the Complex, Jones holding Brundle back. *Motoring News* reported that "the Brazilian quite simply buckled straight down to the job and began to pull away in a relaxed fashion. Bothered by nothing mechanical or human, Senna swiftly vanished into the blue yonder." Behind this lay a potent ploy which almost cost everything.

Senna's team had taped over the oil radiator outlet to heat the oil more quickly, giving Senna a chance to wield The Tactic. "It was perfect. The oil was up to proper temperature within a lap or so rather than the usual six or seven." On lap 6, as anticipated, the water temperature climbed. Senna loosened his seat belts enough to reach out with his right arm and tear the tape away.

He'd practiced this the week before. "By the time I looked back up I was almost at the chicane. I thought I had lost it for a minute. All of a sudden I was not part of the car. I was sliding around inside. It was quite hairy." (Ambrose remembers the tape over the radiator incident. She wondered *what is he doing?* but "assumed he knew"). He got through the chicane and, as he did, settled the race and the championship. He hammered out a lead of seven seconds over Jones, with Brundle – down on power – powerless in third. "Everything was under control from the start."

Ambrose went to the West Surrey truck and "it was getting dark. Eventually I got my chance and dived in to congratulate him on his victory. Anyone who ever glibly said he was cold or unfeeling should have seen him that evening. He was as genuinely overwhelmed as anyone I have ever seen. As I trudged out of the circuit I was torn between awe and the elation of knowing I'd witnessed history being made – and being grateful for it – and the knowledge that with Formula 1 beckoning it could never be the same again."

- **Podium:** Senna 18m 39.78s, Jones at 5.43, Brundle at 8.53.
- **Fastest lap:** Senna.
- **Championship:** Senna 132, Brundle 127 (123 counting), Jones 77.

Macau Grand Prix, Macau,
20 November 1983.
Qualifying: 2m 23.47 (2); 2m 22.02 (1). Pole.
Result: First.

This was described as "the World Championship" of Formula 3. Senna had not confronted a street circuit so far and arrived only the night before the meeting began. Would jet-lag weaken him? Roberto Guerrero, a Grand Prix driver, went quickest in the first session. After three laps Senna had been third quickest before wrecking all four wheels in two brushes with the barriers. In the second session he bent a gear selector but the session was red flagged and that gave time for repairs. In three more laps Senna had pole.

He dominated the two heats (aggregate counting) with The Tactic. Interestingly he led the opening lap of both heats by 2.5 seconds. Senna's precision or coincidence? Senna's precision, surely. In the first heat, Guerrero assumed he'd be safe if he took the initial corner tight and he did take it tight. Then Senna "came past me down the alley between the two corners. I couldn't believe what he was able to do on cold tyres," Guerrero said. (Ambrose "stood outside a TV shop in Tottenham Court Road, London, for about half an hour watching Senna win Macau. I walked away with a sense of rightness I experienced so many times later.") There's a charming anecdote about the fastest lap, initially awarded to Berger who felt sure he hadn't done it and checked. He found Senna had, of course, and they fell to talking about that. It was the first time they had spoken. The beginnings of a friendship were born there and it endured. Gerhard Berger was among the last people to see Ayrton Senna alive.

- **Heat 1:** Senna 35m 44.65s, Guerrero at 06.00, Berger at 20.83.
- **Heat 2:** Senna 35m 50.31s, Guerrero at 01.32, Berger at 16.85.
- **Podium:** Senna 1h 11m 34.96s, Guerrero at 7.32, Berger at 1m 14.38.
- **Fastest lap:** Senna, both heats.

Mastery at Macau. Dick Bennetts, running West Surrey Racing, is standing on the right *Autosport*.

Senna at his first Grand Prix, Brazil 1984 *Formula One Pictures*.

Chapter 4

Toleman

Ayrton Senna signed for the Toleman Formula 1 team on Friday 9 December 1983. He'd tested a Williams, a McLaren and a Brabham but only Toleman made an offer. Once he'd signed he flew immediately to Brazil in search of sponsorship.

Toleman were small, ambitious and enthusiastic. Under team director Alex Hawkridge they'd won the European Formula 2 Championship in 1980 and entered Formula 1 in 1981 with Brian Henton and Derek Warwick. In 1984 Johnny Cecotto, World 350cc motor bike champion in 1975 and who had been driving for the Theodore team, would partner Senna.

Toleman were powered by Hart engines and initially ran Pirelli tyres.

The other front-runners: Niki Lauda and Alain Prost (Marlboro McLaren), Piquet (Brabham), Rosberg (Williams), de Angelis and Nigel Mansell (Lotus), Michele Alboreto and Rene Arnoux (Ferrari), Warwick and Patrick Tambay (Renault).

✳ ✳ ✳

RACE 72

Brazil, Rio, 25 March 1984
Qualifying: 1:36.867 (21); 1:33.525 (17). Row 8.
Pole: de Angelis 1:28.392.
Race weather: hot, dry.
Warm-up: 1:39.746 (12).
Result: Retired after 8 laps, turbo.

It began modestly, almost flawed, this problematic and intensively complex journey towards mastering Formula 1. Senna could cope with the Toleman in all its aspects but in qualifying he met a problem he could not control. Sustained speed chewed chunks of tread from the Pirellis and if you cannot deal in sustained speed what can you deal in? That partially modified his delight at making his F1 debut in Brazil and, by a pragmatic organisation of his entry passes, he enabled his family to have access to the pits. That shared the delight. He qualified as well as he could, not good, not bad. Truly, modestly.

A brief race, a vignette easily unseen. He gained four places on the opening lap and, for the record, this opening lap of so many lasted

one minute 51.452 seconds. What he achieved pointed towards the future as it confirmed the present, but under the sheer pace he fell away: fourteenth on laps 2 and 3, fifteenth on 4, 5 and 6, sixteenth on 7 before the turbo choked and he fell into an abyss, twenty-fourth on lap 8. In the race history of Senna, this represented something – and nothing.

- **Podium:** Prost, Rosberg, de Angelis.
- **Fastest lap:** Prost 1:36.499.
- **Senna:** 1:42.286.

RACE 73

South Africa, Kyalami, 7 April 1984
Qualifying: 1:07.657 (14); 1:06.981 (11). Row 7.
Pole: Piquet 1:04.871.
Race weather: hot, dry.
Warm-up: 1:11.944 (14).
Result: Sixth.

Senna judged that "overall, the car feels pretty good here." After the Friday session he estimated he'd go seven-tenths quicker on the morrow. This is the first recorded instance of

Senna's ability to predict exactly what he could do in Formula 1. And next day he did it. Moreover he risked a prophecy, itself unusual in your second Grand Prix with a little team. "If we have no mechanical problems I'm quite confident we can finish in the points." You can read that as bravado, as driver-speak, and that would be a mistake. When he spoke he had his reasons.

Early in the race a sliver of the Toleman's nose cone loosened and wrenched off but he slogged forward feeling how the car handled without it and he made his decision. Better to live with it than sacrifice time pitting for repairs. No magical, mystical decision, a simple calculation but one he already felt confident enough to make. From fifteenth on the opening lap he ran solidly in sixteenth, no matter that the leader, Lauda, lapped him on 25. Senna wasn't in the Lauda world yet, and knew. Retirements mounted and he rose to ninth on lap 42 to unlapping himself on 49, being lapped again on 53. He understood the rhythm method, replicating laps at one minute 13 seconds and, with profound exhaustion sweating his strength into childlike weakness, summoned a 1:12 on his final lap. He was three laps down. Preconceived perceptions of the spoilt Latin who played by mood and temperament and whim were disproved, perhaps forever: Senna gouged a finish and had to be helped from the cockpit by mechanics. He was taken to hospital with dehydration. He might be anything – nobody knew yet – but he could wring completion from himself. He looked a slight man, too slender to manacle a bronco and restrain it for an hour and a half – but he'd just done that, against his own body.

- **Podium:** Lauda, Prost, Warwick.
- **Fastest lap:** Tambay 1:08.877.
- **Senna:** 1:12.124.

The Toleman-Hart on the grid *Formula One Pictures*.

Belgium, Zolder, 29 April 1984.
Qualifying: 1:18.914 (15); 1:18.876 (18). Row 10.
Pole: Alboreto 1:14.846.
Race weather: sunny.
Warm-up: 1:21.282 (14).
Result: Sixth.

A difficult qualifying. He managed only two laps on the Friday, an electrical problem in the morning session forcing the spare car to be readied and used. Next day a misfire coughed and, worse, a back pain stabbed – he'd hurt himself testing.

He got the start wrong, completing the opening lap twenty-fourth, only Jonathan Palmer (RAM) and Mauro Baldi (Spirit) behind. He set himself to a long flog again: lap 2 twenty-third; lap 3 twenty-second; lap 5 twenty-first; lap 9 eighteenth; lap 12 seventeenth; lap 35 fifteenth (pit stop); lap 40 thirteenth; lap 43 eleventh; lap 50 tenth; lap 52 ninth; lap 59 eighth; lap 67 seventh, which he held to the end. Stefan Bellof (Tyrrell), sixth, subsequently had his points confiscated (as all Tyrrell's points were over the season because the FIA Court of Appeal ruled the team guilty of fuel irregularities). It elevated Senna to sixth and another point.

- **Podium:** Alboreto, Warwick, Arnoux.
- **Fastest lap:** Arnoux 1:19.294.
- **Senna:** 1:22.633.

Team-mates, 1984. Johnny Cecotto was injured at Brands Hatch *Formula One Pictures*.

San Marino, Imola, 6 May 1984.
Qualifying: did not run; 1:41.585 (26).
Result: Did not qualify.

The way it goes. Just when you think you're building nicely somebody shifts the foundation. Toleman were in open dispute with Pirelli over money. Hence neither Senna nor Cecotto had tyres on the Friday. Senna was new to Imola and rain fell during the Saturday morning untimed session, giving him a minimum chance to learn it. In the afternoon "I suffered a problem with the fuel system. The car just wasn't working at all, the engine misfiring all the time." He covered 10 laps, the 1:41.585 coming on the eighth. It left him a chasm away from qualifying for the race. This is the first instance of such a thing. It will be the last instance of such a thing.

Toleman were changing to Michelin tyres. ("I was not upset that we changed, I was upset that we didn't have the opportunity to race in Imola. I was upset for that but it was a good decision because the Michelin tyre was the better tyre.") On the Monday Senna tested the Toleman with Michelins at Dijon. He covered a full race distance and spoke of Toleman's decision as "fully justified." Hawkridge once told me that within five laps Senna told *him* "we're on the pace."

Stefan Johansson took over from Cecotto late in the season *Formula One Pictures*.

RACE 76

Mercedes-Benz Cup, Nurburgring, 12 May 1984.
No qualifying
Race weather: murky.
Result: First.

The old immortal Nurburgring had had a new circuit superimposed, or rather added, and to celebrate the opening of it Mercedes-Benz – who that week unveiled their 190 saloon – invited 20 drivers to compete in a twelve-lap race. They were Klaus Ludwig, Senna, Lauda, Prost, John Watson, Rosberg (World Champion 1982), Laffite, de Angelis, James Hunt (World Champion 1976), Jody Scheckter (World Champion 1979), Stirling Moss (the greatest driver never to win the championship), Jack Brabham (World Champion 1959, 1960, 1966), Phil Hill (World Champion 1961), Denny Hulme (World Champion 1967), John Surtees (World Champion 1964), Hans Herrmann (who'd driven 18 Grands Prix between 1953 and 1966), Carlos Reutemann (who'd driven 146 Grands Prix between 1972 and 1982), Manfred Schurti, Udo Schutz and Alan Jones (World Champion 1980).

A fun race, surely. *Autosport* reported that "everyone behaved for at least one lap but then it was discovered that the ess-bend after the pit straight was much more fun if you drove across it rather than round it! Several people adopted this wheeze, some accidentally and some 'accidentally.'" Reutemann took an early lead from Jones, who dropped out after three laps. Senna moved up and took Reutemann before he came under sustained pressure from Lauda, Watson and Scheckter. He held on. Some drivers did go out to have fun but beyond question Senna saw this seemingly innocuous occasion as a chance to announce himself by beating so many champions.

- **Podium:** Senna 26m 57.7s, Lauda at 1.4, Reutemann at 3.7.
- **Fastest lap** Scheckter.

RACE 77

France, Dijon, 20 May 1984.
Qualifying: 1:05.744 (13); 1:28.225 (16). Row 7.
Pole: Tambay 1:02.200.
Race weather: overcast.
Warm-up: 1:09.530 (14).
Result: Retired after 35 laps, turbo.

Toleman introduced their new car and on the Friday Senna said "really you cannot compare it with the old one. It seemed to me that I could gain on anybody through the corners but we lose out on power up the hill and onto the straight past the pits." A wet Saturday and Michelin gave Toleman their oldest (and certainly slowest) rain compound tyres. Senna could make no further evaluation of the car's potential with them.

The race is quickly told, Senna twelfth, rising to ninth when the turbo failed. It was true and remains true that Senna had an unremarkable, meagre French Grand Prix, his doings obscured in the groundswell of Lauda tightening up to Prost in the championship. Senna was a young man with an undetermined future. He would reach out and seize the future in exactly 14 days and never let go. He would bring the perception of himself into the present tense.

- **Podium:** Lauda, Tambay, Mansell.
- **Fastest lap:** Prost 1:05.257.
- **Senna:** 1:10.100.

The United States Grand Prix at Dallas was hot, very hot.

RACE 78

Monaco, Monte Carlo, 3 June 1984.
Qualifying: 1:27.865 (15); 1:25.009 (13). Row 7.
Pole: Prost 1:22.661.
Race weather: heavy rain.
Warm-up: 1:59.892 (7).
Result: Second.

It's the wrong place for a motor race and everybody knows that. It's the right place for a motor race for the wrong reasons and everybody knows that, too. Monaco is contradictions. Most racing folk dislike every cramped, hostile inch of it but it remains an extreme examination of a driver, not least in his accuracy. Brian Hart produced a new engine management system which gave, Senna insisted, better response but not more power. Early in first qualifying he made a mistake and thumped a barrier, wrecking the car's suspension. He retreated to the spare. Overall he covered 16 laps, setting his best time on the eighth. Next day, learning and absorbing, he covered 25 laps – more than anyone else.

A vicious rain fell on race day, three cars gone on the opening lap: Warwick and Tambay (crash) and Andrea de Cesaris (Ligier/accident damage). Completing that lap Senna was up to ninth. Prost, loathing the wet, led from Mansell but on lap 11 Mansell overtook him before he skimmed into the barrier. By then Senna lay third, catching Prost at a vast rate.

	Prost	Senna
Lap 13	1:58.234	1:56.280
Lap 14	1:58.130	1:56.596
Lap 15	1:58.462	1:57.181

Senna had taken 12 laps to reach the 1:56's – he'd been running regular 1:58's – because the car was extremely difficult with full turbo boost. In the deluge, and overtaking people, Senna simultaneously examined this problem and reached a solution. Progressively he turned the boost down until it was completely off. On lap 16: Prost, Lauda, Senna, who caught Lauda by lap 18. On the start-finish 'straight' Senna placed the Toleman exquisitely to Lauda's left – no matter that he could barely see in the spray – and sliced by. Lauda would write (in *To Hell*

An entirely new type of challenge. Senna samples the Joest Porsche at the Nurburgring, the only time he'd drive a big sportscar competitively. *Autosport.*

and Back) that while overtaking Arnoux on lap 6 "I hang on tightly behind him in the Mirabeau and move out to his left coming up to the next corner...I brake later...I still have to cope with my excess speed. Braking so late puts me into a skid." Near the barrier the "tyres grip again...and Arnoux is behind me. After pulling off a manoeuvre like that, it is criminal to throw away the points. I am in second position, behind Prost. I have to let Senna past..."

At lap 16 the Prost-Senna gap had been 30.102. Senna cut that to 26.141 in ten laps. Lauda meanwhile spun out, Bellof hunting Senna as Senna hunted Prost.

	Prost	Senna	*Gap*
Lap 27	1:59.669	1:55.232	*21.704*
Lap 28	2:00.193	1:56.628	*18.139*
Lap 29	1:59.436	1:56.666	*15.369*
Lap 30	2.02.598	1:59.008	*11.779*

As Prost passed the pits, he gesticulated towards the front of the car indicating a brake problem. "It might have looked easy from the outside," Prost said, "but in the cockpit it was hell. The rain, big problems with the brakes, Senna and his Toleman/Hart on my heels – I was on the limit everywhere."

	Prost	Senna	*Gap*
Lap 31	2:03.766	1:59.433	*7.446*

At this point the race director, Jacky Ickx, decided enough was enough. It proved a highly controversial decision to stop the race and caused much dark muttering, Prost French, Monaco all but French. (Years later Ickx defended the decision to me by pointing out that it was taken on the overall situation, nothing to do with Senna catching Prost. In the control room Ickx had a bank of TV monitors covering the course and he'd seen too many cars spinning too often.) An irony, however. If Senna had caught Prost, Prost had decided not to resist. And a further irony. Completing lap 32 Prost slowed his McLaren at the start-finish line, Senna passing it at full bore a couple of seconds later thinking *I've won*. The race had officially ended at the completion of lap 31.

There are differing accounts of Senna's mood afterwards. One describes him as "furious" although Hawkridge insists Senna wasn't furious enough to get out and kick the car. Senna later judged that the circumstances of the second place made the world's perception of him much sharper than if it had been an ordinary win. Anyway, he'd entered the present tense and we'd entered The Senna Era.

- **Podium:** Prost 1h 1m 7.740s, Senna at 7.446, Bellof at 21.141 (later disqualified).
- **Fastest lap:** Senna 1:54.334.

RACE 79

Canada, Montreal, 17 June 1984.
Qualifying: 1:29.282 (9); 1:27.448 (9). Row 5.
Pole: Piquet 1:25.442.
Race weather: hot, dry.
Warm-up: 1:33.062 (12).
Result: Seventh.

Nigel Roebuck wrote in *Autosport*: "Only a fraction slower than the second McLaren (Lauda) was the first Toleman/Hart, Ayrton Senna qualifying in the top 10 for the first time. As in Monte Carlo, the Brazilian – who now appears to be on the shopping list of every team manager in the business – ran with the Hart engine management system on the opening day, reverting to normal mechanical injection thereafter. If we accept that the Hart engine does not have the power of BMW, Renault or Ferrari then it becomes clear – in the light of Ayrton's overall lap time – that the TG184 chassis is working extremely well. Into corners Senna looked as quick as Prost, with the same fluent ease that we see from the Frenchman. Ninth, on yet another new circuit to him, was a superb performance and he finished up four clear seconds faster than Johnny Cecotto."

In the race Senna rose to sixth on lap 15, fell back to ninth, rose to seventh but two laps adrift of the winner.

- **Podium:** Piquet, Lauda, Prost.
- **Fastest lap:** Piquet 1:28.763. Senna 1:31.822.

During the Saturday morning session at the British Grand Prix, Brands Hatch, Senna had a spectacular turbo fire at Clearways. He got the car back to the pits and directed operations *Zooom*.

USA-East, Detroit, 24 June 1984.
Qualifying: 1:47.188 (7); 1:42.651 (7). Row 4.
Pole: Piquet 1:40.980.
Race weather: hot, dry.
Warm-up: 1:49.347 (9).
Result: Retired after 21 laps, accident.

A fraught practice. On the Friday, Senna clipped the kerbing on the entry to the chicane before the pits. It looked nasty, a flash fire and the Toleman bouncing from barrier to barrier like a pinball. The rear of the car took most of the impact. Toleman repaired it overnight and Senna used it again for the seventh place, his highest in any qualifying so far. Meanwhile Toleman kept the car with the management system – the only car they had with it – for the race.

A multiple-crash at the start, Piquet striking a wall and wrenching his right front wheel off. It flew towards Senna, who was accelerating, and landed on the Toleman with such ferocity that it wrecked the front suspension. Senna took the spare to the re-start and ran tenth for 13 laps, up to eighth by lap 20 but skimmed the tyre wall into turn one.

- **Podium:** Piquet, Brundle (later disqualified), de Angelis.
- **Fastest lap:** Warwick 1:46.221.
- **Senna:** 1:47.444.

RACE 81

USA, Dallas, 8 July 1984.
Qualifying: 1:38.256 (5); did not run. Row 3.
Pole: Mansell 1:37.041.
Race weather: hot, dry.
No warm-up session.
Result: Retired after 48 laps, driveshaft.

Second qualifying, did not run? Ah, a story about that. On the Friday the track began to break up under immense heat – over 100 degrees, so hot the Toleman mechanics poured ice cubes into Senna's overalls. He covered 10 laps, three of them fast. In the Saturday morning untimed session "I didn't tighten my helmet strap enough in the pits and when I went out the helmet slipped over my eyes the first

time I braked hard! In those circumstances, I preferred to go down the escape road." By second qualifying the track surface was disintegrating. Senna changed into his overalls and made his way towards the car. Peter Gethin, the Toleman team manager, decided neither Senna nor Cecotto should go out. Hawkridge explained that, as team manager, Gethin made the decisions. Senna replied, as Hawkridge remembers, "well, if you don't change it I'll act accordingly" – a veiled threat to leave Toleman. Senna defended his desire to go out by saying he'd driven the circuit that morning and who knew the conditions better than he? He added that he felt the decision had been put to him as an order rather than after reasoned discussion. It created a tension, never resolved.

Senna completed the opening lap fourth but hit a wall next lap and pitted for tyres, dropping him to twenty-first. Nine laps later he hit a wall again, pitted and ran last until lap 38 when he overtook Palmer. By lap 47 he'd taken Manfred Winkelhock (ATS). Then the driveshaft failed. There's a strange footnote, all unseen. For most of the race Senna had undone his seat belts – those around the crotch were too tight, affecting his circulation and making his legs feel numb. He explained that it was a risk, of course, but after all he'd been taking it "comparatively easy" down the field.

- **Podium:** Rosberg, Arnoux, de Angelis.
- **Fastest lap:** Lauda 1:45.353.
- **Senna:** 1:46.419.

Despite Cecotto's crash – which upset Senna visibly – he was disciplined enough to finish third at Brands Hatch.

RACE 82

World Sportscar Championship round 4.
Nurburgring, 15 July 1984. Partnering Stefan
Johansson and Henri Pescarolo.
Qualifying: 1:32.07 (9); 1:37.27 (6).
Pole: Bellof/Derek Bell 1:28.68.
Race weather: becoming wet.
Result: Eighth.

Senna told a friend he'd like to try sportscar
racing and the friend organised it with Reinhold
Joest, who ran the Joest Racing Porsche 956
team. Senna arrived as a complete stranger to
this team and this branch of the sport. While
Johansson and Pescarolo monopolised
qualifying in the dry, Senna had a go in the wet
and, according to folklore, completed his first
lap, came in and asked what all the dashboard
dials meant! He also found the Porsche lighter
than he expected. (Joest says that there were
many similarities with a Formula 1 car.) Senna
set a quick time in the wet.

A wet race, too, the car had problems and
Senna couldn't run full boost when his turn at
the wheel came, which Joest judges a prudent
thing – although Joest still savours Senna
overtaking another car on the outside. They lost
eight laps in the pits when the clutch failed and
the car ran twelfth, water on the electrics,
finished 10 laps behind the leaders.

• **Podium:** Bell/Bellof, Thierry Boutsen/David Hobbs,
Sandro Nannini/Paolo Barilla.

RACE 83

Britain, Brands Hatch, 22 July 1984.
Qualifying: 1:11.890 (4); 1:13.991 (13). Row 4.
Pole: Piquet 1:10.869.
Race weather: hot, dry.
Warm-up: 1:16.256 (8).
Result: Third.

Ten minutes into the Friday morning session
Cecotto struck a guardrail virtually head on, a
crash which Senna saw. Cecotto sat trapped in
the car, his legs mauled. Senna returned to the
pits and his face betrayed his feelings, no words
necessary. The session did not resume for more
than an hour and when it did Senna went

One of the great panoramas of Grand Prix racing: the rise to Druids at Brands Hatch *Zooom*.

fastest. On the Saturday morning he had a turbo fire going into Clearways and in the afternoon couldn't sustain his Friday pace.

Within five laps Senna was sixth, cutting past Mansell and Alboreto, but Palmer crashed, halting the race. The re-start: aggregate times to count and grid positions as when it had been stopped. Senna overtook Alboreto again and ran seventh to lap 34 when Tambay pitted. It made him sixth. He settled to a long pursuit of those immediately ahead.

	Warwick	de Angelis	Senna
Lap 35	1:16.398	1:15.527	1:16.212
Lap 36	1:15.325	1:14.646	1:15.081
Lap 37	1:15.845	1:15.731	1:15.703
Lap 38	1:16.354	1:15.005	1:15.487

This lasted until lap 66 when Senna overtook de Angelis at Paddock. Prost, leading, retired on lap 38, gearbox, so Senna became fourth the instant he dealt with de Angelis. On lap 67 Piquet toured, the turbo gone, Senna third. Only he and Warwick finished on the same lap as Lauda.

- **Podium:** Lauda 1h 29m 28.532s,
  Warwick at 42.123, Senna at 1m 03.328.

- **Fastest lap:** Lauda 1:13.191.
- **Senna:** 1:13.951.

RACE 84

Germany, Hockenheim, 5 August 1984.
Qualifying: 1:49.395 (5); 1:49.831 (9). Row 5.
Pole: Prost 1:47.012.
Race weather: dry.
Warm-up: 1:58.553 (2).
Result: Retired after 4 laps, accident.

Rumours abounded that Lotus wanted Senna and these intensified over the weekend. Had he actually signed? Neither Senna nor Lotus would comment but it deepened the tension. Senna did not permit this to affect his driving, although on the Saturday the engine was 1000 revs adrift and he could do no more than the fifth row.

On the second lap he moved smoothly past Tambay and ran fifth for the next three laps. Approaching the first chicane on lap 5 Tambay saw the Toleman's rear bodywork fail. "I couldn't tell what happened," Senna said. "I was flat in fifth but the speed was steady, not accelerating. Then I felt something happen behind me. I didn't want to brake hard to unsettle the car but it spun anyway, twice. Then I was off the road and into the guardrail, sliding

The podium at Brands: Niki Lauda, who won, has his arm raised by Senna while Derek Warwick, second, looks pleased, too *Autosport*.

along it, and the car just wouldn't stop. It seemed to go on and on. A real pity because it felt fabulous in the race, really quick."

- **Podium:** Prost, Lauda, Warwick.
- **Fastest lap:** Prost 1:53.538.
- **Senna:** 1:55.712.

RACE 85

Austria, Osterreichring, 19 August 1984.
Qualifying: 1:29.463 (10); 1:29.200 (10). Row 5.
Pole: Piquet 1:26.173.
Race weather: warm, dry.
Warm-up: 1:32.978 (6)
Result: Retired after 35 laps, engine.

In both qualifying sessions Senna's car was down on revs despite having larger turbos. In direct comparison, for example, Piquet's speed crossing the start-finish line in first qualifying was 181.656 mph (292.347 kph) against Senna's 174.588 (280.972). Senna cranked that up to 176.453 (283.974) on the Saturday but it remained a big difference. Incidentally, during the Saturday morning untimed session Senna judged his race car's chassis better but the spare car's engine better: the team couldn't change the engine in time for second qualifying but did for the race.

Senna raced: seventh for the first four laps, three of them behind de Angelis. At the Hella Licht chicane at the top of the hill after the start-finish straight Senna suddenly darted through catching de Angelis by surprise; a move which de Angelis repeated on him three laps later (and no doubt chuckled about: he was that kind of man). De Angelis took Warwick, who Senna caught by lap 15. Next lap Senna tried to take Warwick at the chicane but Warwick blocked; Warwick's engine failed, leaving Senna fifth, to become fourth on lap 28 when de Angelis pitted, engine expired. A lap later that became third when Prost spun on oil de Angelis had deposited and roared into the barrier. Senna felt the Hart engine tightening and by lap 32 could not resist Tambay, who took third from him. Rather than risk destroying the engine Senna brought the car in.

- **Podium:** Lauda, Piquet, Alboreto.
- **Fastest lap:** Lauda 1:32.882.
- **Senna:** 1:34.348.

RACE 86

Holland, Zandvoort, 26 August 1984.
Qualifying: 1:16.951 (13); 1:15.960 (13). Row 7.
Pole: Prost 1:13.567.
Race weather: dry.
Warm-up: 1:20.607 (5).
Result: Retired after 19 laps, engine.

We can dispense with qualifying quickly, a misfire on Friday, a blown engine on Saturday morning. On the Sunday morning Senna warned the Toleman team-members closest to him that there would be some action this day, and not just on the track. Lotus announced that Senna would be joining them in 1985 and Toleman were enraged.

Not much of a race to balance that, Senna working up to ninth before the turbo blew. He pulled off after Tarzan and all that remained was a short stroll to the pits.

- **Podium:** Prost, Lauda, Mansell.
- **Fastest lap:** Arnoux 1:19.465.
- **Senna:** 1:21.683.

RACE

Italy, Monza, 9 September 1984.
Result: Did not take part.

Strictly speaking, this 'race' ought not to be included. Toleman, threatening litigation against Senna, took the car off him because they felt the only way to reach Senna was to do that. Senna went to Monza and, seeming wearied and saddened, said "I intended to keep quiet about the whole thing and deal with the people who were involved at Toleman. I don't want any more aggravation. I just want to go motor racing."

- **Podium:** Lauda, Alboreto, Riccardo Patrese (Benetton) – Stefan Johansson (making his Toleman debut) fourth.

Europe, Nurburgring, 7 October 1984.
Qualifying: 1:22.439 (12); 1:43.747 (12). Row 6.
Pole: Piquet 1:18.871.
Race weather: cool.
Warm-up: 1:25.066 (6).
Result: Retired 0 laps, accident.

By now the eyes of the world were firmly on the contest between Prost and Lauda for the championship. Lauda led 63 – 52.5 (the half from Monaco). The Hart engine had newer and bigger turbos and Senna said he was pleased with how much speed they gave him exiting the corners. He had a difficult Friday untimed session because a wire in the electronic control box severed, forcing him to the spare car. He covered no more than a lap and a half in that before the engine failed. The wiring was repaired in time for first qualifying. It rained on the Saturday.

Race morning warm-up was infinitely more interesting. Senna went sixth quickest but – in outright speed crossing the start-finish line – a lot slower than Johansson: Senna at 139.228 mph (224.066 kph), Johansson at 141.788 (228.185); interesting because Johansson came only thirteenth in the session. Clearly Senna was squeezing time from the rest of the bland, boring new Nurburgring. Senna's race lasted

seconds. In the first corner, a right-left already notorious for accidents in any kind of racing, he claimed that Eddie Cheever (Alfa Romeo) pincered him and he had no option but to go into Rosberg's Williams. Some felt Senna had braked too late, others that he'd been tapped by another car. The Toleman rode onto the Williams leaving dark, foreboding tyre marks on the bodywork.

- **Podium:** Prost, Alboreto, Piquet.
- **Fastest lap:** Alboreto and Piquet 1:23.146.
- **Senna:** no lap.

Portugal, Estoril, 21 October 1984.
Qualifying: 1:30.077 (6); 1:21.936 (3). Row 2.
Pole: Piquet 1:21.703.
Race weather: hot, dry.
Warm-up: 1:26.147 (5).
Result: Third.

The championship decider, Lauda 66, Prost 62.5, all others supporting cast. That produced a sub plot because Lauda qualified eleventh and, assuming Prost won, needed to finish second which meant overtaking (in grid order) Johansson, Warwick, Alboreto, Tambay, Mansell, de Angelis, Rosberg, Senna and Piquet. Senna felt comfortable in Portugal for reasons of history and language. Hadn't the Portuguese cheered him as one of their own when he'd raced this same Estoril in the 1979 World Karting Championship?

In *Autosport* Roebuck wrote that "you felt the big occasion immediately. Most people – including the drivers – flew into Lisbon on Wednesday afternoon and evening, and immediately beyond Customs were local press, TV and radio people seeking an audience. 'Ayrton!' went up the cry as the Brazilian emerged, and the fans rushed forward with their autograph books and programmes." Because the circuit was new to Formula 1, an introductory session was run on the Thursday, Prost quickest from de Angelis and Senna. Rain fell on the Friday making a chaotic session but Senna went quickest in the Saturday untimed session and

Power and poise in Portugal, his last race for Toleman.

began to suggest to the team he might win. Saturday afternoon finished

Piquet	1:21.703
Prost	1:21.774
Senna	1:21.936

He was fifth in the Sunday morning warm-up and thereby hangs a tale that I've recounted before but which stands repetition. Many drivers expressed unease at their predicament with Lauda needing to overtake them. These drivers held, as it might prove, the outcome of the championship in their own hands. At least one driver I spoke to said he'd get out of Lauda's way rather than find a place in history as the idiot who spoiled the whole thing. I approached Senna and asked if he'd get out of the way. "No." He'd come to win, and let Lauda take care of himself.

Prost led by lap 9, Senna fourth, Lauda ninth and coming. On lap 19 Senna took Rosberg for third, where he remained until lap 33. Lauda wrote in *To Hell and Back* "things are moving along nicely now. I am reeling them in one after the other every second round. Finally, I overtake Senna. I think I am in second position." Senna, hampered by a misfire, ran unobtrusively to the end an unnoticed third. He looked sombre on the podium. Perhaps he was tired. Perhaps he accepted that the moment belonged to Lauda (and Prost), not him; but he'd be back here soon enough for his own moment.

- **Podium:** Prost 1h 41m 11.753s, Lauda at 13.425, Senna at 20.042.
- **Fastest lap:** Lauda 1:22.996.
- **Senna:** 1:24.373.
- **Championship:** Lauda 72, Prost 71.5, de Angelis 34, Senna joint ninth 13.

Lauda has taken the championship from Alain Prost. Senna would be back on the Estoril podium soon enough, and on the top step.

Senna in 1985, his Lotus era ready to open.

Chapter 5

Lotus
1985

Senna joined de Angelis at Lotus and their relationship seems to have been one of content. They even holidayed together and Senna wouldn't do that again for years, until he partnered Berger. Lotus, once a great team but now trying to arrest decline, believed Senna was the man around whom to build the effort. They had Renault turbo engines. The other front-runners: Lauda and Prost (Marlboro McLaren), Rosberg and Mansell (Williams), Piquet (Brabham), Alboreto and Arnoux (Ferrari), Tambay and Warwick (Renault). In due course there will be much talk of tyre compounds. Goodyear supplied five, from A (the hardest) to E (for qualifying).

* * *

RACE 89

Brazil, Rio, 7 April 1985.
Qualifying: 1:28.705 (2); 1:28.389 (3). Row 2.
Pole: Alboreto 1:27.768.
Race weather: hot, dry.
Warm-up: 1:38.194 (8).
Result: Retired after 48 laps, engine electronics.

Lotus went strongly for pole and de Angelis took it provisionally from Senna on the Friday. Here, already, was a shift in Senna's career. Lotus, much bigger than Toleman, gave him a car which allowed him to run with the leaders regularly.

Autosport reported that the Sunday was "the hottest day so far, the sun shining down from a clear blue sky. The huge stands lining the back straight were already packed as the teams began arriving at 7.30 am and when the cars rolled around on their warm-up lap at 12.30 pm there wasn't much doubt who they had all come to cheer home as a great roar of voices and a sea of waving arms followed Senna's Lotus down the main straight." He ran fourth, third when Rosberg's turbocharger failed. "The hard-charging Lauda moved ahead of de Angelis on lap 11 and took Senna four laps

later in a heart-stopping finely judged out-braking manoeuvre going into the fast left-hander at the end of the straight." Lauda's engine electronics failed after 27 laps, leaving Senna a long thrust towards the end. He didn't make it. He was disappointed the car had been off the winning pace but insisted he felt fit and fine despite some spectators noticing that "the young Brazilian looked very tired, with his head rolling around a lot through the corners."

- **Podium:** Prost, Alboreto, de Angelis.
- **Fastest lap:** Prost 1:36.702.
- **Senna:** 1:38.440.

RACE 90

Portugal, Estoril, 21 April 1985.
Qualifying: 1:21.708 (1), 1:21.007 (1). Pole.
Race weather: very wet.
Warm-up: 1:27.337 (7).
Result: First.

If the global mythology of Senna began at Monaco in the Toleman, it increased massively here. He dominated qualifying except for the Friday morning untimed when de Angelis went quicker. Thereafter the destruction of de Angelis

anything behind me. It was even difficult to keep the car in a straight line sometimes and for sure the race should have been stopped. It was much worse than Monaco last year. Once I nearly spun in front of the pits and I was lucky to stay on the road." This was his only mistake, if it can be termed a mistake. By comparison, 17 of the 26 starters didn't finish.

- **Podium:** Senna 2h 00m 28.006s, Alboreto at 1m 02.978, Tambay at one lap.
- **Fastest lap:** Senna 1:44.121.

His 1985 team-mate, the lamented Elio de Angelis *Formula One Pictures*

begin — he'd take a single pole position from 1985 and leave Lotus. In starkest contrast, this was the first of Senna's 65 poles and achieved with an economy of effort. On the Friday he went out early and had a look, readied himself, covered a further warm-up lap and did the 1:21.708. On the Saturday he made his statement: the pole time on his first run and 1:21.797 later, itself good enough for the front row.

The race was so wet it was aquatic. Senna made a smooth start, de Angelis up past Prost but Senna lapping a clear second quicker. The Tactic. By lap 10 Senna led de Angelis by 12 seconds, cars spinning everywhere like a crazed carousel. Alboreto took de Angelis for second place on lap 43, the gap 58.066 to Senna. Senna did not permit this gap to close. Within 10 laps he increased it to 1m 09.983 and kept increasing it until he backed off near the end. As he approached the finishing line some of the Lotus team sprang over the pit lane wall onto the track to acclaim him. Senna slowed further and steered away from the mechanics but Mansell, two laps adrift, arrived hard and went onto the grass to avoid Senna. It might have been nasty. "The big danger was that conditions changed all the time. Sometimes the rain was very heavy, sometimes not. I couldn't see

RACE 91

San Marino, Imola, 5 May 1985.
Qualifying: 1:27.589 (1); 1:27.327 (1). Pole.
Race weather: overcast.
Warm-up: 1:53.317 (11).
Result: Retired after 57 laps, out of fuel.

Senna expressed "surprise" to be on pole. What he added can haunt you in view of Imola nine years later. "I like the atmosphere at this circuit but not the track itself. It needs more fast corners. It seems to be all straight, chicane, straight, chicane...brake, turn in, not very interesting. It's a pure horsepower circuit." On the Saturday he did a lot of running on race tyres. "I used my qualifiers last and they were nearly a second slower. There was rain, but the biggest problem was that we couldn't get enough heat into the qualifiers. I was driving very hard – any harder would have been verging on the dangerous – but I improved only because the track was a bit faster." Fuel regulations limited each car to 220 litres and everybody knew Imola's thirst. We'll come to that, just as Senna would come to that...

He made a good start, de Angelis behind and working visibly harder to stay with him: the classic confrontation, a fast young man hammering out a career and an older man defending one.

	Senna	de Angelis
Lap 2	1:35.539	1:34.855
Lap 3	1:34.430	1:34.387
Lap 4	1:34.439	1:34.352
Lap 5	1:33.825	1:34.314

De Angelis suffered brake problems. Senna and Prost duelled for the first time in a race, a further classic confrontation: a young man measuring himself against the champion elect. Once Prost nosed the McLaren in front through the Villeneuve curve but Senna, moving instantly from defence to attack, re-took him at Tosa. It was, although nobody could know it, a very precise vision of virtually the next decade. They came up to lap Tambay (Renault) and Senna got through but Prost didn't immediately – another precise vision of the next decade, too. With Prost hemmed behind Tambay, Senna seized his chance. "I went away from Prost not because I pushed the engine *but* because I pushed the tyres and brakes." This amazing man was conserving fuel and finding the speed through late-braking, through working the tyres harder. "I hadn't been pushing before that because the car was too heavy on fuel. I had saved everything until that point, and after I made my break I turned the boost down and cut my revs by a thousand, thinking only of saving fuel. I thought I had no problem then to win. I *never* expected to run out."

- **Podium:** Prost (later disqualified), de Angelis, Thierry Boutsen (Arrows).
- **Fastest lap:** Alboreto 1:30.961.
- **Senna:** 1:31.549.

RACE 92

Monaco, Monte Carlo, 19 May 1985.
Qualifying: 1:21.630 (1); 1:20.450 (1). Pole.
Race weather: overcast.
Warm-up: 1:25.195 (7).
Result: Retired after 13 laps, engine.

The Senna qualifying mythology, especially here, was born. Meanwhile, Roebuck pointed out that "believe it or not, the Brazilian has topped every single timed qualifying session since the circus left Rio to head back for the European season, and there are signs of resentment from some of his colleagues." On the Saturday Senna set his time early and, as it would seem, then defended it by holding up Lauda and Alboreto – holding up is easy around narrow streets. Alboreto became so

enraged he knee-jerked through at Rascasse offering Senna the choice of conceding or crashing. Senna confessed he "felt bad" about Lauda. "I think I'm one of the drivers who uses his mirrors the most but I didn't see him in time. It was my fault. I went to apologise to him afterwards." Lauda, reportedly, declined to accept this.

"As for Alboreto, I don't understand him. If I was holding him up, why didn't he ease back for half a lap and then go for it? It wasn't down to me to make it clear for him, it was down to him to find a clear lap, just as I had to." Overall, Senna estimated "I drove closer to the limit on my quick laps than ever before."

Immediately before the race the electric blankets warming Senna's tyres short-circuited, blistering the fronts which had to be replaced. It meant, said Peter Warr, the man running Lotus, that he started on cold fronts and warm rears. Senna led but "until the fronts came properly up to temperature the car was very unbalanced." Alboreto vainly chased him – he led by four seconds after 12 laps – then the engine failed.

- **Podium:** Prost, Alboreto, de Angelis.
- **Fastest lap:** Alboreto 1:22.637.
- **Senna:** 1:24.803.

RACE 93

Canada, Montreal, 16 June 1985.
Qualifying: 1:25.399 (2); 1:24.816 (2).
Front row.
Pole: de Angelis 1:24.567.
Race weather: overcast.
Warm-up: 1:30.530 (7).
Result: Sixteenth.

"Some drivers don't like Montreal but it's one of my favourites. No challenge here? What about the blind corners after the pits. For sure they're a challenge – for me, anyway. I'm not completely flat through there yet, although I know I can do it. No, I like this place. Very hard to go quickly and save the car." De Angelis, only sixth on the Friday, took the third and last pole of his life on the Saturday.

De Angelis led from Senna who had to pit on lap 6, a turbo problem and no boost. "Everything was too hot to touch for a while." He sat impotent while five laps uncurled without him, emerged and ran to the end at real, venomous pace. During this Rosberg reached him and they went, as they were always going to go, head-to-head. "I really enjoyed it. Keke is fantastic, driving on the limit all the time. It was a good experience for me. He takes some amazing chances." To which Rosberg responded "he's really good. I was impressed, but Jesus *he* take some risks..."

- **Podium:** Alboreto, Johansson, Prost.
- **Fastest lap:** Senna 1:27.445.

RACE 94

USA-East, Detroit, 23 June 1985.
Qualifying: 1:42.051 (1); did not run. Pole.
Race weather: hot, dry.
Warm-up: 1:44.877 (1).
Result: Retired after 51 laps, accident.

Senna complained that the infamous bumps (and manhole covers) were worse than the year before. He didn't mind the circuit layout "too much, but how you can be happy between walls when you're spinning the wheels in fifth gear I don't know." He set his time on his fourth lap, a stunning thing a full second faster than Mansell, next. Deep into the session Senna sat bare-headed in the Lotus watching a timing monitor perched in front of him, ready in case he had to go out again. He must have known he wouldn't. Rain on Saturday brought standing water.

Senna led but pitted on lap eight, the surface gnawing the tyres. That made him thirteenth. Within six laps he'd risen to eighth, risen to seventh when he pitted for more tyres. He didn't lose a place during this stop and after it constructed a monumental assault, moving on to the pace and then

	Bellof	Senna
Lap 42	1:50.368	1:47.362
Lap 43	1:50.309	1:46.731
Lap 44	1:50.287	1:48.075
Lap 45	1:50.779	1:47.114

Next lap Senna went through and set off after Alboreto.

	Alboreto	Senna
Lap 46	1:50.631	1:45.839
Lap 47	1:49.515	1:47.664
Lap 48	1:50.416	1:45.825
Lap 49	1:49.021	1:46.749

By lap 51 – Senna setting fastest lap of the race – he was full on Alboreto, third, and a freakish possibility loomed. Senna might win. Then he tried to overtake Alboreto into turn three, "hit the tyre barrier and it was my own fault. I'd been pushing and touched the wall several times but the car was still perfect. My only problem was with the carbon brakes. They began to go soft and I was having to pump. I went to pass Alboreto and I forgot to pump. The pedal went to the floor and when I knew what was going to happen I was a little worried about my legs. I pulled them as far back into the cockpit as I could, but the Lotus is very strong and there was no problem with that. I jarred my hand on the steering wheel, nothing more."

- **Podium:** Rosberg, Johansson, Alboreto.
- **Fastest lap:** Senna 1:45.612.

RACE 95

France, Paul Ricard, 7 July 1985.
Qualifying: 1:32.835 (1); 1:33.677 (4).
Front row.
Pole: Rosberg 1:32.462.
Race weather: hot, dry.
Warm-up: 1:41.020 (8).
Result: Retired after 26 laps, accident.

Friday candour: "I missed a gearchange on my first run and at the end of the lap the tyres were still in good shape so obviously I wasn't driving hard enough(!) The second run was better. I was flat out. No problem really except that the wind at Signes [at the end of the immense Mistral straight] made the corner difficult, all the time trying to push you off the road." On the Saturday, trying to better Rosberg's time, the engine blew. Senna judged it would have been a good lap and quite possibly good enough.

In the race he ran second to Rosberg for six laps before Piquet slipstreamed past along the Mistral. Senna slowed on lap 9 and pitted, the gear selectors jammed, he came out twentieth and gained five places by lap 26 before the engine blew. The Lotus careened off on its own oil at the approach to Signes and plunged through the catch fencing. Senna was unhurt.

- **Podium:** Piquet, Rosberg, Prost.
- **Fastest lap:** Rosberg 1:39.914.
- **Senna:** 1:41.552.

RACE 96

Britain, Silverstone, 21 July 1985.
Qualifying: 1:06.324 (3); 1:06.794 (4). Row 2.
Pole: Rosberg 1:05.591.
Race weather: overcast.
Warm-up: 1:12.065 (7).
Result: Retired after 60 laps, out of fuel.

Qualifying belonged entirely to Rosberg who became the first man to lap Silverstone at 160 miles an hour. Contrast Senna. On the Friday he suffered engine problems on his qualifying car and "had to use the other one." He went into a vast slide at Woodcote on some oil. On the Saturday he suffered fuel feed problems. "On my first run the engine actually cut out at Woodcote and the left rear tyre was gone before the end of the lap." He tried again later, warming to 1:07.408 overall and expressed delight with the handling of the car but "I was blocked by the same guy at Club and Woodcote" (de Cesaris).

Senna made a massive start, Rosberg briefly harrying him before they travelled in tandem from the pack. Senna drew away, Rosberg accepting that he'd destroy his tyres if he tried to stay with him. Prost accelerated and took Rosberg, Senna nine seconds ahead. Prost closed. Senna responded although "I had the boost right down, the switch at its lowest point." Senna profited from traffic to create a small gap but the engine misfired, allowing Prost by, and with five laps left he parked it, the fuel all swallowed and gone.

- **Podium:** Prost, Alboreto, Laffite.
- **Fastest lap:** Prost 1:09.886.
- **Senna:** 1:10.032.

Portugal and Senna's first victory. Michele Alboreto (left) and Patrick Tambay join in the fun *Zooom*.

Germany, Nurburgring, 4 August 1985.
Qualifying: 1:18.792 (5); 1:36.471 (4). Row 3.
Pole: Teo Fabi (Toleman) 1:17.429.
Race weather: overcast.
Warm-up: 1:23.398 (3).
Result: Retired after 27 laps, CV joint.

A rubber washer came loose and went into the mechanical fuel pump, allowing Senna only one run on the Friday; a wet Saturday.

The race was a re-run of Silverstone in reverse, Rosberg leading, Senna in tandem, both drawing away. On lap 16 Senna pressed the power at the hairpin, slotted the car to the inside and forced Rosberg to concede. Senna maximised that.

	Senna	Rosberg
Lap 17	1:24.671	1:25.092
Lap 18	1:24.841	1:25.236
Lap 19	1:24.553	1:24.895
Lap 20	1:24.270	1:24.887

After another seven laps Senna raised his arm – warning those behind *I'm slowing, miss me* – and journeyed towards the pits, the CV joint gone. The frustration factor: Senna had led Imola, Monaco, Detroit, Silverstone and here for not a single point.

- **Podium:** Alboreto, Prost, Laffite.
- **Fastest lap:** Lauda 1:22.806.
- **Senna:** 1:24.270.

Austria, Osterreichring, 18 August 1985.
Qualifying: 1:28.123 (10); 3:04.856 (22). Row 7.
Pole: Prost 1:25.490.
Race weather: overcast.
Warm-up: 1:32.352 (5).
Result: Second.

A delicate Friday. "If we cannot get the balance of the car better tomorrow I may as well stop after five laps in the race. I've driven my own car and the spare today and they're both

The European Grand Prix where Senna had a lively disagreement with Rosberg *Formula One Pictures.*

impossible. Also I had engine problems on both, but an engine you can change." On the Saturday he waited at the end of the pit lane for the session to start, intent on an immediate time because the weather threatened. He managed a single lap and a turbo failed. He could not disguise his anger. Rain fell soon after...

The race had to be restarted after a crash. Senna completed the opening lap tenth and worked his way up so effectively that when Lauda, leading, dropped out after 39 laps (turbo) he ran second behind Prost. "The car was good in the corners at the beginning but I was very down on power *so* I decided to save the tyres until the fuel load lightened. That worked well. Then I got a big vibration from the front tyres at about half-distance. I thought of stopping but I decided to keep going." Unbelievably – in the true sense of the word – this represented only the second time Senna had taken points for Lotus.

- **Podium:** Prost 1h 20m 12.583s, Senna at 30.002, Alboreto at 34.356.
- **Fastest lap:** Prost 1:29.241.
- **Senna:** 1:31.666.

RACE 99

Holland, Zandvoort, 25 August 1985.
Qualifying: 1:11.837 (4); did not run. Row 2.
Pole: Piquet 1:11.074.
Race weather: warm, dry.
Warm-up: 1:17.997 (7).
Result: Third.

Throughout his career officialdom found Senna unyielding and uncompromising. In the Friday morning untimed session Senna's Lotus caught fire and, needing a marshal with an extinguisher, he took to the slip road at the hairpin. This represented a short cut to the paddock, something the Stewards deemed dangerous. They fined him $5,000 and gave him a severe warning about his future conduct. It stung. "I wanted to save the car. When Marc Surer's Brabham caught fire in the Nurburgring testing it burnt out because no-one acted quickly enough. Who paid for that?" A wet Saturday, no more to be said.

Piquet stalled on the grid and so did Boutsen's Arrows but everyone got through, Rosberg leading from Senna. Prost and Lauda went by on lap 14 but Rosberg departed after 19 laps, engine, and Lauda pitted for tyres. It made Senna second to Prost. After their pit stops Lauda led and Prost, chasing the championship voraciously, strove to overtake. Senna could not make the Lotus live with this and for a reason. "My engine was terrible for the whole race. I thought for sure I wouldn't finish." On the final lap Alboreto caught him and wanted his third place. They 'met' at the chicane. Alboreto claimed that Senna baulked him; Senna said "he just drove straight into the back of me, trying to push me straight on. For sure it was deliberate. I tell you, that Ferrari is one strong car. He really hit me hard."

- **Podium:** Lauda 1h 32m 29.263, Prost at 0.232, Senna at 48.491.
- **Fastest lap:** Prost 1:16.538.
- **Senna:** 1:17.835.

RACE 100

Italy, Monza, 8 September 1985.
Qualifying: 1:27.009 (4); 1:25.084 (1). Pole.
Race weather: overcast.
Warm-up: 1:32.639 (11).
Result: Third.

Senna, remember, had not driven Monza before because Toleman took the car off him the previous year. He went seventh fastest in the Friday untimed. "It's quite a difficult track, I think, and I haven't had much time to learn it. I arrived at the chicane flat in fifth on one lap simply because I'd forgotten it was there!" This is the first recorded instance of Senna forgetting something so important, and the last. On the Saturday he made an early thrust (1:26.404) and retreated to the pits until 10 minutes remained. At that point Rosberg and Mansell filled the front row. Senna came out and went for it, almost lost control. He had too much understeer into the chicane before the Lesmo curves. "The car bounced over the kerb and onto the grass. To be honest I thought it was gone. When I got back on the track my tyres were covered with grass and stones *so* through the second Lesmo I eased off." Eased off needs to be tempered against the knowledge that, over the lap, he averaged 152.487 mph (245.405 kph).

The start was alarming, Senna leading but, into the jaws of the first chicane, Rosberg thrust the Williams alongside on the outside, poked its snout in front. Rosberg turned in. Senna stabbed the brakes and that pitched the Lotus across the kerb – it just missed the rear of the Williams. Senna dug a sandstorm from the area beyond the kerb, still in second place. The Honda power of the Williams was too much and Mansell went by on that opening lap, followed by Prost. Senna completed a quiet race. Rosberg and Mansell dropped out (engine problems both), Prost led and Piquet overtook Senna with 10 laps left. I wonder what he thought about that.

- **Podium:** Prost 1h 17m 59.451s, Piquet at 51.635, Senna at 1m 00.390.
- **Fastest lap:** Mansell 1:28.283.
- **Senna:** 1:31.703.

RACE 101

Belgium, Spa, 15 September 1985.
Qualifying: 2:00.710 (18); 1:55.403 (2). Front row.
Pole: Prost 1:55.306.
Race weather: wet, drying.
Warm-up: 2:26.732 (3).
Result: First.

The Belgian Grand Prix ought to have been run on 2 June but the surface had been newly relaid and it broke up completely in places. Even Senna pronounced it impossible. The race, uniquely, was postponed. Now, on the Friday, Senna found no consolation. "In the morning I was stuck in second gear – a broken selector – and it took most of the session to sort it out." In the afternoon "my car was having an engine change so I decided to run in the spare on race tyres, then run qualifiers on my own when it was ready. We had a fire in the pits which burned an oil line. They changed that, I went

out and the left-hand turbo broke." Saturday was better although on his flying lap – his fourth – he locked the brakes at La Source hairpin. "I braked very late. I gained time because I was so late on the brakes but lost it again because I got sideways. Then I lost out some more because the tyres didn't last the full lap. I tell you, the right-hander – flat in fifth – before the last chicane, it was, mmmm, very twitchy. Here you need a car with perfect balance if the tyres are going to last and that's what we didn't have."

A wet race, and Senna made a gorgeous start. He led clearly on the climb after Eau Rouge while Prost, mindful of the championship (65 – 33 up on Alboreto) decided on playing percentages, particularly when the clutch on Alboreto's Ferrari failed after only three laps. Prost did not resist a strong attack from Mansell on the next lap. The weather drying, these three came in for slicks on lap 8. Senna flowed sinuously from Mansell, holding the Lotus with such poise and certainty that he made the conditions look better. That was deceptive, as we shall see.

	Senna	Mansell
Lap 10	2:13.871	2:14.536
Lap 11	2.11.558	2:15.450
Lap 12	2:08.457	2:08.944
Lap 13	2:06.616	2:08.749

It settled the race. Deceptive? "The engine started missing occasionally halfway through. At first it was happening only on the straights but later it was in the corners, too. It was getting worse. Because of the conditions it was quite a slow race *so* I knew I wasn't low on fuel or anything. I thought maybe an exhaust was breaking. This was a difficult race because the track was never completely dry, and particularly bad when there was rain in only one part."

- **Podium:** Senna 1h 34m 19.893s, Mansell at 28.422, Prost at 55.109.
- **Fastest lap:** Prost 2:01.730.
- **Senna:** 2:03.700.

Senna in 1986.

RACE 102

Europe, Brands Hatch, 6 October 1985.
Qualifying: 1:08.020 (1); 1:07.169 (1). Pole.
Race weather: cool, dry.
Warm-up: 1:14.995 (9).
Result: Second.

Provisional pole on the Friday and decisively, Piquet next on 1:09.204 – a difference of 1.184. "Was a good lap, but not a perfect one. We still have a bit of understeer we need to get rid of, and in two places I was not that precise, but the car is the best I've had all year. This is not a place for accidents, you know, but when the car is so safe you can still go more – it offers you the possibility to go more." On the Saturday he dipped into the 1m 7's and only Piquet could follow him there. This, however, was but a prelude. Senna made a second run and conjured and soothed and pounded a lap of the kind you never forget. Brands in autumn, a cool and dry day, russet leaves on the trees. Prost was on the circuit and Senna reached him at Hawthorn, the big right in the country. Senna didn't seem to lift at all as travelled so swiftly by. At Westfield, the

next big right, he put a wheel off. The rest of the lap moved into the realms of the hypnotic. When he crossed the line he'd averaged 140.100 mph and nobody had done that at Brands before. He dissected it dispassionately. "I lost maybe a fraction with Prost – not his fault – and I made a mistake at Paddock. I was a little bit wide. Otherwise in the one minute 6's no problem. Understeer is gone. The car is perfect. I pushed, you know, tried very hard, but maybe I did not get the most out of the car..."

Senna led, Rosberg, roused, after him like a terrier. Thereby hangs a tale or three. Repeatedly Rosberg tried to overtake and on lap 7 – trying again – spun. Piquet, helpless, rammed him. Rosberg made his way back to the pits and at the instant he emerged, a lap down, Senna was coming round followed by Rosberg's team-mate Mansell. Rosberg decided to help Mansell and show Senna what blocking looked like when you're on the receiving end. Rosberg justified this by citing what Senna had been doing to him: "You get big eyes when someone starts weaving at 180mph. I'll admit it, I didn't have the balls to start banging wheels at that speed, and that's what it would have led to if I hadn't backed off on the occasions when I was going to go by." (Later, when Rosberg broached this interesting topic, Senna said "come on, I was in front, I do my own line.") Senna did not feel Rosberg needed to block him for Mansell to win. Mansell would have done that anyway, Senna said, because Mansell's Honda engine had too much power to be resisted.

- **Podium:** Mansell 1h 32m 58.109s, Senna at 21.396, Rosberg at 58.533.
- **Fastest lap:** Laffite (Ligier) 1:11.526.
- **Senna:** 1:12.601.

RACE 103

South Africa, Kyalami, 19 October 1985.
Qualifying: 1:04.517 (4); 1:02.825 (4). Row 2.
Pole: Mansell 1:02.366.
Race weather: hot, dry.
Warm-up: 1:08.296 (2).
Result: Retired after 8 laps, engine.

The Renault engine wasn't giving enough straight line speed, a crippling disadvantage because Kyalami had an enormous straight. On the Friday Senna was down on boost but felt better after the Saturday: more boost and the car better balanced.

A nothing of a race, fourth on the first two laps, fifth for the next three, fourth on lap 6, third on lap 7; and that was it.

- **Podium:** Mansell, Rosberg, Prost.
- **Fastest lap:** Rosberg 1:08.149.
- **Senna:** 1:10.077.

RACE 104

Australia, Adelaide, 3 November 1985.
Qualifying: 1:22.403 (2), 1:19.843 (1). Pole.
Race weather: hot, dry.
Warm-up: 1:23.854 (1).
Result: Retired after 63 laps, engine.

How mature was Senna? This race called that into question, to put it mildly. Senna went out early on the Friday, "made a few mistakes" and claimed Mansell blocked him on his second run. On the Saturday Senna did 1:21.053 and

Mansell promptly bettered that, 1:20.537. What would Senna find now? Roebuck wrote that "live coverage in the pits followed his lap, which was sensational, 'ET' [that was naughty, Nigel] using the kerbs to set up his car and stop the drifts in a perfect display of car control." Senna was sure "I couldn't have gone 100th of a second quicker. I was so busy trying to balance the power and the wheelspin I didn't even know if it was a good lap." He made a third run later but simply to follow Mansell and remember what lines Mansell was taking.

Mansell gripped the lead from Senna but on a left-hander at the back of the circuit Senna lunged down in the inside and hoofed Mansell off. (When Senna subsequently mounted a robust defence of the move he was virtually alone in seeing it as he did.) A tumult of a race. Rosberg led from Senna who, trying to hold Alboreto at bay, had the Lotus at wild angles. Alboreto did overtake him – Senna sideways under braking – but Senna re-took him a couple of corners later. Rosberg pitted for tyres on lap 42 and did it suddenly. Senna, tight on him, couldn't react fast enough and the Lotus lost its front right wing. Senna ought to have pitted next time round for repairs but it seemed a strange, almost out-of-mind mood gripped him. He rushed on, the car a bronco of understeer and it plunged off at the hairpin. He caught it before it crashed into the wall. He did pit next time round for a new nose cone, caught and passed Lauda for second place and set off after Rosberg. Inevitably Rosberg put the hammer down, he and Senna murdering their rear tyres. Rosberg pitted for more, Senna leading from Lauda; and Lauda noted the state of Senna's tyres. Lauda applied pressure, Rosberg travelling like a tornado at both of them. Lauda overtook Senna on lap 56 but had brake problems and crashed almost immediately. Senna led again until blue smoke and dribbling oil announced the end of the engine and the end of his first season with Lotus.

- **Podium:** Rosberg, Laffite, Philippe Streiff (Ligier).
- **Fastest lap:** Rosberg 1:23.758.
- **Senna:** 1:24.140.
- **Championship:** Prost 76 (73 counting), Alboreto 53, Rosberg 40, Senna 38.

1986

De Angelis departed for Brabham and Senna invoked the wrath of many by making sure Lotus did not sign Warwick to replace him but Dumfries, a debutant, instead. The other front runners: Prost and Rosberg (Marlboro McLaren), Mansell and Piquet (Williams), Teo Fabi and Berger (Benetton), Alboreto and Johansson (Ferrari).

* * *

RACE 105

Brazil, Rio, 23 March 1986.
Qualifying: 1:26.983 (2) 1:25.501 (1). Pole.
Race weather: hot, dry.
Warm-up: 1:36.556 (10).
Result: Second.

The Friday belonged to Piquet who put together the fastest lap ever driven at the circuit. The Saturday belonged to Senna although his first run was no more than 1:27.403 – Mansell had done 1:26.800. Senna sat silent in the crowded, noisy pit and contemplated. He spoke briefly about a change in the wing setting, sat silent again. When he was ready he emerged and stole pole on the final lap of the session.

A front row of Senna and Piquet stirred divergent passions in a country prey to passions. Competing groups chanted "Senna" or Piquet" and Senna's supporters won on volume. Senna away quickest from Mansell, and Mansell pulled out to take the inside line at the fast left-hander. Senna granted him just enough space and they went in side-by-side. They touched, the Lotus quivering but Senna steadied that. His supporters adored the moment of regaining control and the volume swelled by decibels. *Autosport* reported that when Piquet had taken Mansell he "shadowed the Lotus [of Senna] down the straight and then, to the delight of the crowd, an orange-gloved arm appeared out of the Lotus cockpit and Senna pointed behind him most of the way down the straight as if to say 'see who's number two?'" Piquet's response? He went through on lap 3 and they ran like that to the end. I wonder what Senna thought about that.

- **Podium:** Piquet 1h 39m 32.583s, Senna at 34.827, Laffite at 59.759.
- **Fastest lap:** Piquet 1:33.546.
- **Senna:** 1:34.785.

The familiar face of contemplation and concentration.

Spain, Jerez, 13 April 1986.
Qualifying: 1:21.605 (1); 1:21.924 (1). Pole.
Race weather: hot, dry.
Warm-up: 1:28.964 (3).
Result: First.

On the Friday Senna insisted the Lotus was "bottoming everywhere." This is the sort of devastating thing he did say because against him Mansell, next, could do no better than 1:23.024. Senna watched most of the Saturday session on a television in the Lotus motorhome, which is also devastating. With 20 minutes remaining Mansell thrust 1:22.760, which had Senna striding to the Lotus. He managed the 1:21.924 despite traffic, felt sure otherwise he'd have beaten his Friday time...

Senna led to lap 39, Mansell taking him as they came upon a back-marker. Mansell led for 10 laps and built a four second cushion. Senna tore the cushion apart. They grappled and Senna overtook Mansell at the uphill hairpin. Mansell risked pitting for fresh tyres and, hungry, devoured the circuit.

	Senna	Mansell	*Gap*
Lap 66	1:31.490	1:28.967	*12.843*
Lap 67	1:32.671	1:28.504	*8.676*
Lap 68	1:31.591	1:29.039	*6.124*

A beautiful balance, Senna forcing what he could from tired tyres, Mansell forcing everything.

	Senna	Mansell	*Gap*
Lap 70	1:30.037	1:28.197	*5.354*
Lap 71	1:32.170	1:28.405	*1:589*

One to go and all through it Mansell closed, closed, closed. As they braked for the hairpin before the screaming sprint to the line Mansell was on him, hungrier. Out of the hairpin and they sprinted. Senna crossed the line and Mansell crossed it a fraction of a fraction later – the noses of the cars so symmetrical that Mansell imagined he'd won.

- **Podium:** Senna 1h 48m 47.735s, Mansell at 0.014, Prost at 21.552.
- **Fastest lap:** Mansell 1:27.176.
- **Senna:** 1:28.801.
- **Championship:** Senna 15, Piquet 9, Mansell 6.

San Marino, Imola, 27 April 1986.
Qualifying: 1:25.050 (1); 1:25.286 (1). Pole.
Race weather: overcast.
Warm-up: 1:32.225 (2).
Result: Retired after 11 laps, wheel bearing.

Senna wasn't completely happy with the brakes on the Friday and said he hadn't driven well, another devastation. He was quickest (by 0.840 from Piquet). Traffic hampered him on the Saturday.

He moved swift away from the green light but, by Villeneuve, Piquet overtook. Piquet's Honda had a lot of power. On lap 4 Prost went by into Tosa and Rosberg went by on the exit to Tosa. On lap 12 the failed wheel bearing brought a smoke-cloud from the Lotus and Senna, slowing, edged sharply aside to grant Alboreto rites of passage. Then he pitted.

- **Podium:** Prost, Piquet, Berger.
- **Fastest lap:** Piquet 1:28.667.
- **Senna:** 1:31.999.
- **Championship:** Senna and Piquet 15, Prost 13.

Monaco, Monte Carlo, 11 May 1986.
Qualifying: 1:25.222 (1); 1:23.175 (3). Row 2.
Pole: Prost 1:22.627.
Race weather: warm, sunny.
Warm-up: 1:28.376 (6).
Result: Third.

Familiar territory and small, fleeting nuances magnify to large nuances on the unforgiving streets. On the Thursday Senna "missed a gear at the chicane and on my second run I got held up by Johansson. I don't think he meant to do it but it happened." On the Saturday he led the queue waiting for the second session to begin but each lap was hampered by traffic. That familiar territory.

His 1986 team-mate, Johnny Dumfries *Formula One Pictures.*

Prost led from Senna and Mansell, Senna holding second until Prost pitted for tyres on lap 35. Quickly Prost caught Senna but chose to wait behind until Senna pitted on lap 42, Rosberg up to second place. It remained static – more familiar territory – Prost from Rosberg from Senna. "Very tough, very stressing race but nothing to do against those two and that [McLaren] car."

- **Podium:** Prost 1h 55m 41.060s, Rosberg at 25.022, Senna at 53.646.
- **Fastest lap:** Prost 1:26.607.
- **Senna:** 1:26.843.
- **Championship:** Prost 22, Senna 19, Piquet 15.

RACE 109

Belgium, Spa, 25 May 1986.
Qualifying: 1:55.776 (5); 1:54.576 (3). Row 2.
Pole: Piquet 1:54.331.
Race weather: hot, dry.
Warm-up: 2:01.950 (10).
Result: Second.

One of those things pockmarked the Friday. Rosberg embarked on his second flying lap and Senna held him up out of Eau Rouge, which compelled Rosberg to find Senna afterwards and explain the facts of life. It must have been an – er – illuminating though brief encounter. Senna reportedly remained unrepentant. Balance changes improved the Lotus on the Saturday but during Senna's big attempt third gear jumped out twice.

Senna tracked Piquet early but Piquet departed without ceremony (engine). After the pit stops Mansell led from Senna. "I had big understeer all through *so* the car was very hard on the front tyres and in the last few laps I just didn't have the front end to work with. Like Mansell I was worried about fuel and I knew that only he, of all the World Championship contenders, was in a good position for points. Therefore I decided to have six rather than risk having nothing."

- **Podium:** Mansell 1h 27m 57.925s, Senna at 19.827, Johansson at 26.592.
- **Fastest lap:** Prost 1:59.282.
- **Senna:** 1:59.867.
- **Championship:** Senna 25, Prost 23, Mansell 18.

Canada, Montreal, 15 June 1986.
Qualifying: 1:27.422 (1); 1:24.188 (2).
Front row.
Pole: Mansell 1:24.118.
Race weather: hot, dry.
Warm-up: 1:30.168 (11).
Result: Fifth.

A wet but drying Friday, Piquet, Mansell and Rosberg quick and everything fairly ordinary. In the final minutes Senna went out on wet tyres to gauge the conditions and returned for qualifiers. At this point he was subjected to a random weight check. That done he motored urgently to the pit, urgently the qualifiers went on. Was there time for a run? Out he went and crossed the line less than one second before session's end; or, putting it more prosaically, the Longines timing beam was switched off precisely at the end of the hour and if he'd been a second slower he wouldn't have had the time – worth provisional pole – at all. On the Saturday he couldn't find quite enough speed or acceleration. "I'm not too disappointed about missing pole because here it is not so important. The only real advantage is to be clear of any kind of accident at the start." Hmmm.

Montreal was, and is, naggingly awkward for overtaking. In the years to come Senna would demonstrate that – to Nigel Mansell's extreme irritation.

Now Mansell led from Senna, but into lap five Prost pressed the McLaren alongside in the sweepers and gained the racing line. It forced Senna to lift and skitter over the kerbing which in turn allowed Rosberg, Piquet and Arnoux through, Senna sixth. (Subsequently Senna did not dispute the fairness of Prost's move. Interesting. He would have done a couple of years later.) Senna overtook Arnoux for fifth and spent the rest of the afternoon fending him off.

- **Podium:** Mansell, Prost, Piquet.
- **Fastest lap:** Piquet 1:25.443.
- **Senna:** 1:27.503.
- **Championship:** Prost 29, Mansell and Senna 27.

USA-East, Detroit, 22 June 1986.
Qualifying: 1:40.301 (2); 1:38.301 (1). Pole.
Race weather: hot.
Warm-up: 1:42.499 (3).
Result: First.

Senna couldn't match Mansell on the Friday but did on the Saturday, whereupon he departed to his hotel room to watch France v Brazil in the World Cup quarter finals in Guadalajara, Mexico, rather than attend the mandatory pole press conference. (France won 4 – 3 on penalties which pleased those who were not pleased with Senna.) He sent a tape recording of his thoughts and they played that over the loudspeakers. In one way it was explicable, the consuming passion to see his beloved Brazil, and Senna a football fan anyway. In another way it reeked of arrogance. Maybe he was held between the two ways.

The race turned on tyres (no pun intended). Senna chose B compounds. "I spent a lot of time trying both in practice and there was no doubt that the Cs gave better grip for a few laps but after that they started to go off." Mansell went for Cs all round. Senna nipped the start but into lap 3 missed a gear, ceding the lead to Mansell. Senna, of course, knew Mansell had a temporary tyre advantage and didn't allow that to disturb him. Severe brake problems crippled Mansell and in a flurry Senna, Arnoux and Laffite overtook. Senna pitted for tyres on lap 14 – "the car had been behaving strangely. I was going nearly sideways in a straight line sometimes. My left rear had punctured." He wanted more Bs and within the concrete walls the hunt was on. In a couple of laps he passed Johansson, then Alboreto and ran behind Piquet, everyone jerking up a place when Arnoux pitted for tyres. Order at lap 30: Laffite, Piquet, Senna. Laffite pitted next lap, Piquet nine laps later and Senna led to the end. "My biggest problem was probably my foot. It's all brake, brake, brake, very hard all the time and after a few laps my foot began to hurt. The car was not perfect but there were no serious problems. When I had my slow puncture in the early laps my stop was quick and I could catch

On his way to second place in the Brazilian Grand Prix – but Nelson Piquet won, which can't have pleased Senna at all.

The trick was always to relax when you could.

them again. I enjoyed today because fuel consumption did not come into it. This was more a fighting race."

- **Podium:** Senna 1h 51m 12.847s, Laffite at 31.017, Prost at 31.824.
- **Fastest lap:** Piquet 1:41.233.
- **Senna:** 1:41.981.
- **Championship:** Senna 36, Prost 33, Mansell 29.

RACE 112

France, Paul Ricard, 6 July 1986.
Qualifying: 1:06.526 (1); 1:06.807 (1). Pole.
Race weather: overcast.
Warm-up: 1:11.982 (6).
Result: Retired after 3 laps, accident.

The circuit had been truncated after the death of de Angelis in testing in 1985. Senna had a revised Renault engine and covered a lot of laps in both untimed sessions in his race car. By Saturday he expressed satisfaction. "The track conditions were quite good, particularly in the new loop, where more rubber had gone down, but the heat was working against the engines. The car itself felt better."

Senna led immediately but Mansell out-braked him into the first corner. On lap 4 de Cesaris's engine blew on his Minardi and laid oil in Signes. Mansell's Williams shivered on it but Mansell caught that; Senna couldn't and cuffed the tyre barrier. "I didn't see the oil in time and I lost it. No excuses."

- **Podium:** Mansell, Prost, Piquet.
- **Fastest lap:** Mansell 1:09.993.
- **Senna:** 1:12.882.
- **Championship:** Prost 39, Mansell 38, Senna 36.

RACE 113

Britain, Brands Hatch 13 July 1986.
Qualifying: 1:09.042 (4); 1:07.524 (3). Row 2.
Pole: Piquet 1:06.961.
Race weather: hot, dry.
Warm-up: 1:13.095 (4).
Result: Retired after 27 laps, gearbox.

Roebuck wrote that, just this once, Senna was "never convincing as a contender for pole. His

hot laps were awesome but also untidy. The Lotus wagged its tail at every opportunity, seemed to tag every piece of kerbing on the circuit."

The race had to be restarted after a crash and Mansell fought a mind-over-matter contest with Piquet, Senna fourth until the gearbox failed.

- **Podium:** Mansell, Piquet, Prost.
- **Fastest lap:** Mansell 1:09.593.
- **Senna:** 1:14.024.
- **Championship:** Mansell 47, Prost 43, Senna 36.

RACE 114

Germany, Hockenheim 27 July 1986.
Qualifying: 1:45.212 (8); 1:42.329 (3). Row 2.
Pole: Rosberg 1:42.013.
Race weather: hot, dry.
Warm-up: 1:51.863 (9).
Result: Second.

Pressured, precious time in the domain of precious time. On the Friday the balance of the Lotus wasn't quite right, but better on the Saturday. However 10 minutes before the second session began a fuel pump proved defective on Senna's qualifying car. The mechanics set to and in 35 minutes removed the engine, replaced the pump, put the engine back. He made a run in the race car with 10 minutes left and did 1:44.887, thirteenth. He pitted with five minutes left, the mechanics completing work on the other car. He bustled into it and constructed the lap.

At the green light Senna bored between the McLarens and led for a lap before Rosberg went through, then Piquet, then Prost. The sting would be in the tail. Rosberg ran out of fuel and Senna risked some of his in overtaking Prost – who also ran out. Approaching the finishing line Senna weaved the Lotus from side to side to slosh whatever fuel remained into the engine.

- **Podium:** Piquet 1h 22m 08.263s, Senna at 15.437, Mansell at 44.580.
- **Fastest lap:** Berger 1:46.604.
- **Senna:** 1:49.424.
- **Championship:** Mansell 51, Prost 44, Senna 42.

RACE 115

Hungary, Hungaroring, 10 August 1986.
Qualifying: 1:32.281 (3); 1:29.450 (1). Pole.
Race weather: hot, dry.
Warm-up: 1:35.048 (6).
Result: Second.

Formula 1 moved effortlessly behind (what was then) the Iron Curtain. Formula 1 liked Hungary, a very civilised and agreeable country, and Hungary liked Formula 1. Inevitably the new circuit lacked enough rubber on it and in the Thursday introductory session cars spun everywhere, Senna quickest, however. "I think I've spun here more times than in the rest of my career. The organisation has been fantastic but one thing that worries me is the marshalling. I don't blame them because I know it's only inexperience but when you spin off they take a long time getting to you." On the Saturday most teams laid their bets each way – running on race tyres then qualifiers – except Senna who chose qualifiers both times. He was right.

At home in Brazil.

Senna led from Mansell into turn one, the fearsome, snapping corner at the end of the start-finish straight. Piquet overtook Mansell on lap 3 but, on lap 7, Patrese spun and next lap Senna and Piquet came upon Patrese's car straddling the track. Worse, a lap after that, the rescue car towing the Brabham almost lurched into Senna. Piquet advanced upon him

	Senna	Piquet
Lap 9	1:36.498	1:36.264
Lap 10	1:37.138	1:37.734
Lap 11	1:36.912	1:36.428

Piquet overtook him on the straight on lap 12 and "that was really the problem for me through the whole race. The Lotus was as quick as the Williams in the corners, maybe even a little better in some places, but Piquet was much faster in the straights." Piquet pitted for tyres on lap 35, Senna into the lead and pressing his advantage: ending lap 41 the gap stood at 30.826, sufficient for Senna to pit and emerge before Piquet reached him. From lap 49 Piquet gained a couple of seconds a lap and caught Senna by lap 56. They had a rare, wonderful, electrified moment in turn one, Piquet forging in front, Senna reacting instantly and taking the lead back. Somehow it was postponing the inevitable. Into lap 57 – and at turn one again – Piquet described an arc round the outside, gave Senna a brake test and shook his fist at him. You meet the nicest people in Formula 1.

• **Podium:** Piquet 2h 00m 34.508s, Senna at 17.673, Mansell at one lap.
• **Fastest lap:** Piquet 1:31.001.
• **Senna:** 1:31.261.
• **Championship:** Mansell 55, Senna 48, Piquet 47.

RACE 116

Austria, Osterreichring, 17 August 1986.
Qualifying: 1:26.650 (9); 1:25.249 (7). Row 4.
Pole: Fabi 1:23.549.
Race weather: hot, dry.
Warm-up: 1:31.824 (12).
Result: Retired after 13 laps, engine.

A mundane weekend, no more, no less: on the Friday Senna had engine problems and used Dumfries's car, on the Saturday he had his own car but was unhappy with its balance and grip.

He ran seventh early on, pitted for tyres on lap 8, pitted again three laps later with a misfire, managed a 1:52.440 (an eternity off the pace), struggled round in 3:35.788 and pitted again, game over.

Podium: Prost, Alboreto, Johansson.
Fastest lap: Berger 1:29.444.
Senna: 1:33.437.
Championship: Mansell 55, Prost 53, Senna 48.

RACE 117

Italy, Monza, 7 September 1986.
Qualifying: 1:25.363 (1); 1:24.916 (5). Row 3.
Pole: Fabi 1:24.078.
Race weather: hot, dry.
Warm-up: 1:30.482 (10).
Result: Retired no laps, clutch.

Fastest on the Friday, Senna couldn't hold on to that. His opening gambit – a 1:24.916 – was second fastest (when it was done) on the Saturday but a blown engine blew his later gambit, whatever that might have been.

At the green light the clutch broke and as the Lotus edged slowly, slowly forward. Senna waved a frenzied arm to those behind. *Miss me!* They did.

• **Podium:** Piquet, Mansell, Johansson.
• **Fastest lap:** Fabi 1:28.099.
• **Senna:** No lap.
• **Championship:** Mansell 61, Piquet 56, Prost 53, Senna 48.

RACE 118

Portugal, Estoril, 21 September 1986.
Qualifying: 1:19.943 (5); 1:16.673 (1). Pole.
Race weather: overcast.
Warm-up: 1:22.844 (4).
Result: Fourth.

Mundane, again. On the Friday he didn't like the balance of the car. On the Saturday Roebuck wrote of the pole performance that "it was a visually spectacular lap, reviving memories of early season qualifying sessions at such as Jerez and Imola. All the way round the black car was shrouded in sparks. And it brought from rival teams and drivers a selection of comments, some ribald – 'I see that the Lotus has let her stays down again' – and some cynical – 'amazing how the sparks seem to appear when he laps a couple of seconds faster than he has before..."'

Mansell claimed the first corner after the start. Although Senna flirted with a move on him out at the back of the circuit, Estoril being Estoril, the order congealed.

Piquet would spend a long afternoon trying to get at Senna, Senna wielding the traffic like a shield, cutting past back-markers at places where he knew Piquet couldn't follow. Into the final lap Senna was safe – and ran out of fuel. He was classified fourth.

- **Podium:** Mansell, Prost, Piquet.
- **Fastest lap:** Mansell 1:20.943.
- **Senna:** 1:21.283.
- **Championship:** Mansell 70, Piquet 60, Prost 59, Senna 51.

RACE 119

Mexico, Mexico City, 12 October 1986.
Qualifying: 1:18.367 (4); 1:16.990 (1). Pole.
Race weather: hot, dry.
Warm-up: 1:20.962 (3).
Result: Third.

Mansell could have taken the championship at this arid, unloved place. The previous Mexican Grand Prix had been 16 years before and the surface remained corrugated with bumps. Senna couldn't avoid one on his pole lap. "I hit a bump, got off line and had to lift from the throttle. It seemed to take for ever until the power came back on again. I could have been half a second quicker."

Mansell struggled to get the Williams into first gear, Piquet fast from Senna who challenged him at the first corner and brought smoke from his tyres when he braked violently, Piquet ceding nothing. It stayed like that for 31 laps when Piquet pitted, Senna leading for four laps until he pitted, too. Berger would complete the race without a stop and led, Senna behind. Senna pitted a second time, no chance of catching Berger now.

- **Podium:** Berger 1h 33m 18.700s, Prost at 25.438, Senna at 52.513.
- **Fastest lap:** Piquet 1:19.360.
- **Senna:** 1:20.237.
- **Championship:** Mansell 72 (70 counting), Prost 65 (64 counting), Piquet 63, Senna 55.

RACE 120

Australia, Adelaide, 26 October 1986.
Qualifying: 1:21.302 (6); 1:18.906 (3). Row 2.
Pole: Mansell 1:18.403.
Race weather: overcast.
Warm-up: 1:22.698 (1).
Result: Retired after 43 laps, engine.

An overhanging weekend with Mansell favourite for the championship but Prost and Piquet guarding their own chances. On the Friday Senna crashed in the qualifying car and set his time in the race car. On the Saturday he improved using race tyres but during the session the track lost grip.

After race morning warm-up he expressed concern about fuel consumption if he tried to run with the McLarens and Williamses. He felt a prisoner of his possibilities.

Mansell made the better start, Senna harrying into the first chicane – the power of the Renault made the Lotus twitch – then obediently assuming a position behind. They moved through the left-sprint-right and Senna placed the Lotus inside. Mansell did not contest this. Piquet broke through and on lap 2 Rosberg overtook Senna as well. Mansell, pacing himself, made his move on lap 4 and overtook, then Prost did on lap 7. Senna ran fifth to lap 42 and the engine ended the second season with Lotus.

- **Podium:** Prost, Piquet, Johansson.
- **Fastest lap:** Piquet 1:20.787.
- **Senna:** 1:24.149.
- **Championship:** Prost 74 (72 counting), Mansell 72 (70 counting), Piquet 69, Senna 55.

1987

Dumfries, who had scored three points in 1986, departed Lotus to be replaced by Satoru Nakajima, a pleasant Japanese who, we assumed, came as part of a package: Lotus secured Honda engines. The other front-runners: Prost and Johansson (Marlboro McLaren), Piquet and Mansell (Williams), Patrese and de Cesaris (Brabham), Boutsen and Fabi (Benetton), Alboreto and Berger (Ferrari).

✳ ✳ ✳

RACE 121

Brazil, Rio, 12 April 1987.
Qualifying: 1:29.002 (3); 1:28.408 (3). Row 2.
Pole: Mansell 1:26.128.
Race weather: hot, dry.
Warm-up: 1:33.547 (3).
Result: Retired after 50 laps, engine.

Senna had an active suspension car and said: "Gerard Ducarouge (the designer) believes it is the way to go. Look at the regulations: we have a limit on horsepower, a limit on weight and a limit on tyres in that we all use Goodyears so this is maybe the one area where some advantage could be gained. We decided two weeks ago that we would run only 'active' throughout this season, and I agree completely. In fact, I don't want to drive a car with a normal suspension again. Yes, the system has a weight penalty [it weighs more] but when it works well it's incredible." This system, which Lotus pioneered, proved complex and not a complete advantage. On the Friday Senna complained that the car felt terrible and not much better on the Saturday. His lap times came from himself rather than the car.

Piquet led Senna by three seconds after a couple of laps, Mansell moving up. Piquet pitted because he'd picked up some waste paper which coated his radiators and threatened to boil the engine breathless. Senna led, pitted for tyres on lap 13 and worked up to second place, slipped back. "I felt the engine was going to seize."

- **Podium:** Prost, Piquet, Johansson.
- **Fastest lap:** Piquet 1:33.861.
- **Senna:** 1:35.312

Senna in 1987 and a new livery because Lotus had new sponsors.

San Marino, Imola, 3 May 1987.
Qualifying: 1:27.543 (3); 1:25.826 (1). Pole.
Race weather: hot, dry.
Warm-up: 1:32.416 (7).
Result: Second.

Senna professed surprise to be on pole, pointing to the complexities of the 'active' system. "We have so much to learn about it. The car is really not handling that well." The lap, on his second run, contained much twitching-darting, even over the kerbs. Senna professed doubts about lasting the race distance and matching the McLarens and Williamses. Nothing seemed to have changed since 1986.

He led through Tamburello but Mansell slotted out approaching Villeneuve and overtook. Senna resisted Prost for three laps and drifted into a swap shop sort of afternoon: third, second, fourth and when Patrese fell away on lap 50, third. A lap later he overtook Alboreto, the Ferrari losing boost.

- **Podium:** Mansell 1h 31m 24.076s, Senna at 27.545, Alboreto at 39.144.
- **Fastest lap:** Fabi 1:29.246.
- **Senna:** 1:30.851.
- **Championship:** Mansell 10, Prost 9, Johansson 7, Senna and Piquet 6.

His 1987 team-mate, Satoru Nakajima *Camel*.

RACE 123

Belgium, Spa, 17 May 1987.
Qualifying: 2:08.450 (5); 1:53.426 (3). Row 2.
Pole: Mansell 1:52.026.
Race weather: overcast.
Warm-up: 2:02.000 (12).
Result: Retired, no laps, accident.

Traditional Spa, the Friday wet and cold, the Saturday wet and dry. "Yes, I am quick in the wet but that doesn't mean I like it. In the rain two years ago the Renault engine was perfect here because the power came in so smoothly. The Honda has more power but arrives more brutally. The balance of the car is not too bad but it doesn't feel as stable as I would like at a circuit as quick as this. It's been difficult to evaluate the suspension because the conditions have been changing so quickly."

A race of extreme brevity and trauma. Senna led from Mansell but at a right-hander out in the country Mansell came alongside and they touched, pirouetted. Mansell was able to rejoin, Senna not. When Mansell retired after 17 laps he strode to the Lotus pit and grasped Senna round the throat. Two Lotus mechanics manhandled Mansell off. In his autobiography Mansell has described how he felt "raging with fury" because he sensed he'd win the race and had done nothing wrong.

Senna said: "I couldn't believe what he was trying to do – overtake on the outside at a place like that. When I saw what he was doing I tried to get out of the way, brake as much as possible, but you can only do so much in a situation like that. I was committed to the corner and there was no way I could stop."

I remember Senna after Mansell strode from the Lotus pit: completely calm and standing on the pit wall watching Nakajima go by. Sometimes Senna's self-control could amaze you, just as sometimes his lack of it could, too.

- **Podium:** Prost, Johansson, de Cesaris.
- **Fastest lap:** Prost 1:57.153.
- **Senna:** no lap.
- **Championship:** Prost 18, Johansson 13, Mansell 10, Senna and Piquet 6.

RACE 124

Monaco, Monte Carlo, 31 May 1987.
Qualifying: 1:25.255 (2); 1:23.711 (2).
Front row.
Pole: Mansell 1:23.039.
Race weather: warm, dry.
Warm-up: 1:26.796 (1).
Result: First.

After the drivers' meeting on Thursday Senna and Mansell had a talk and although (typically) neither retracted from their position over the crash at Spa they decided to let it rest. Mansell, rampant in the car, couldn't be caught in either session.

After Spa, a front row of Mansell and Senna offered ominous prospects at Ste Devote. As (typically) happens in the real world – and when the cars set off it is a very real world – the great hate-hype-horror dissolves quite naturally away. Mansell travelled clean through followed by Senna who concentrated on finding "a pace, a rhythm I could sustain for the whole race." He let Mansell go.

	Mansell	**Senna**
Lap 1	1:36.709	1:38.735
Lap 2	1:31.613	1:32.328
Lap 3	1:31.275	1:31.756

Senna understood that Monaco is invariably a destructive race. Therefore, in his logic, he gazed at a whole picture: the 78 laps. You can be brave and challenging, which may not solve the conundrum of passing the car in front, or you can wait and see. Mansell slowed. On lap 28 he'd led by some 11 seconds, down to six next lap, Senna through the lap after that, Mansell out with a broken exhaust. Senna led Piquet by 16.607 seconds and it would be enough. "Towards the end I was having trouble with the selection of second and third gears and there was one bad moment near the swimming pool. I couldn't get the gear in and suddenly realised I had to get on the brakes! The car got a little bit sideways but it was OK, no problem."

- **Podium:** Senna 1h 57m 54.085s, Piquet at 33.212, Alboreto at 1m 12.839.
- **Fastest lap:** Senna 1:27.685.
- **Championship:** Prost 18, Senna 15, Johansson 13.

USA-East, Detroit, 21 June 1987.
Qualifying: 1:42.985 (2); 1:40.607 (2).
Front row.
Pole: Mansell 1:39.264.
Race weather: overcast.
Warm-up: 2:12.754 (12).
Result: First.

Mansell bestrode the Friday and Saturday, fastest in both. Roebuck wrote that "after the race in Monte Carlo, it was remarkable to see that Ayrton's hands, often in the past bruised and blistered after a street race, were in fine condition. The 'active' 99T, he said, gave the driver a much easier ride. No small thing, this, in a race of this kind." Senna (briefly) held pole on the Saturday but Mansell battered that.

As the race unfolded they replayed Monaco.

	Mansell	Senna
Lap 1	1:53.904	1:54.753
Lap 2	1:48.410	1:49.726
Lap 3	1:47.440	1:48.664

Mansell led by five seconds after 10 laps, Alboreto almost half a minute distant in third. Around lap 30 Mansell still held a substantial lead but the gap down from 18 seconds to 13. Mansell, tyre stop imminent, sought to increase it and on lap 33, just before the stop, delved into the one minute 42's for the first time. It was fastest lap of the race until Senna crossed the line. 1:41.057. "Early in the race I was in trouble with a soft brake pedal and I backed off. Two years ago I had the same problem and finished up in the wall *so* this time I knew better. And maybe slowing helped me on tyre wear. The team gave me excellent information on what was happening with the others." Mansell, enjoying the supposed advantage of new tyres, mounted his assault on Senna's citadel.

	Senna	Mansell
Lap 35	1:42.228	1:47.599
Lap 36	1:42.170	1:40.535
Lap 37	1:41.585	1:42.013

This effort by Senna to resist climaxed on lap 39 when he did 1:40.464, fastest of the race. Mansell was hampered by traffic and suffered cramp and exhaustion. Would Senna stop for tyres at all? A leading question. "I was intending to stop at half-distance. Then I decided to stay out another 10 laps. The tyres were still in good shape so it seemed better to continue on them to the end. Things can go wrong in pit stops so there is no point in coming in unless it is necessary."

- **Podium:** Senna 1h 50m 16.358, Piquet at 33.819, Prost at 45.327.
- **Fastest lap:** Senna 1:40.464.
- **Championship:** Senna 24, Prost 22, Piquet 18.

The car of 1987, everything gambled on active suspension.

RACE 126

France, Paul Ricard, 5 July 1987.
Qualifying: 1:07.303 (4); 1:07.024 (2). Row 2.
Pole: Mansell 1:06.454.
Race weather: hot, dry.
Warm-up: 1:10.797 (3).
Result: Fourth.

Mansell dominated qualifying again. On the Friday Senna had a troubled session, although quickest at the timing beam on the Mistral Straight with 205.664 mph (330.985 kph), Piquet next at 200.983 mph. Senna professed that the car lacked downforce, work needed to be done on the gearbox; and he went off at Signes. On the Saturday he liked the car's balance better but, chasing Prost's Friday time of 1:06.877 – beating that would have put him on the front row – the engine tightened.

He ran fourth from the start and remained there until the pit stops, ran fourth again. The balance of the car, evidently, had been the problem.

• **Podium:** Mansell, Piquet, Prost.
• **Fastest lap:** Piquet 1:09.548.
• **Senna:** 1:12.231.
• **Championship:** Senna 27, Prost 26, Piquet 24.

RACE 127

Britain, Silverstone, 12 July 1987.
Qualifying: 1:09.255 (4); 1:08.181 (3). Row 2.
Pole: Piquet 1:07.110.
Race weather: hot, dry.
Warm-up: 1:13.450 (7).
Result: Third.

On the Friday Senna remained unhappy about the balance and the team experimented with different settings. His chances of a major lap perished when, tracking in Mansell's wake, the Williams cast back a piece of metal which another car had deposited on the circuit and it smote Senna's left front wing. The piece of metal was ragged and sharp – what if it had struck Senna's helmet? – and Senna radioed to Warr, both assuming it had come from the Williams. When Senna returned to the pits Patrick Head, the Williams designer, examined the metal and

said "sorry, not ours!" The car felt better on the Saturday.

Piquet made a crisp start, Mansell negating that under gathering acceleration but Prost went outside both of them into Copse, Senna fourth. By Woodcote Piquet and Mansell retook Prost and Senna probed at him. Cut and thrust, chance and counter chance. On lap 2 Senna claimed the inside at Copse and overtook. Three laps later Prost claimed the inside at Copse and overtook. Senna circled fourth. He dare not do more than proceed evenly because of fuel consumption fears. Prost pitted for tyres on lap 29 and Senna ran third to the end. Whatever championship chances are, they don't look like this.

• **Podium:** Mansell 1h 19m 11.780s, Piquet at 1.918, Senna at one lap.
• **Fastest lap:** Mansell 1:09.832.
• **Senna:** 1:11.605.
• **Championship:** Senna 31, Mansell and Piquet 30.

RACE 128

Germany, Hockenheim, 26 July 1987.
Qualifying: 1:42.873 (2); no time. Front row.
Pole: Mansell 1:42.616.
Race weather: overcast.
Warm-up: 1:49.718 (7).
Result: Third.

Senna liked the balance better on the Friday – evidently the 'active' suspension had a new programme – although he damaged the underside of the qualifying car. "As I came into the second chicane the car jumped out of fourth gear. Therefore I arrived in neutral and I had to go over the kerb." He transferred to the race car but it bottomed so badly he spun in the Stadium. On the Saturday, in terrible weather, he ventured out for a single uncompleted lap.

He made a superb start, Mansell tardy, but out into the country Mansell screamed by and Senna had Prost behind him. On this lap 2 Prost flicked inside into the Stadium entry. A lap later Piquet sailed by and Senna settled for the art of the possible: fourth, becoming third when Prost's alternator failed. "Right from the start we were hopeless on top speed. They all passed me on the straight and there was nothing I could

Preparing for the Belgian Grand Prix, Spa.

do about it. Then I found that the boost control switch had no effect on the boost – and all the time I had terrible understeer."

- **Podium:** Piquet 1h 21m 25.091s, Johansson at 1m 39.591, Senna at one lap.
- **Fastest lap:** Mansell 1:45.716.
- **Senna:** 1:49.187.
- **Championship:** Piquet 39, Senna 35, Mansell 30.

RACE 129

Hungary, Hungaroring, 9 August 1987.
Qualifying: 1:31.387 (8); 1:30.387 (6). Row 3.
Pole: Mansell 1:28.047.
Race weather: hot, dry.
Warm-up: 1:35.096 (8).
Result: Second.

An unhappy qualifying despite Lotus's revised rear bodywork to improve the airflow. Senna couldn't find enough grip and on the Saturday his engine cut in too quickly. The 1:30.387 compared to his pole time in 1986 in the non-'active' Lotus of 1:29.450. Progress? Regress? These were questions Senna was asking himself.

He ran fifth early, fourth when Berger went (differential), and third when Alboreto went (engine). That was lap 44. Senna lay 12.312 seconds behind Piquet who was in second place. Six laps to go and Mansell went (a loose wheel nut). Piquet first and Senna second. "Everything in the car got tired, including me. I'm amazed

that the car held together. I had a big pain in my back and side."

- **Podium:** Piquet 1h 59m 26.793s, Senna at 37.727, Prost at 1m 27.456.
- **Fastest lap:** Piquet 1:30.149.
- **Senna:** 1:32.426.
- **Championship:** Piquet 48, Senna 41, Mansell and Prost 30.

RACE 130

Austria, Osterreichring, 16 August 1987.
Qualifying: 1:25.492 (7); 1:39.647 (4). Row 4.
Pole: Piquet 1:23.357.
Race weather: hot, dry.
Warm-up: 1:29.153 (6).
Result: Fifth.

A difficult qualifying, the elusive search for balance continuing. "It is poor here and the car feels unstable on some parts of the circuit."

A shambolic sequence of starts on the narrow grid. Cars crashed and bashed three times before they finally got away, Senna eighteenth, a place behind Prost and a place ahead of Alboreto. All started from the pit lane, Prost's engine dying on the formation lap, Senna in the spare (a CV joint broken), Alboreto because a wheel hadn't been put on properly. This became a race within a race as they stampeded through the slower cars, Senna gaining six places on lap 2. Then, in sequence: tenth on lap 3, ninth on lap 6, eighth on lap 7, seventh on lap 12, into the points on lap 13. Alboreto rose with Senna and overtook him at Hella Licht on lap 15. After the pit stops Senna ran sixth, caught Alboreto and they quarrelled. This lasted two laps, Senna making a heave at Hella Licht. They touched. Senna pitted for new front wings. "Alboreto weaved in front of me and hit the brakes. There was nothing I could do." Senna, ninth, stampeded again: eighth on lap 41, seventh on lap 43, sixth on lap 44 and fifth on the final lap by overtaking Prost, who had an electrical problem.

- **Podium:** Mansell, Piquet, Fabi.
- **Fastest lap:** Mansell 1:28.318.
- **Senna:** 1:28.559.
- **Championship:** Piquet 54, Senna 43, Mansell 39.

Italy, Monza, 6 September 1987.
Qualifying: 1:25.535 (7); 1:24.907 (4). Row 2.
Pole: Piquet 1:23.460.
Race weather: hot, dry.
Warm-up: 1:29.308 (3).
Result: Second.

Everything changed. Marlboro McLaren announced that Senna was joining them to partner Prost in 1988, and McLaren would have Honda engines. In qualifying Senna could only get to slightly less that a second from Berger, who was third on the Saturday. Senna knew he'd reached the limit of what the Lotus could be made to do. "I was trying to brake as late as possible and as a result the brakes overheated. I let them cool and I must have overdone it because I found they were locking into the chicane."

A poor start, sixth across the opening four laps before he opened up. "I wanted to win this one or be nowhere." He took Prost on lap 5 and amidst the pit-stops led – and he didn't come in. "The plan was to change tyres like everyone else *but* I knew if I stopped the race was lost. When they called me I radioed back about the possibility of staying out." Warr checked with Goodyear who murmured hmmm, maybe a set will survive to the end. Warr radioed that to Senna who "decided it was worth taking a chance." The art of the possible. On lap 25, the other pit stops completed, Senna had a gap of 14.084 to Piquet. It left Piquet 25 laps to make it up and initially he seemed to be doing that. It stabilised at 6 from laps 33 to 36, edged into the

5's for three laps, into the 4's for three. On lap 43 Senna pushed hard toward the Parabolica, drawing up to Piercarlo Ghinzani (Ligier).

"I had a lot of trouble with back-markers through the race. There could have been many accidents before, and with Ghinzani it was just the same except that it went wrong. I wanted to pass him under braking but he was right in the middle of the road, not on the left [the normal turn-in point for the right-hander]. I couldn't stop the car enough for the corner and I went straight on." The Lotus bounded over the run-off area, almost skirmished with the tyre barrier and when Senna hauled it back Piquet was through. Senna abandoned all caution, all thoughts of fuel, all thoughts of worn tyres. He had eight laps and went quicker and quicker

Lap	Gap
45	5.5
46	3.8
47	2.8
48	2.6
49	2.5

That 49 represented total commitment. Piquet did 1:26.858, fastest of the race but only until Senna crossed the line – 1:26.796. Even that didn't bring him close enough for an attempt on the final lap.

- **Podium:** Piquet 1h 14m 47.707s, Senna at 1.806, Mansell at 49.036.
- **Fastest lap:** Senna 1:26.796.
- **Championship:** Piquet 63, Senna 49, Mansell 43.

A brief race at Spa. Senna crashed with Nigel Mansell and *then* the action started.

Portugal, Estoril, 20 September 1987.
Qualifying: 1:18.382 (3); 1:18.354 (4). Row 3.
Pole: Berger 1:17.620.
Race weather: hot, dry.
Warm-up: 1:22.877 (8).
Result: Seventh.

More difficulties. On the Friday he spun twice, one of them to avoid a spinning car, and on the Saturday he had an engine fire. He retreated to the spare. It rained.

The race was re-started after a crash on the opening lap. Grid.

Berger

Mansell

Prost

Piquet

Senna

Alboreto

The loneliness of Estoril, where the Lotus broke down in qualifying.

And a long way to turn one, the hard right. At the green light Berger slewed to mid-track and Mansell, abreast, did too. Senna flicked fully to mid-track between Prost to his right and Piquet ahead and left. This happened within 10 metres of the line. Prost stayed right, Piquet level with Berger. Piquet put two wheels on the grass and Berger kept adjusting left, left, left. Instantaneously Senna angled the Lotus to the gap between Prost and Berger and went into it round Piquet. In turn one Senna was third behind Mansell and Berger. Piquet harassed and on lap 11 sneaked by on a slingshot. Senna pitted on lap 14 – an intermittent engine cutout – and emerged twenty-second. From that he produced a vehement, insistent charge so that he finished only four seconds behind Eddie Cheever (Arrows), sixth.

- **Podium:** Prost, Berger, Piquet.
- **Fastest lap:** Berger 1:19.282.
- **Senna:** 1:20.217.
- **Championship:** Piquet 67, Senna 49, Mansell 43.

Spain, Jerez, 27 September 1987.
Qualifying: 1:25.162 (6); 1:24.320 (2). Row 3.
Pole: Piquet 1:22.461.
Race weather: hot, dry.
Warm-up: 1:31.170 (14).
Result: Fifth.

On the Friday the engine on Senna's qualifying car misbehaved and on the Saturday morning he damaged the underbelly over a kerb. In the afternoon he covered 24 laps – only Ghinzani (25) did more – shaving fractions as best he could. The art of the possible.

Mansell led from Piquet, Senna third and clearly holding the others up. That was their problem, not his. He hugged the racing line lap upon lap. Mansell pitted for tyres on lap 42, Piquet on lap 45, Senna now second behind Mansell. "I knew that if I came in the best I could hope for was maybe fourth or fifth. I only had a real problem in the slow corners – in the quick ones I was OK and there was no problem on the straights *so* I decided to stay out, fight, and hope that the tyres would last." They did and they didn't. Late on he couldn't resist moves by Piquet, Johansson and Prost. The championship had virtually gone.

- **Podium:** Mansell, Prost, Johansson.
- **Fastest lap:** Berger 1:26.986.
- **Senna:** 1:30.088.
- **Championship:** Piquet 70, Mansell 52, Senna 51.

RACE 134

Mexico, Mexico City, 18 October 1987.
Qualifying: 1:21.361 (7); 1:19.089 (7). Row 4.
Pole: Mansell 1:18.383.
Race weather: hot, dry.
Warm-up: 1:25.367 (18).
Result: Retired after 54 laps, spun off.

The 'active' suspension helped over the Mexican corrugation but the Lotus lacked grip. While its straight-line speed was immense – 4mph quickest at a timing point out on the circuit, 1mph quickest over the start-finish line – the slow corners slowed Senna to a crucial degree. On the Saturday, urging hard and with only moments of the session left, he bounded a bump in the Peraltada corner, the vast spoon onto the start-finish line. "The wheels came off the ground and the car slid sideways." He rammed the tyre wall, clambered out, wandered a few steps and sank by the tyre wall, didn't seem to know where he was.

He ran consistently in the race, rising to second behind Mansell on lap 21 before Piquet overtook him on lap 38. The clutch failed and, nine laps to go, he tried to change down without it. His brakes locked and he spun, the car stalling. Roebuck wrote that Senna "beseeched the marshals to come and give him a shove. This they failed to do to his satisfaction and, after stepping from the Lotus, he proceeded to slug one of them. Or was it two? Well, whatever, it cost him a 15,000 dollar fine from the Stewards afterwards." The mystifying self-control and lack of it.

- **Podium:** Mansell, Piquet, Patrese.
- **Fastest lap:** Piquet 1:19.132.
- **Senna:** 1:20.586.
- **Championship:** Piquet 73, Mansell 61, Senna 51.

The deceptive delight of Adelaide, Senna moving towards second place, then disqualification – the brake-ducting on the Lotus was ruled illegal *Formula One Pictures.*

RACE 135

Japan, Suzuka, 1 November 1987.
Qualifying: 1:44.026 (9); 1:42.723 (7). Row 4.
Pole: Berger 1:40.042.
Race weather: overcast.
Warm-up: 1:47.740 (6).
Result: Second.

A crash by Mansell on the Friday gave the championship to Piquet. For Senna the familiar fate: lack of balance, lack of grip. Moreover Nakajima recorded a greater maximum speed on the back straight timing point on the Friday (197.319 mph against 196.261), enough to raise an eyebrow or two.

Berger led from Boutsen, Senna third, Piquet fourth. The dislike between Senna and Piquet no doubt deepened because Senna had expressed the profound hope that Mansell would be champion. Now Piquet complained that Senna went off the track and returned to it with less than decorum. "I had to back off to avoid being hit by him," Piquet said, and added that, rather than call Senna the "Sao Paulo taxi driver" as he habitually did, he intended to call him "handbrake." Senna said "I had to go around Piquet at the start because he was so slow getting away. I went to the right of him *because* if I'd gone to the left there might have been an accident. Alboreto was stalled there. What else could I do?" After the pit stops Senna ran third behind Berger and Johansson until, on the final lap, fuel problems slowed Johansson.

- **Podium:** Berger 1h 32m 58.072s, Senna at 17.384, Johansson at 17.694.
- **Fastest lap:** Prost 1:43.844.
- **Senna:** 1:45.805.
- **Championship:** Piquet 73, Mansell 61, Senna 57.

RACE 136

Australia, Adelaide, 15 November 1987.
Qualifying: 1:18.508 (4); 1:18.488 (4). Row 2.
Pole: Berger 1:17.267.
Race weather: hot.
Warm-up: 1:23.701 (8).
Result: Disqualified.

Senna savoured the prospect of a street race and second row of the grid opened up possibilities – no matter that he was alongside Piquet.

A sad, angered end to three years with Lotus. Senna didn't make a pit stop, enabling him to finish second to Berger. Benetton successfully protested the brake-ducting on the Lotus. Senna was neither understanding nor sympathetic. After all, he'd been wasting his time, all 1h 53m 30.989s of it. He could not or would not bring himself to say goodbye to the team, something he'd not done before and never would again.

- **Podium:** Berger, Senna (later disqualified), Alboreto.
- **Fastest lap:** Berger 1:20.416.
- **Senna:** 1:20.456.
- **Championship:** Piquet 76 (73 counting), Mansell 61, Senna 57.

The Adelaide podium, before the disqualification.

Chapter 6

McLaren
The first championship
1988

*P*rost, World Champion in 1985 and 1986, had been in Grand Prix racing since 1980. How would he cope with Senna as a team-mate? Would he cope? None had so far, but none had had the stature of Prost. It became the central question of the season, and the next season, too. McLaren had Honda turbo engines. The other front-runners: Mansell and Patrese (Williams); Piquet (Lotus); Boutsen and Sandro Nannini (Benetton); Alboreto and Berger (Ferrari).

* * *

RACE 137

Brazil, Rio, 3 April 1988.
Qualifying: 1:30.218 (1); 1:28.096 (1). Pole.
Race weather: overcast.
Warm-up: 1:45.165 (1).
Result: Disqualified after 31 laps.

The Friday morning untimed session said a great deal, Prost quickest, Senna next and an eye blink between them, Prost 1:31.234, Senna 1:31.761. Maybe that set the tone for the relationship. The tone sharpened in first qualifying, Senna on provisional pole but Prost fourth. "We have not had any serious problems. Our car is virtually brand new and we are still finding out about it *so* it is only to be expected that we will be adjusting both the chassis and the engine. The circuit is still developing grip so I think we can improve quite a lot." A vast, noisy, exuberant crowd came to witness that on the Saturday and got what they wanted to see, Senna improving by the two seconds. "I was quite lucky with the traffic but the most important thing is that we seem to be more than competitive in spite of the

inevitable minor problems that are to be expected with a brand new car."

Senna brought them round slowly on the parade lap and, settled on the grid, began to wave his arms vigorously. The gear linkage had broken when he tried to snick the McLaren into first. Four rows behind him Ivan Capelli's March belched smoke. The start was aborted, and Senna began it from the pit lane in the spare. He completed the opening lap twenty-first, gained three places next lap and rushed. On lap 13 he tracked Alboreto down the start-finish straight, positioned himself calmly inside for the right-hander and went through. Three laps later he'd taken Boutsen. Piquet lay ahead. Senna drew up down the back straight, nipped out and went to mid-track, came back squeezing Piquet, assumed the racing line and was third. They pitted for tyres on laps 26 and 27, Senna sixth. He ran there for four laps. The Stewards had decided to disqualify him for changing cars after the first start, a decision which Ron Dennis of McLaren had been vehemently disputing. Senna was black-flagged.

Senna in 1988

- **Podium:** Prost, Berger, Piquet.
- **Fastest lap:** Berger 1:32.943.
- **Senna:** 1:34.657.

RACE 138

San Marino, Imola, 1 May 1988.
Qualifying: 1:41.597 (2); 1:27.148 (1). Pole.
Race weather: warm, dry.
Warm-up: 1:32.544 (2).
Result: First.

Each qualifying became an examination of man against man – of Prost, long a McLaren 'family' member, against the newcomer. The Friday was wet, the Saturday overcast but dry. Senna had a problem before he set the pole time on Saturday. "The pop-off valve was giving trouble, obliging the Honda engineers to fit a new one. Although I knew the valve was not operating correctly I did not come into the pits immediately because I was worried that it might rain."

At the green light Prost, who'd felt a problem with the engine, almost stalled, or as Dennis said "unfortunately the car is quite difficult to get away from the line. Alain didn't get it right and he had to work hard to catch up." This is a lovely example of the fabled Ron Dennis management-speak. What happened? Prost hiccuped, crawled and when the engine fired he'd been engulfed by the pack, Senna crisp into the lead. Prost completed the lap sixth. What would Prost do? By lap three he was fifth, by lap 5 fourth, by lap 8 second. Prost knew "Ayrton would be very difficult to beat." And was. At lap 11 Senna led Prost by 11.5 seconds, enough. "I was never really confident I would finish. The balance of the engine was beautiful, consumption good, sure, but quite early in the race I had smoke – together with a burning smell – coming into the cockpit, which worried me. Later on the gearbox started to feel loose and I thought perhaps the linkage would break but everything stayed OK. The only other problem was traffic, but I guess all the quick guys had that."

- **Podium:** Senna 1h 32m 41.264s, Prost at 2.334, Piquet at one lap.
- **Fastest lap:** Prost 1:29.685.
- **Senna:** 1:29.815.
- **Championship:** Prost 15, Senna 9, Piquet and Berger 8.

RACE 139

Monaco, Monte Carlo, 15 May 1988.
Qualifying: 1:26.464 (1); 1:23.998 (1). Pole.
Race weather: warm, dry.
Warm-up: 1:44.159 (1).
Result: Retired after 66 laps, accident.

Senna recounted his inner thoughts to Gerry Donaldson in a famous interview which appeared in *Grand Prix People*. "Monte Carlo, '88, the last qualifying session. I was already on pole and I was going faster and faster. One lap after the other, quicker, and quicker, and quicker. I was at one stage just on pole, then by half a second, and then one second...and I kept going."

3rd lap	1:27.014
5th lap	1:25.592
7th lap	1:24.439
9th lap	1:23.998

His 1988 team-mate, Alain Prost. The partnership started smoothly enough *Marlboro*.

101

Homage in Brazil, but Senna would be black-flagged for changing cars at the re-start of the race.

These laps were on the same run. "Suddenly I was nearly two seconds faster than anybody else, including my team-mate with the same car. And I suddenly realised that I was no longer driving the car consciously. I was kind of driving it by instinct, only I was in a different dimension. It was like I was in a tunnel, not only the tunnel under the hotel, but the whole circuit for me was a tunnel. I was just going, going – more, and more, and more, and more. I was way over the limit but still able to find even more. Then suddenly something just kicked me. I kind of woke up and I realised that I was in a different atmosphere than you normally are. Immediately my reaction was to back off and I didn't want to go out any more that day. It frightened me because I was well beyond my conscious understanding."

Senna led, Berger uncompromising on the inside into Ste Devote, Prost third. Senna uncoiled the McLaren round the Monaco coil, Berger holding up Prost. By the time Prost took Berger (lap 54!) Senna led by more than 46 seconds. Dennis radioed Senna and Prost to relay the position, weighing no doubt the prospect of a comfortable 1-2 result. Senna relaxed his pace, Prost relaxed his pace. On lap 67 Senna lost concentration in the right-hander before the tunnel and punted the barrier. A television crew caught Senna as he walked from the car and he wasn't crying yet. He'd do that, but only in private, and still be crying five hours later. He dipped his head, a gesture of self-immolation. He tugged absently at the straps of the helmet he'd just removed, hands working subconsciously, eyes narrowed now. He was consumed by the fate he had invoked upon himself. He blinked, a nervous mechanism – half the face twitching – and fiddled on with the straps, tapped his forehead, set the helmet down, unzipped his overalls. His eyes roved, he licked his lower lip, he grimaced. He was in that other dimension, the one we can't reach. He was incanting to himself *I will never lose concentration again, never.* And maybe – surely – never did.

- **Podium:** Prost, Berger, Alboreto.
- **Fastest lap:** Senna 1:26.321.
- **Championship:** Prost 24, Berger 14, Senna 9.

Senna taking provisional pole on a damp Thursday at Monaco *Formula One Pictures.*

RACE 140

Mexico, Mexico City, 29 May 1988.
Qualifying: 1:17.468 (1); 1:17.666 (1). Pole.
Race weather: overcast.
Warm-up: 1:20.121 (1).
Result: Second.

Senna set the pace in the Friday untimed session, Prost next. In fact the only session when Senna wasn't quickest was Saturday morning untimed – Prost first, Senna fourth. "Everything is fine."

The race was settled at the start, Prost and Piquet off faster. Senna tracked Piquet to Peraltada and overtook him on the start-finish straight, but – the McLarens evenly matched – such a short delay proved too much to recapture. All afternoon they circled 1-2. "By the time I got myself into a rhythm Alain was already some way clear. He drove very fast and he deserved the race. The pop-off valve opened unexpectedly when I took second gear from the start and for most of that lap I was behind Piquet seeing Prost pull away. I knew already it would be difficult to catch him. Like Imola, but the other way round."

- **Podium:** Prost 1h 30m 15.737s, Senna at 7.104, Berger at 57.314.
- **Fastest lap:** Prost 1:18.608.
- **Senna:** 1:18.776.
- **Championship:** Prost 33, Berger 18, Senna 15.

RACE 141

Canada, Montreal, 12 June 1988.
Qualifying: 1:22.392 (1); 1:21.681 (1). Pole.
Race weather: dry.
Warm-up: 1:26.645 (6).
Result: First.

Straight Senna, his fifth consecutive pole. He took it provisionally on the Friday (from Prost, of course) with a run just before the end. "For most of the session I had too much understeer. We managed to improve the car but the session was stopped by accidents so it was difficult to keep a rhythm going." He set the pole early in the Saturday session.

Prost made the more assertive start, Senna angry that he'd been given the wrong side of the grid for pole: on the right but the first corner a left, favouring Prost. This is the first recorded instance of Senna complaining about such a matter. He would again, as we shall see and the whole world would see. Senna was within striking distance of Prost but where to overtake? That's a perennial problem round the Ile Notre Dame. Senna created the move at the hairpin on lap 19, nicely inside and Prost giving him room. Senna had outbraked him.

"For all 69 laps we were on the limit of the fuel so Alain and I were pacing each other. Passing him is never easy but when I saw an opportunity everything came good." Senna accelerated.

The McLarens were in a class of their own. Here Senna tracks Prost in the French Grand Prix.

Strictly symbolic. Senna leads Piquet, now with Lotus, at Silverstone *Formula One Pictures*.

	Senna	Prost
Lap 20	1:26.922	1:27.411
Lap 21	1:26.718	1:27.048
Lap 22	1:26.495	1:27.135

And that settled it.

- **Podium:** Senna 1h 39m 46.618s, Prost at 5.934, Boutsen at 51.409.
- **Fastest lap:** Senna 1:24.973.
- **Championship:** Prost 39, Senna 24, Berger 18.

RACE 142

USA-East, Detroit, 19 June 1988.
Qualifying: 1:40.606 (1); 1:41.719 (3). Pole.
Race weather: hot, dry.
Warm-up: 1:42.409 (2).
Result: First.

Senna didn't venture out for most of the Friday session and complained about the difficulty of getting a clear lap. "The tyres were most effective only in the first two or three laps." The track, recently resurfaced, broke up on the Saturday. It meant more straight Senna, consecutive six now.

Senna's chances were spiced by Berger and Alboreto lining up between himself and Prost. Berger almost outdragged Senna into turn one but Senna responded to that and led. Prost, prudent because he loathed Detroit, crossed the

line to complete the opening lap in fifth but picked them off exquisitely – Boutsen, Alboreto, Berger – and by lap 7 was second. Any hopes of a race within the race, Prost catching Senna, ebbed as gearbox problems hampered Prost. Senna pitted for tyres on lap 39. "When the crew told me to come in I did not want to *but* when I saw that Alain had stopped [for tyres] I was happy to do the same." Senna's overview: "This race is very hard mentally and physically. You're racing against the heat and the walls."

- **Podium:** Senna 1h 54m 56.035s, Prost at 38.713, Boutsen at one lap.
- **Fastest lap:** Prost 1:44.836.
- **Senna:** 1:44.992.
- **Championship:** Prost 45, Senna 33, Berger 18.

RACE 143

France, Paul Ricard, 3 July 1988.
Qualifying: 1:08.456 (2); 1:08.067 (2). Front row.
Pole: Prost 1:07.589.
Race weather: hot, dry.
Warm-up: 1:10.135 (1).
Result: Second.

Prost quickest both sessions, the first pole Senna hadn't taken this season. Senna held it fleetingly on the Saturday before Prost countered. "On my first set of tyres I couldn't get a clear lap until my ninth and the tyres, I think, are at their best for four laps." Senna thought like that: absolute adjudication of the temporal and the transient brought to his judgement.

Prost led, Senna swiftly overtaking Berger. Prost siphoned a gap of a second, Berger lurking around Senna. Crossing the line into lap 2, Prost eked out one and half seconds. Then, stalemate. Prost had a long stop (10.68), Senna led. Prost caught him but two back-markers were wedged between. Prost had them on the Mistral, tracked, drew up, Senna locking his brakes at the end of the start-finish straight – twice. Back-markers loomed on lap 61 at Beausset, a right. From a long way back Prost mounted an enormous and unexpected run down the inside channel, hugging the kerbing and was through, Senna still behind the back-markers. Almost invariably from Paddock Hill 1 March 1981 to here it had been the other way round.

- **Podium:** Prost 1h 37m 37.328s, Senna at 31.752, Alboreto at 1m 06.505.
- **Fastest lap:** Prost 1:11.737.
- **Senna:** 1:11.856.
- **Championship:** Prost 54, Senna 39, Berger 21.

RACE 144

Britain, Silverstone, 10 July 1988.
Qualifying: 1:10.787 (3); 1:10.616 (3). Row 2.
Pole: Berger 1:10.133.
Race weather: wet.
Warm-up: 1:17.264 (1).
Result: First.

A Ferrari festival in qualifying, both days. "Because of trying to get the handling right we haven't done as much 'fuel running' as usual so we don't really know what the position is with consumption." On the Saturday Senna spun through 360 degrees twice, rotations of absolute ferocity, and both times he continued at tremendous speed as if nothing had happened.

"The car was not handling very well there and I was more on the limit than I had been yesterday." It was a typically downbeat description and the searching out of a reason why it happened. You'd never have known it was wild, wondrous. The rotations, moreover, make me speculate. Gilles Villeneuve, they say, had an inborn ability to know where the track was going regardless of where his car pointed and there's a photograph of him slewed at Monaco but his eyes locked onto the track, not the direction of the car. Did Senna also have this? If you were at Silverstone on 9 July 1988 you know the answer.

Officially a wet race. Berger led, Senna manipulating wide around Alboreto at Maggotts for second place. Senna attacked into Stowe but Berger blocked that and Senna existed within the spray Berger cast back. "At the speed Berger was running I couldn't make the finish on fuel. I was pretty sure he couldn't, either, so I thought I'd sit back for a bit. I couldn't see much when the rain was really bad and I was getting water behind my visor which made it mist up." Prost chugged losing place after place, the McLaren ill-handling and Prost

Moving into other-worldly concentration, Hungary.

more and more convinced the conditions were unacceptable. On lap 14 Senna overtook Berger towards Woodcote and went mid-track into the mouth of Woodcote to lap Prost, who turned in. "Alain and I almost touched. It was a bad moment because the visibility was so bad. Then we had some unexpected problems with fuel consumption which was worrying until I got the fuel situation under control again."

- **Podium:** Senna 1h 33m 16.367s, Mansell at 23.344, Nannini at 51.214.
- **Fastest lap:** Mansell 1:23.308.
- **Senna:** 1:23.595.
- **Championship:** Prost 54, Senna 48, Berger 21.

RACE 145

Germany, Hockenheim, 24 July 1988.
Qualifying: 1:44.596 (1); 1:50.002 (10). Pole.
Race weather: damp, cloudy.
Warm-up: 1:48.674 (1).
Result: First.

On the Friday the Honda engines were down on power though not that far down. Saturday was hot and humid, no improvement possible. Senna decided to concentrate on race set-up, running with a full fuel load. "The worst that was going to happen was that Alain might knock me off pole position *but* I wasn't too worried about that at this circuit so we figured it would be more worthwhile running through some chassis settings for the race."

On a damp track virtually everyone began on wet tyres. Senna led but Prost, fourth, needed 11 laps to reach second place. By then Senna was an unassailable 13 seconds ahead. "Alain was pushing hard to get back to me so I concentrated on maintaining the gap. With wet tyres over a full race distance, and without a stop, it was a bit difficult so my fifth win feels good."

- **Podium:** Senna 1h 32m 54.188s, Prost at 13.609, Berger at 52.095.
- **Fastest lap:** Alessandro Nannini (Benetton) 2:03.032.
- **Senna:** 2:05.001.
- **Championship:** Prost 60, Senna 57, Berger 25.

Victory, Hungary.

RACE 146

Hungary, Hungaroring, 7 August, 1988.
Qualifying: 1:30.422 (5); 1:27.635 (1). Pole.
Race weather: hot, dry.
Warm-up: 1:32.379 (8).
Result: First.

A dank Friday – "at the end of the session when the track was almost completely dry it was just a matter of getting a clear lap and I didn't get one" – and a cut and thrust Saturday. Senna came out after 11 minutes and flung the car at the hairpin. His 1:29.405 beat Prost's provisional pole. Prost summoned 1:29.299, then 1:29.231, then 1:29.185. Senna summoned 1:28.212. Mansell placed himself squarely into the equation, 1:27.743, and that stood until five minutes from the end when Senna beat it. "Hard work."

On the fourth row Prost prepared to apply his logic to the problem of gaining places. Senna out-rushed Mansell into turn one, Prost tenth. Two races were going on concurrently: Senna

Italy, trying to escape the mind-games Prost wove.

versus Mansell for the lead, Prost versus the rest to reach Senna and Mansell. Prost gained places at the favoured place, the long start-finish straight, Mansell drifted back. At lap 30: Senna, Patrese, Boutsen, Prost. Everything changed like an upheaval. Prost picked off Patrese on the straight and, freed, set about catching Boutsen.

Lap 31	1:36.598
Lap 32	1:33.701
Lap 33	1:31.533

On lap 47 Prost darted past Boutsen into the mouth of turn one and set about catching Senna, who was fleetingly baulked by two back-markers onto the straight, Prost behind now. Into turn one they produced a mosaic of movement. Senna went right, Prost further right and inside. Prost's impetus heaved him across the track – his rear seemed to brush Senna's front – and Senna grabbed it back. "Alain was pushing hard and he was quicker than me. He managed to go through and we avoided each other but for an instant I thought we could both go off the road." Soon after Prost felt a "huge vibration" from the front of the car. He pushed on, keeping the race taut and alive to the end.

- **Podium:** Senna 1h 57m 47.081s, Prost at 0.529, Boutsen at 31.410.
- **Fastest lap:** Prost 1:30.639.
- **Senna:** 1:30.964.
- **Championship:** Senna and Prost 66, Berger 28.

RACE 147

Belgium, Spa, 28 August 1988.
Qualifying: 1:53.718 (1); 2:15.196 (4). Pole.
Race weather: dry, sunny.
Warm-up: 1:59.988 (1).
Result: First.

Japan, and the first World Championship. Prost is left and Thierry Boutsen right.

Senna got pole, as it transpired, on the Friday. "The last lap with the second set of tyres was really good and I think I might have been able to go quicker on a later lap if I had not been forced to back off" – an accident ahead. A wet Saturday.

Senna and Prost, filling the front row, made a pact not to take each other off at La Source in the jostle from the lights. Once through they'd race. This seemed a mature and prudent arrangement. Nobody really knew about it except them and they did not know its foreboding quality. Senna churned too much wheelspin, giving La Source to Prost but out in the country Senna went by. He applied The Tactic. He covered this opening lap in 2:08.003, Prost 2:09.480, Berger third, 2:09.768. Prost spent the race trying to stay with Senna and couldn't. "Today was not as hard as Hungary, for example, but the car's handling deteriorated because of oil on the circuit and I had to keep it consistent."

- **Podium:** Senna 1h 28m 00.549s, Prost at 30.470, Boutsen at 59.681 (later disqualified).
- **Fastest lap:** Berger 2:00.772.
- **Senna:** 2:01.061.
- **Championship:** Senna 75, Prost 72, Berger 28.

RACE 148

Italy, Monza 11 September 1988.
Qualifying: 1:26.160 (1); 1:25.974 (1). Pole.
Race weather: hot, dry.
Warm-up: 1:29.820 (1).
Result: Retired after 49 laps, accident.

Pressure point for Prost in the verdant parkland. On the Friday Senna "only used one set of tyres on the race car *because* I wanted to check that everything was OK with the T-car [the spare] that I am using this weekend. The traffic was not too bad but I made a mistake in the T-car and went straight on at the second chicane." On the Saturday he improved by two-tenths for his 26th pole and the tenth of the season, beating the record of nine held jointly by Piquet (1984), Ronnie Peterson (1973) and Lauda (1974 and 1975).

The mystery of what happened in the race endures, although Monza lay strewn with clues. By lap 2 Senna led by 3.4 seconds from Prost, who had a misfire. Prost sensed the engine wouldn't last and decided to push Senna, who didn't know about the misfire, of course. Prost pushed. The reasoning: Senna, forced to respond, might use too much fuel. Prost completed 34 laps before the misfire claimed him and now the two Ferraris, Berger and Alboreto, took up the chase. With two laps to go the Ferraris were visible in Senna's mirrors and closing to within striking distance. Senna had lapped in the 1:33's but now he had to force into the 1:30's. Did he have enough fuel? He'd insist he did. "I had it under control. There was no pressure on me." At the first chicane on lap 50, second last lap, he encountered Jean-Louis Schlesser, deputising for Mansell (ill). The race perished in a frenetic flurry. Into the chicane Schlesser twisted from Senna's path and lost control under braking. Senna saw the gap and plunged for it but Schlesser wrestled the Williams. It returned and harpooned Senna, pitching him over the far kerbing and beached him there. Had the presence of the Ferraris forced Senna to plunge? The question endures, unanswered, and always will.

- **Podium:** Berger, Alboreto, Cheever.
- **Fastest lap:** Alboreto 1:29.070.
- **Senna:** 1:29.569.
- **Championship:** Senna 75, Prost 72, Berger 37.

Before the implosion. Senna and Prost still cordial at the beginning of 1989.

A wet race in Canada, 1989. He was leading when the engine failed with three laps to go.

RACE 149

Portugal, Estoril, 25 September 1988.
Qualifying: 1:18.032 (1); 1:17.869 (2).
Front row.
Pole: Prost 1:17.411.
Race weather: hot, dry.
Warm-up: 1:22.601 (9).
Result: Sixth.

Prost bedded in a new car on the Friday and still the McLarens were the only cars into the 1:18's. On the Saturday Prost professed that "I wasn't terribly interested in getting pole – no point in taking any more risks just for the sake of a tenth of a second." That makes his pole time more remarkable. Senna said his car was working well although he'd had a repeat of an electrical failure from the day before, making the dashboard instruments go blank.

The race had to be re-started after a crash. Prost scampered across and squeezed Senna, forcing him to place two wheels on the kerb. Senna did not appreciate that. They flowed abreast towards turn one, Prost mid-track and better placed. Senna carved round the outside. Out at the back Prost used the looping corners to close. Along the start-finish straight he positioned himself directly behind Senna, both cars over to the left. Prost jinked right as they accelerated towards 190 mph and Senna jinked at him. There is no question Senna did this. Their wheels virtually touched, Prost wedged between Senna and the pit lane wall. Within the wedge Prost managed a tiny wriggle away from Senna. "It was very dangerous," Prost said, "because I was very close to him and very close to the wall. If I'd backed off I might have hit his rear wheel." It seemed nothing had changed since Formula Ford 1600: Senna could still not tolerate defeat. His fuel read-out soon gave alarming readings and he settled to an economy run.

• **Podium:** Prost, Capelli, Boutsen.
• **Fastest lap:** Berger 1:21.961.
• **Senna:** 1:22.852.
• **Championship:** Prost 81, Senna 76, Berger 37.

Spain, Jerez, 2 October 1988.
Qualifying: 1:24.775 (1); 1:24.067 (1). Pole.
Race weather: hot, dry.
Warm-up: 1:29.299 (5).
Result: Fourth.

The pressure shifted onto Senna. On the Friday he found it "quite difficult to get the car to work. We changed the chassis set-up after the morning session which made an improvement and I was lucky to get my one clear lap when I did because the car and the engine were working well then." He and Prost improved on the Saturday but "we have to concentrate on getting the chassis set-up to be right through the full distance."

Prost made an instantaneous start, Senna hesitant, Mansell into second. Senna attacked Mansell, wove a path through at a right-hander, drifted wide and Mansell nipped back at him. The McLaren used too much fuel and by lap 39 was fourth. Senna pitted late for tyres – seventh – and flogged into the points.

- **Podium:** Prost, Mansell, Nannini.
- **Fastest lap:** Prost 1:27.845.
- **Senna:** 1:28.273.
- **Championship:** Prost 90 (84 counting), Senna 79, Berger 38.

Japan, Suzuka, 30 October 1988.
Qualifying: 1:42.157 (1); 1:41.853 (1). Pole.
Race weather: wet, dry.
Warm-up: 1:46.372 (1).
Result: First.

They say he read The Bible on the flight. They say he was withdrawn during the flight. He prepared to vindicate his life and, as it seemed, retreated far into himself to arrange himself for that. The permutations favoured him, not Prost. A driver could count his 11 best finishes from the 16 rounds and Prost had already finished in 12, lowest place second. The most he could leave Suzuka with was 81 and, winning Australia, the most he could total was 84. Senna had finished in the points 11 times but could discard the one point from Estoril. If he won Suzuka he totalled 87.

Prost stated his intentions by going fastest in the Friday morning untimed session, Senna second. Senna took provisional pole in the afternoon, setting the time on his first set of tyres. "Unfortunately on the second set I could not get a clear lap before the tyres were too far worn." On an overcast Saturday afternoon he took pole in a five-lap run of gathering momentum, feeling his way through the 1:50's into a blitz. *Motoring News* reported that "impressive though the Brazilian's on-track performance was, he earned little kudos off-track for the brusqueness that characterised his weekend as he focussed relentlessly on his championship quest."

The start went wrong. "The clutch was very sensitive and I got the jump on the green light only for the engine to stall. It was partly the clutch, partly my fault. I thought it was all over for me." He was saved by the simplest thing in the world: the track sloped. The car dribbled forward. "I dropped the clutch and got going and the engine stalled again but I managed to pick it up a second time and staggered away. I was really lucky." He was eighth after lap 1.

	Prost	Senna	Overtaking
Lap 2	1:51.028	1:51.579	Patrese, Nannini
Lap 3	1:49.431	1:52.210	Boutsen
Lap 4	1:49.837	1:50.490	Alboreto
Lap 5	1:49.190	1:49.474	
Lap 6	1:48.425	1:48.104	

He ran fourth reeling in Berger – the gap to Prost 11.628 at lap 10 – and on lap 11 overtook Berger, Capelli pressuring Prost. Senna needed 10 laps to take Capelli, rain falling. The electrics on Capelli's March failed after 19 laps. It restored a symmetry to the whole season and the championship, Prost and Senna unhindered – and Senna came hard, probed at Prost for eight laps, got by. He would not be caught. Prost dug a warrior's effort towards the end, cutting the gap to 1.5 but, the rain heavy, had no further chance. Senna spent the final laps gesturing to have the race stopped. He was on

The body language of defeat. Senna walks back to the pits, Canada.

slick tyres, after all, and the car might have floated from him at any instant.

During the last lap in the last corner he'd say he saw God.

- **Podium:** Senna 1h 33m 26.173s, Prost at 13.363, Boutsen at 36.109.
- **Fastest lap:** Senna 1:46.326.
- **Championship:** Senna 88 (87 counting), Prost 96 (84 counting), Berger 41.

On the Friday "the good lap was clear but I made a mistake at the hairpin when I went a bit wide under braking." He'd hurt his right wrist on holiday and "it's a bit painful and I am having it treated." A frantic Saturday finale. With four minutes remaining Senna did 1:18.140, shaving Prost's 1:18.247. Two

Preparing to win the German Grand Prix at Hockenheim from Prost.

minutes later Prost shaved that, 1:17.880. As the flag was to fall Senna shaved that, 1:17.748 – his thirteenth pole of the season.

Prost made the better start and Berger overtook Senna on lap 3. Berger even overtook Prost on lap 14 but crashed into Arnoux while lapping him. Prost led and increased the gap; that was all.

- **Podium:** Prost 1h 53m 14.676s, Senna at 36.787, Piquet at 47.546.
- **Fastest lap:** Prost 1:21.216. Senna 1:21.668.
- **Championship:** Senna 94 (90 counting), Prost 105 (87 counting), Berger 41.

1989

Could Prost survive Senna? The question sharpened and quickly. The other front-runners: Boutsen and Patrese (Williams), Piquet (Lotus), Nannini and Herbert (Benetton), Mansell and Berger (Ferrari). Turbos and the fuel restriction had been banned.

The pole came on the Saturday. "I wouldn't say I took any risks, because the car felt safe to drive. The most difficult thing is to believe that you can go through the corners at the sort of speeds you need to produce this sort of time. There are a lot of long, very fast corners which are extremely difficult."

At the green light Senna moved to mid-track, Berger out from behind, Senna flicking towards Berger forcing Berger to flick clear, two wheels off the track. They reached the first corner, a right, three abreast: Berger, Senna, Patrese. The Ferrari and the McLaren clouted each other. "The only way out of the problem would have been to go straight up in the air. Patrese and Berger trapped me and I lost the nose section." Berger claimed that "Senna chopped across twice to try to make me back off but he shouldn't try that with me. Never in my life will I back off in that situation." Senna pitted for a new nose cone, making him last. He ran to the end two laps down.

- **Podium:** Mansell, Prost, Mauricio Gugelmin (March).
- **Fastest lap:** Patrese 1:32.507.
- **Senna:** 1:33.685.

RACE 154

San Marino, Imola, 23 April 1989.
Qualifying: 1:42.939 (2); 1:26.010 (1). Pole.
Race weather: warm, sunny.
Warm-up: 1:28.571 (2).
Result: First.

Senna explored the nuances of qualifying. On the Friday "it was all a question of being out and ready for a quick lap in the last few minutes because the circuit was getting drier all the time. I slightly fumbled a gearchange under braking for Tosa which put me into a quick spin." On the Saturday "I managed to get a clear lap on race tyres but on qualifying tyres I came up behind two other cars – the Arrows, I think – running slowly on the straight down towards Tosa. I had to aim between them, flat out, and at the last moment I found myself taking a 'confidence' lift from the throttle. It was also frustrating to miss the last few minutes of the session because a bent front suspension pull-rod had to be changed. When the jack was slipped under the front of the car the qualifying rubber was still so hot that the car was literally stuck to the tarmac. Their efforts with the jack tweaked the pull-rod."

The race was quite normal until lap 4 – Senna leading from Prost – when Berger crashed at Tamburello, the Ferrari exploding in flames. At the re-start Prost out-gunned Senna onto the power and led through Tamburello but, into Tosa, Senna curved round the outside. "The car wasn't going too well under heavy braking at first and with Alain pushing me hard it took a while to settle into a rhythm but once the gap

reached six seconds I was able to maintain that pace and after Alain spun [on lap 47] the pressure was really off." Afterwards Prost could not conceal his anger – but at what? Remember Spa and La Source. It was the same pact and subsequently Prost claimed Senna broke it by overtaking him at Tosa. Senna defended his action to me by pointing out that Prost was relatively slow into Tosa and that annulled the pact. From this moment the relationship disintegrated, dangerously.

- **Podium:** Senna 1h 26m 51.245s, Prost at 40.225, Nannini at one lap.
- **Fastest lap:** Prost 1:26.795.
- **Senna:** 1:27.273.
- **Championship:** Prost 12, Senna and Mansell 9.

RACE 155

Monaco, Monte Carlo, 7 May 1989.
Qualifying: 1:24.126 (1); 1:22.308 (1). Pole.
Race weather: warm, sunny.
Warm-up: 1:26.214 (1).
Result: First.

On the Saturday Senna confessed to "a slight mistake at Casino Square" but got a "clear run" and took pole. No-one had ever driven a lap of the circuit quicker and, crushingly, Prost was a full second slower for the other place on the front row.

The race needed two starts – Warwick stalled, aborting the first – and Senna reacted to the green light superbly, embracing Ste Devote. For the first three laps – The Tactic – he fashioned a gap but Prost set fastest lap and drew up. "At the beginning I didn't want to push too hard but when we came to lapping traffic I began to pull away, perhaps rather more than I had expected. It was just as well because I suffered gearbox problems in the second half, losing second then first. It made the car extremely difficult to drive in traffic *but* I kept pressing on as hard as I could because I didn't want to give Alain any indication that I was in trouble." Prost felt that an old team-mate and adversary – Arnoux (Ligier) – blocked him beyond the call of duty, permitting Senna to escape. Worse, Prost came upon a crash between

Piquet and de Cesaris at the Loews hairpin which covered the track and obliged Prost to come to a complete halt. For the first time in his career Prost sat motionless in a Formula 1 car – in neutral.

- **Podium:** Senna 1h 53m 33.251s, Prost at 52.529, Stefano Modena (Brabham) at one lap.
- **Fastest lap:** Prost 1:25.501.
- **Senna:** 1:26.017.
- **Championship:** Prost and Senna 18, Mansell 9.

RACE 156

Mexico, Mexico City, 28 May 1989.
Qualifying: 1:19.112 (1); 1:17.876 (1). Pole.
Race weather: hot, sunny.
Warm-up: 1:21.461 (3).
Result: First.

"It's a lot easier in a way than driving a turbo because the altitude means we have less power than normally so to compensate we have run less wing and the car is obviously much lighter in the corners. Combined with the slippery surface it makes a big challenge." That was the Friday. On the Saturday he equalled Jim Clark's record of 33 poles. Clark had done this in 72 Grand Prix meetings, Senna 82. Senna also established a new record of seven consecutive poles, beating his own total – which he shared with Stirling Moss and Lauda – of six in 1988.

At the green light Senna went full over to the left and hugged the kerbing to turn perfectly into turn one, the right. A tale of tyres. Senna chose Bs for the left, Cs for the right, Prost Cs all round, Senna correct, Prost incorrect. That was evident after only a handful of laps. Prost pitted on lap 20 and wanted the same as Senna but the team fitted Cs all round again by mistake. Prost would finish fifth. "My choice of tyres was fundamental to success. It was a compromise which proved correct for my car."

- **Podium:** Senna 1h 35m 21.431s, Patrese at 15.560, Alboreto at 31.254.
- **Fastest lap:** Mansell 1:20.420.
- **Senna:** 1:20.585.
- **Championship:** Senna 27, Prost 20, Mansell 9.

RACE 157

USA, Phoenix, 4 June 1989.
Qualifying: 1:30.108 (1); 1:30.710 (1). Pole.
Race weather: hot, sunny.
Warm-up: 1:33.949 (1).
Result: Retired after 44 laps, electrics.

Past Clark's 33. Senna described the Friday as "obviously extremely hard work on what was a very low grip surface." It proved sufficient, the track markedly slower on the Saturday. "I feel rather light-headed with no weight on my shoulders now that I have established this new record. I take the record from Jim Clark, a man I never saw racing but by his results obviously a very special driver. It is a big moment for me. In the conditions I felt that nobody could get close to my Friday time *so* perhaps I was not as wound up as I might have been."

Prost almost headed Senna into the first corner but, as Prost explained, "I was on the right where there's a bad bump. I changed up just as I went over it, got wheelspin and hit the rev limiter. Momentarily the engine just stopped and Senna overtook me on the left." Senna meanwhile explained that "everything was perfect from the start. I was leading quite comfortably, keeping a cushion over Alain when the engine began to misfire slightly..."

	Senna	**Prost**
Lap 30	1:35.166	1:35.407
Lap 31	1:35.422	1:35.589
Lap 32	1:35.178	1:34.957
Lap 33	1:38.746	1:36.152

"At first [when the problem arose] I thought I could drive round it but eventually it got bad enough for me to come into the pits." That was lap 34. "Initially it was rectified and I went back out pressing really hard – and not with fresh tyres – and had no difficulty running much quicker than I had been in the early stages." He set fastest lap on lap 38. "Then the misfire returned and I came in for good."

- **Podium:** Prost, Patrese, Cheever (Arrows).
- **Fastest lap:** Senna 1:33.969.
- **Championship:** Prost 29, Senna 27, Patrese 12.

Canada, Montreal, 18 June 1989.
Qualifying: 1:21.049 (2); 1:21.269 (1).
Front row.
Pole: Prost 1:20.973.
Race weather: wet.
Warm-up: 1:47.149 (4).
Result: Seventh.

On the Friday shod with race tyres "I could not go any quicker and on my last run I had a slight problem with third gear jumping out a couple of times – I think one of the dog rings may have been damaged – and that meant things were a bit of a handful through the fast ess-bend section. As things turned out qualifying rubber was fractionally quicker for me but I don't think we got the best from it." On the Saturday "the circuit conditions were a lot worse so the fact that I almost equalled my Friday time indicates how well the car was working." And, unstated, the driver, too.

A drying track for the race, although not dry enough to tempt drivers onto slick tyres. Prost slithered across Senna for the lead and squeezed a little gap completing the opening lap. On lap 2 Senna surged by – Prost thought he had a puncture and pitted. Senna pitted for dry tyres on lap 4. "Stopping early avoided destroying the wet tyres." Rain fell from lap 5, Senna fifth, up to second by lap 11 and by lap 15 had caught Patrese, leading and on wet tyres. Once at the hairpin Senna skimmed off, returned splashing through a puddle – on the dry tyres. On lap 21 Senna had to come in to change. From sixth he was up to second behind Warwick. On lap 39 Senna went by at the esses, Warwick tip-toeing politely and prudently aside, then with three laps to go he felt the engine tighten.

• **Podium:** Boutsen, Patrese, de Cesaris.
• **Fastest lap:** Palmer (Tyrrell) 1:31.925.
• **Senna:** 1:32.143.
• **Championship:** Prost 29, Senna 27, Patrese 18.

The podium Hockenheim: entrances and exits.

France, Paul Ricard, 9 July 1989.
Qualifying: 1:07.920 (1); 1:07.228 (2).
Front row.
Pole: Prost 1:07.203.
Race weather: hot, sunny.
Warm-up: 1:10.951 (3).
Result: Retired, no laps, differential.

On the Friday "I made a mistake and dropped a wheel over one of the kerbs. That spoilt my chances so I slowed and came in immediately." The wind dropped on the Saturday and Senna mingled with "a lot of traffic on my first run". The second was "fine but just a shade away."

Senna led but Gugelmin was involved in a crash. At the re-start "I was just about changing from first to second gear when the drive simply vanished. There was nothing I could do." He parked the McLaren by the side of the track and walked across tugging his gloves off. He looked sanguine.

- **Podium:** Prost, Mansell, Patrese.
- **Fastest lap:** Gugelmin 1:12.090.
- **Senna:** no lap.
- **Championship:** Prost 38, Senna 27, Patrese 22.

RACE 160

Britain, Silverstone, 16 July 1989.
Qualifying: 1:09.124 (1); 1:09.099 (1). Pole.
Race weather: warm, sunny.
Warm-up: 1:12.530 (3).
Result: Retired after 11 laps, gearbox/spin.

Straight Senna. A strong run on the Friday "but I had to ease off slightly for yellow flags at Woodcote when Alesi spun his Tyrrell." On the Saturday he revealed that "I had lots of problems throughout both days, all involving problems with the engine oil system."

A convulsive start, Prost away hard enough to judge that by the entry to Copse he could safely turn in across Senna. Wrong. Senna went inside and gripped the corner and produced The Tactic – 1:20.039 against Prost's 1:20.836, but Prost stayed. "I had difficulty selecting third gear on the downchange," Senna said, "almost from the start." At Becketts into lap 12 he

slewed and spun onto the gravel trap. A marshal wanted him out of the cockpit and to a safe place. When Senna did get out he tapped the marshal on the shoulder. Thanks for your help. "Four or five laps before, I almost went off at the same place. Eventually I couldn't get the gear and that was that. I couldn't take the corner in neutral."

- **Podium:** Prost, Mansell, Nannini.
- **Fastest lap:** Mansell 1:12.017.
- **Senna:** 1:13.737.
- **Championship:** Prost 47, Senna 27, Patrese 22.

RACE 161

Germany, Hockenheim, 30 July 1989.
Qualifying: 1:42.300 (1); 1:42.790 (1). Pole.
Race weather: warm, cloudy.
Warm-up: 1:46.433 (1).
Result: First.

Potentially a pivotal weekend because the half way point in the season had passed and Prost was the 20 points ahead. In the Friday untimed Senna made a mistake and spun. "I damaged the car and the mechanics had to work very hard to repair it, a task they managed with 20 minutes of the qualifying session left. The spin was my fault. I put a wheel onto the kerb under braking and the car snapped round on me. It was a stupid mistake. It was quite a big impact and I had a slight headache." Pole on the Saturday? "No problem!"

From his grid position on the right Berger made an astonishing start. He flung the Ferrari diagonally left round Senna on the outside into the lead. It couldn't last and didn't. In the country Senna went by and Prost went by. Senna led to lap 19 when he pitted for tyres, a long stop. Ron Dennis explained that "the mechanic on the right rear wheel was not completely certain that he had secured Ayrton's wheel correctly so it was taken off and refitted. In the event he had done it correctly the first time but it was safer to be sure." Senna emerged three seconds behind Prost and Prost built a cushion. Senna countered, soothing fractions from each lap. "I did not have any particular strategy to pass Alain. I was concentrating on getting as close to him as possible. I was easing towards him with two laps to go and anything could happen." Approaching the Stadium complex Prost slowed and Senna fled past. "I lost top gear," Prost explained.

- **Podium:** Senna 1h 21m 43.302s, Prost at 18.151, Mansell at 1m 23.254.
- **Fastest lap:** Senna 1:45.884.
- **Championship:** Prost 53, Senna 36, Mansell and Patrese 25.

RACE 162

Hungary, Hungaroring, 13 August 1989.
Qualifying: 1:21.576 (6); 1:20.039 (1).
Front row.
Pole: Patrese 1:19.726.
Race weather: warm, overcast.
Warm-up: 1:24.176 (3).
Result: Second.

On the Friday Senna had "balance problems, but my best lap was spoiled when I came up behind Warwick and [Olivier] Grouillard [Ligier] running side-by-side on their first slow lap out of the pits. There was nothing I could do about that." On the Saturday Senna made a point of congratulating Patrese on his "super time from yesterday. It was impossible to beat.

On my quick lap I made a couple of little mistakes because I was trying so hard."

Patrese got the start right, fending off Senna, and, as is the way of the Hungaroring, Patrese would hold this lead for 52 laps until Senna drew up along the start-finish straight, feinted left, flicked right and overtook on the inside. Mansell overtook Patrese, too, and swarmed Senna for five laps. Out at the back of the circuit they came upon the Onyx of Johansson at a corkscrewing right-hander. Johansson, exiting, kept far over to the left. Senna, directly behind, moved quite normally to mid-track to go by. Instantaneously Mansell saw a gap full on the right and corkscrewed the Ferrari into it – utter opportunism and nerve. "It was obviously a good race but I lost the lead when I had to brake behind Johansson and Nigel managed to get by. He might well have passed me towards the end. Perhaps, perhaps not. What matters is that he did it and it was a good race. I eased up towards the end with a bad tyre vibration but that was after Nigel got ahead." No excuses, only reasons.

- **Podium:** Mansell 1h 49m 38.650, Senna at 25.967, Boutsen at 38.354.
- **Fastest lap:** Mansell 1:22.637.
- **Senna:** 1:23.313.
- **Championship:** Prost 56, Senna 42, Mansell 34.

No more than second place in Hungary, 25.967 seconds behind Mansell *Formula One Pictures*.

Belgium, Spa, 27 August 1989.
Qualifying: 2:11.171 (2); 1:50.867 (1). Pole.
Race weather: cold, wet.
Warm-up: 2:16.252 (5).
Result: First.

On the Friday "on my first run the car felt better and better. I ended up only a fraction slower than Berger and I think he must have produced a very good lap under these rainy circumstances. We made some adjustments to the car which gradually improved its feel but I went out far too late." On the Saturday "it was obviously a very busy session after yesterday was effectively rained out. I had been suffering rather too much understeer during the morning but we gradually reduced it. My first run (2:11.171) felt good but not as good as my second, by which time the understeer had almost been dialled out."

A wet race and at the green light Senna moved from Prost and went left, screening the entry to La Source. He built an immediate gap, Prost lost in the spray and hanging back for visibility. This opening lap decided the whole thing, Senna 2:27.369, Prost 2:29.971. After three laps Senna led by more than five seconds and although Prost would draw up – the track subsequently drying – overtaking was an unreachable dimension away. "In conditions like those today there is always a danger of pressing too hard. There is a tendency to want to press on faster than perhaps is prudent so the real key is to suppress your natural instincts slightly and keep well inside the limit. I always find myself wanting to push, push but you have to draw yourself back." Back-markers? "It was really very dangerous and uncomfortable because you couldn't see anything but if you didn't go for it you lost five seconds just like that." Towards the end Senna cut his speed

Senna gets a push in qualifying in Portugal as Piquet goes by *Formula One Pictures.*

drastically. A crisis with the car? No, not at all, he said whimsically, spreading that slow smile. *My understanding of a motor race is that the first across the line wins and that's what I was making sure happened.*

- **Podium:** Senna 1h 40m 54.196s, Prost at 1.304, Mansell at 1.824.
- **Fastest lap:** Prost 2:11.571.
- **Senna:** 2:12.890.
- **Championship:** Prost 62, Senna 51, Mansell 38.

RACE 164

Italy, Monza, 10 September 1989.
Qualifying: 1:25.021 (3); 1:23.720 (1). Pole.
Race weather: warm, sunny.
Warm-up: 1:27.637 (1).
Result: Retired after 44 laps, engine.

On the Friday Berger took provisional pole from Mansell. "I think my absolute best would have been a 1m 24.8, nothing quicker. I missed a gear and made a mistake at one of the chicanes," Senna said. On the Saturday "I missed a gear again on my first run but at least it gave me a reference point for my second try. During my best lap I got a bit sideways onto the kerb going into the first chicane."

A big start, Senna nicely in front of the Ferraris, Prost fourth, although across the opening lap Berger stayed with Senna. Berger could not make the Ferrari maintain this and it solidified into a static mid-race, Senna from Berger and Mansell from Prost. On lap 21 Prost took a 'tow' from Mansell and that sucked him through. Prost advanced on Berger and on lap 41 – Senna 22 seconds ahead – Prost out-powered Berger on the start-finish straight. Three laps later Senna was gone, smoke from the engine and a slow pirouette. He came to rest in the Parabolica facing oncoming traffic and sprang out. The crowd cheered him – or was it jeered him? "From the start I had no need to rev the engine as high as it could go but about five laps before I retired the oil pressure warning light began flashing intermittently. Then it began flashing more and more so I reduced the revs slightly but there was nothing I could really do. The engine broke coming down to Parabolica so

I switched it off and coasted into the corner. I spun on my own oil."

- **Podium:** Prost, Berger, Boutsen.
- **Fastest lap:** Prost 1:28.107.
- **Senna:** 1:28.179.
- **Championship:** Prost 71, Senna 51, Mansell 38.

RACE 165

Portugal, Estoril, 24 September 1989.
Qualifying: 1:15.496 (1); 1:15.468 (1). Pole.
Race weather: hot, sunny.
Warm-up: 1:19.795 (1).
Result: Retired after 48 laps, accident.

Senna had a "slight problem which I was unable specifically to pinpoint" on the Friday but still did a time good enough to remain pole.

The race would be lost in controversy and confusion; and the championship lost too. Berger led, Mansell hustling Senna, Prost fourth. On lap 8 Mansell got a 'tow' down the start-finish straight and slotted by. The order endured to lap 24 when Mansell took Berger.

Mansell pitted for tyres on lap 40 but overshot his pit. The mechanics prepared to haul the Ferrari to the bay but Mansell reversed. He emerged fourth, Senna second to Berger. Mansell was black-flagged for the reversing but claimed he hadn't seen the flag because the low sun shone full into his eyes. He pressed Senna and on lap 49 Dennis used the on-board radio to explain to Senna that Mansell was no longer a factor. As Dennis did that Mansell made a late move to the inside at turn one and Senna turned into him. The McLaren chewed the gravel trap, a front wheel held up like a broken paw. Senna walked to the tyre barrier and dipped his head. "Why did Nigel stay out after he was disqualified? Everyone can see the television transmission of what happened. I don't really want to comment..."

- **Podium:** Berger, Prost, Johansson.
- **Fastest lap:** Berger 1:18.986.
- **Senna:** 1:19.490.
- **Championship:** Prost 77 (75 counting), Senna 51, Mansell 38.

Spain, Jerez, 1 October 1989.
Qualifying: 1:21.855 (1); 1:20.291 (1). Pole.
Race weather: warm, sunny.
Warm-up: 1:25.552 (3).
Result: First.

Senna needed a win or a second place to keep the championship alive. He converted provisional pole to pole itself on the Saturday when "I got a clear run on my second set of qualifiers and I am delighted to have taken the fortieth pole of my career. It was a goal I set myself at the very start of the season."

The real pressure had come. Senna responded to it at the green light with a yearn of a start, power-power-power, Berger tracking, Prost third. Senna would not lose the lead. "It was a very long race on an extremely stressful circuit and that stress was intensified by Gerhard keeping up the pressure from second place in the early stages. I had a few problems with the gearbox for the last 35 laps or so, then with the brakes over the last 20 laps, but it was a very satisfying win."

- **Podium:** Senna 1h 47m 48.264s, Berger at 27.051, Prost at 53.788.
- **Fastest lap:** Senna 1:25.779.
- **Championship:** Prost 81 (76 counting), Senna 60, Mansell 38.

Japan, Suzuka, 22 October 1989.
Qualifying: 1:39.493 (1); 1:38.041 (1). Pole.
Race weather: mild, overcast.
Warm-up: 1:44.801 (3).
Result: First, disqualified.

The discipline of the decider could wait until normal qualifying was completed, and of this qualifying Senna spoke quite normally. On the Friday "I missed second gear coming out of the hairpin. Without that I think I could have managed a 1:39 dead. I also blistered my right front tyre midway round and understeered over a kerb." On the Saturday "my fastest lap wasn't a smooth one but quick, believe me. I fumbled a couple of gearchanges but it was a great lap

nonetheless. Since chassis settings are so important here I chose to use one set of C race tyres and one set of E qualifiers to continue working for the race during second qualifying."

Prost had made a pact, but with himself. He'd moved aside rather than crash with Senna before. Not now. Prost led, Senna holding Berger. It unfolded

	Prost	Senna
Lap 1	1:49.369	1:50.770
Lap 2	1:46.799	1:47.673
Lap 3	1:46.283	1:47.244

During that third lap you could see Prost glancing in his mirror to monitor the gap. Prost increased it to five seconds after 14 laps. Lonely duellists they were, measuring the distance between themselves, Senna cutting this gap, Prost responding. At lap 30 it shrank to one second, at lap 35 it elongated to 3.4 under the response. Prost felt the calm of control.

	Prost	Senna
Lap 37	1:43.647	1:43.300
Lap 38	1:43.729	1:43.025

That was Senna's fastest. He was digging deep to create his challenge.

	Prost	Senna
Lap 39	1:44.222	1:43.705
Lap 40	1:45.335	1:43.995
Lap 41	1:45.643	1:45.767

They ran together, the whole season distilled. Senna would draw up into the corners on late braking, Prost ease away coming out. A flash reading – 0.429 seconds – held no meaning. Prost harboured suspicions that Senna could still not tolerate defeat and might – would – risk everything. Where? When? On lap 47 Senna tried it: a long thrust towards the chicane, Prost following the orthodox line, over to the left, cutting over right-right-right into the chicane, into where Senna now had the McLaren. The inescapable laws of geometry decreed the crash. The cars locked and ebbed down the escape road. Prost levered himself out with the subdued anger of a man who wished to leave this place immediately. Senna, thinking tactically even

Monitoring a television monitor, Japan. Did he see what was coming?

now, gestured for the marshals to push him, restart him. Senna drove down the escape road and rejoined, the nose of the McLaren wounded. He pitted for a new one and emerged, Nannini leading. On lap 51 Senna overtook Nannini at the chicane. Nannini had made no pact with himself to shut doors which might be left open – but it was close, very close. Thirty one minutes after the race the podium ceremony took place without Senna. The Stewards judged he had "avoided the chicane" by using the escape road. Amid the furore, Senna issued a statement: "That was the only place where I could overtake, and somebody who should not have been there just closed the door and that was that." There would be an appeal, of course, the championship technically in abeyance.

- **Podium:** Nannini, Patrese, Boutsen.
- **Fastest lap:** Prost 1:43.506.
- **Senna:** 1:43.025.
- **Championship:** Prost 81 (76 counting), Senna 60, Mansell 38.

The crash with Prost in Japan which virtually settled the World Championship and ignited Formula 1.

Australia, Adelaide 5 November 1989.
Qualifying: 1:17.712 (2); 1:16.665 (1). Pole.
Race weather: wet.
Warm-up: 1:21.306 (1).
Result: Retired after 13 laps, accident.

Between Suzuka and here Senna's disqualification was *not* confirmed by a meeting of the FIA Court of Appeal in Paris. He appeared fatalistic on the Saturday. "My first run was not as smooth as I would have liked but my second produced no problems. That was as much as I could do. If anybody had been able to go faster then so be it."

A deluge descended on Adelaide, the start delayed by half an hour. Senna remained in his cockpit. He had to race, had to win or the championship truly was gone – if he didn't win, re-instatement at Suzuka became irrelevant. Some drivers were frightened and said so. A street circuit with standing water would still produce a fastest lap average speed of more than 85 mph. The start was hopelessly ragged, half the cars nowhere near their grid positions. Prost got away better but he and Senna oscillated towards each other, nearly touched, oscillated apart. Senna seized the first corner and cut a long lead. Prost pitted and got out. His life, he reasoned, was more important than this. On lap 2 the race was stopped, re-started 30 minutes later. Senna led again, the car moving like a nervous breakdown in these conditions. Senna had 28.232 seconds over Boutsen by lap 6. He spun, a carousel ride, the car rotating three times. He kept the lead, now at 24 seconds. On lap 14, unsighted and boring "into the spray" he hammered the rear of Brundle's Brabham. He limped to the pits on three wheels and felt the race should have been stopped there and then. After all, he pointed out, the championship was no longer in play. It left many people with the uneasy feeling that Senna imagined Formula 1 was being run for his benefit alone.

- **Podium:** Boutsen, Nannini, Patrese.
- **Fastest lap:** Nakajima 1:38.480.
- **Senna:** 1:41.159.
- **Championship:** Prost 81 (76 counting), Senna 60, Patrese 40.

Deluge at Adelaide and Prost wouldn't be in the re-start, leaving the number 2 position on the grid vacant.

Senna in 1990.

Chapter 7

McLaren
The great years
1990

*B*erger came to McLaren and after a brief misunderstanding with Senna they grew to like each other. The other front-runners: Prost and Mansell (Ferrari), Boutsen and Patrese (Williams), Piquet and Nannini (Benetton), Alesi (Tyrrell).

✳ ✳ ✳

RACE 169

USA, Phoenix, 11 March 1990.
Qualifying: 1:29.431 (5); 1:52.015 (3). Row 3.
Pole: Berger 1:28.664.
Race weather: cool, overcast.
Warm-up: 1:30.458 (1).
Result: First.

On the Friday "we had some electrical problems with the race car in the morning so we changed the cockpit computer but the engine still misfired slightly in the afternoon. I came in and changed a few things. The engine began making a mechanical noise and lost power. Chassis set-up is not right, not wrong." Rain smothered the Saturday.

Around the concrete-clad channels young Jean Alesi was poised to make his statement. Into the jostle down to the first right-hander – and from the second row – he sliced between Berger and de Cesaris. Alesi urged the Tyrrell clear of Berger, Senna fourth and patient. On lap 4 Senna slotted neatly past de Cesaris and drew up towards Berger who, on lap 9, "was a little bit between the brake and throttle pedal, already braking on the limit, and as I caught

the throttle pedal I lost it." Berger rammed a tyre barrier. By lap 11 Alesi led by eight seconds. Senna decided it was time to make his statement. He looked poised and precise, as he could within the constrictions of a street circuit. He didn't look hurried. He didn't seem to claw time but to caress it. At 23 laps: 2.317. Senna tracked, still patient, a hunter measuring his prey. On lap 34 into a right-hander Senna sneaked the inside line under braking. Alesi ought to have been obedient and let him go. They were in a point-and-squirt 'straight' to a left-hander. Alesi pounced on the inside line and elbowed Senna aside. "I certainly didn't expect Alesi to go round the outside of me when I got inside him." Next lap Senna repeated the move at the right-hander and covered the left heavily. It settled it. "A very exciting battle. Alesi drove really well, very clean and precise, the sort of motor racing I like."

- **Podium:** Senna 1h 52m 32.829s, Alesi at 8.685, Boutsen at 54.080.
- **Fastest lap:** Berger 1:31.050.
- **Senna:** 1:32.178.

His team-mate Gerhard Berger. After initial misunderstandings they'd bond into a strong friendship *Marlboro*.

end I changed to my second set because I felt the conditions were on the verge of improving. I had to go wide on one corner which cost me perhaps a tenth of a second. It was a good lap."

Senna led to his pit stop on lap 33 and led again to lap 41 when he reached Nakajima (Tyrrell). "I followed him through three corners and he seemed to open the door to let me through. As I went inside him he came across and my nose was lost against his rear wheel." Nakajima had moved onto the dusty part of track, couldn't avoid sliding. Senna pitted for a new nose-cone and that cost 23.61 seconds stationary. "My only thought was to finish – although it was my dream to win here."

- **Podium:** Prost 1h 37m 21.258s, Berger at 13.564, Senna at 37.722.
- **Fastest lap:** Berger 1:19.899.
- **Senna:** 1:20.067.
- **Championship:** Senna 13, Prost 9, Alesi, Berger and Boutsen 6.

RACE 170

Brazil, Sao Paulo, 25 March 1990.
Qualifying: 1:17.769 (1); 1:17.277 (1). Pole.
Race weather: hot, sunny.
Warm-up: 1:20.990 (2).
Result: Third.

RACE 171

San Marino, Imola, 13 May 1990.
Qualifying: 1:24.079 (2); 1:23.220 (1). Pole.
Race weather: hot, sunny.
Warm-up: 1:27.497 (1).
Result: Retired after 3 laps, broken wheel.

Senna had not driven in front of his home crowd before, his six Brazilian Grands Prix all at Rio. Whatever the emotion, he dissected qualifying clinically. On the Friday "on my first set of tyres I didn't drive very well. The car felt too light. On my second set I put a little bit more wing on but I still didn't drive very well. I went wide on a couple of corners and caught one of the Brabhams through a corner. I will need a helmet strap tomorrow to support it on one side of the cockpit. I have a slight neck problem and when I hit a bump through a long corner I felt a crack and a pain." On the Saturday "about half an hour into the session I tried to go quickly but the track was still very slippery and I knew that a 1m 18.6s was not very special (he'd done 1:18.512). I went out again on the same set of tyres and the conditions were so-so. A few minutes before the

On the Friday "I had done about half a lap when [Pierluigi] Martini [Minardi] had his accident [he crashed heavily] and the session was stopped. I went out again but my tyres had obviously lost some of their grip. They were OK but not performing to the maximum. The circuit at that stage was slightly quicker, I think." On the Saturday "it is all a question of believing you can do it and not making any mistakes; thinking about it carefully. I believe it would have been possible to be even quicker. A 1:23.0 would have been feasible but anything quicker would have been incautious."

The first corner of the race was the beginning of the end. "I felt something flexing at the right rear. I backed off a little bit and was able to control it." You'd scarcely have known, Senna overtaking Berger for the lead. "Then at the top chicane on lap 4 the car got rather

Testing at Imola.

sideways and I slowed right down. By the time I exited I was on the radio to the pits thinking that I had a deflating tyre but as I came down the hill to Rivazza I realised I was losing my brakes. I couldn't stop the car. It was all over the place. I just tried to get out of the way of the others." The right rear wheel had broken.

- **Podium:** Patrese, Berger, Nannini.
- **Fastest lap:** Nannini 1:27.156.
- **Senna:** 1:30.615.
- **Championship:** Senna 13, Prost and Berger 12.

RACE 172

Monaco, Monte Carlo, 27 May 1990.
Qualifying: 1:21.797 (1); 1:21.314 (1). Pole.
Race weather: warm, overcast.
Warm-up: 1:24.814 (1).
Result: First.

Straight Senna. He didn't quite feel "that I produced my maximum on my first run" on the Friday "so I really had to give it everything on the second just in case we had problems on the Saturday but even though my second run was quicker it was not perfect because I locked a wheel and ran slightly wide at both Portier and the Loews hairpin. I wasn't sure whether a slower car in front of me was going to move over or not." Stunning Senna on the Saturday. As he pointed out, both his runs would have given him pole.

After a re-start he led from Prost although "I was worried because of the possible strain on transmission components" following the two starts.

	Senna	Prost
Lap 1	1:32.746	1:35.287
Lap 2	1:28.115	1:29.284
Lap 3	1:27.972	1:28.337

Senna dealt with the traffic with brutal finesse (no contradiction) and when Prost dropped out – 30 laps, battery – Alesi ran second. Midway through Senna led him by 22 seconds, enough. "My car went perfectly until a few laps from the end when I started losing power very slightly so I cut back the revs and took it easy over the last few laps."

- **Podium:** Senna 1h 52m 46.982s, Alesi at 1.087, Berger at 2.073.
- **Fastest lap:** Senna 1:24.468.
- **Championship:** Senna 22, Berger 16, Alesi 13.

He led the San Marino Grand Prix but spun off *Zooom*.

Champagne cascade, Canada. Piquet was second and Mansell (here behind Senna) third.

Canada, Montreal, 10 June 1990.
Qualifying: 1:20.399 (1); 1:30.514 (5). Pole.
Race weather: wet, drying.
Warm-up: 1:37.394 (3).
Result: First.

On the Friday Senna thought he was on a very good lap when "I lost fifth gear coming out of the fast chicane, then I hooked third." Saturday was drying, no improvement.

Berger jumped the start but amidst plumes of spray Senna led. Berger described his start as "over eager" and insisted it gave him no advantage. Berger pitted for dry tyres on lap 10, Senna on 12 and it settled in that order. "They radioed me very early to say Gerhard had been penalised a minute. That reduced the pressure on me, which was good because it was very slippery in the first part of the race. I concentrated on being smooth and keeping a good average. Lapping people was bad because off the line it was still very wet so you had to be careful. It was a very tough race – first gear broke just after I stopped to change tyres. I used second gear instead in the appropriate places but I was worried that the broken gear might cause other problems." Senna need not overtake Berger, simply stay within that minute of him. Berger was classified fourth.

- **Podium:** Senna 1h 42m 56.400s, Piquet at 10.497, Mansell at 13.385.
- **Fastest lap:** Berger 1:22.077.
- **Senna:** 1:23.375.
- **Championship:** Senna 31, Berger 19, Prost 14.

Mexico, Mexico City, 24 June 1990.
Qualifying: 1:18.417 (4); 1:17.670 (2). Row 2.
Pole: Berger 1:17.227.
Race weather: cool, overcast.
Warm-up: 1:19.930 (2).
Result: Retired after 63 laps, puncture.

Senna off the pace. On the Friday "I only tried one set of qualifying tyres, at the end of the afternoon session when I went for my time. I think I was a little too conservative early in the

lap *because* I was a bit worried that the tyres might go off before the end of it, and apart from that the car did not feel quite right. It was too rough over the bumps." No pole on the Saturday. "We made a slight improvement. The car was more consistent and I could manage a full lap without the tyres losing their edge."

Patrese reached turn one before Senna, who used the lap to close and take him on the start-finish straight, Berger past Patrese next lap. Berger's front left tyre blistered, however, and he pitted after 10 laps. Piquet ran the mid-part second, Senna safely ahead. "About 25 laps from the end I felt the car getting unstable and I thought it was a tyre problem. I called on the radio but they didn't hear me so I did one more lap and called again. I was told to stay out. In part it was my fault for not taking the initiative and deciding myself to come in." He had a slow puncture in the right-rear and Prost went by, next lap Mansell went by. On lap 64 the tyre shredded. "I think we called it wrong," Ron Dennis said, "even though Ayrton's eventual retirement was caused by a puncture rather than tyre wear. We started Ayrton a little lower on pressure than Gerhard and we were confident he would not have a wear problem. With 10 laps to go I thought third place would be better than bringing him in. I was wrong, but you can't win them all."

- **Podium:** Prost, Mansell, Berger.
- **Fastest lap:** Prost 1:17.958.
- **Senna:** 1:19.062.
- **Championship:** Senna 31, Prost and Berger 23.

France, Paul Ricard, 8 July 1990.
Qualifying: 1:04.549 (2); 1:08.886 (30). Row 2.
Pole: Mansell 1:04.402.
Race weather: hot, sunny.
Warm-up: 1:08.711 (5).
Result: Third.

On the Friday "my best lap was clear of traffic, very good, but on my second set of tyres I had to back off a little on the double right-hander beyond Signes when my left front lost grip." On the Saturday "we ran in race conditions, mainly to gain as much data as possible and it proved productive. The higher temperature [precluding improvement] was one factor behind our decision."

Senna made a hesitant start, third into turn one behind Mansell and Berger. On the opening lap Berger overtook Mansell and next lap Senna followed down the back straight. Berger and Senna circled 1-2 and it remained like that until Berger pitted for tyres after 27 laps and then lost first gear, "a real problem on the tight right-hander after the pits." Senna led for two laps. "In the early stages I felt I was slightly quicker than Gerhard but he was running less down-force which ensured he was a little bit quicker in a straight line. I could not get by. Then I made my tyre stop which is where we lost the race." It lasted 16 seconds, a problem with the left rear. Senna, eighth, could only work his way up. "In retrospect I am not certain we needed to change tyres anyway because we did not run better with fresh rubber." The margins which are so maddening to master...

- **Podium:** Prost 1h 33m 29.606s, Capelli (Leyton House) at 8.626, Senna at 11.606.
- **Fastest lap:** Mansell 1.08.012.
- **Senna:** 1:08.573.
- **Championship:** Senna 35, Prost 32, Berger 25.

Britain, Silverstone, 15 July 1990.
Qualifying: 1:08.071 (1); 1:09.055 (8). Front row.
Pole: Mansell 1:07.428.
Race weather: hot, sunny.
Warm-up: 1:11.840 (5).
Result: Third.

On the Friday "on my first run I was slightly baulked going into Copse at the start of the lap. You need a considerable amount of precision not to push too hard too early on a qualifying run, bringing the tyres in gently." On the Saturday he "badly blistered the front tyres" on his first run. "I decided to take off some down-force before the second run but when I turned into Copse I realised the car was dangerously

nervous. As a result there was no real chance of improving and even though I pressed quite hard further round the lap it was unrealistic."

Sometimes there's nothing you can do. At the green light Mansell went to mid-track and Senna, coming hard, nearly nudged him. Senna led into Copse and Mansell would need 12 laps to overhaul him. "When I was leading the car felt quite loose. Mansell tried hard to overtake but the first time [lap 9] he went too deep into the chicane and I immediately re-passed." In fact Mansell drifted wide. "The second time [lap 12] he stayed ahead. I could not keep up with him, I had big difficulty with the rear tyres and when I touched the kerb [at Copse] I spun. I changed tyres a couple of laps later and tried to make a good race but the car was difficult to drive." He'd been as low as tenth after the stop and handled the remainder gently. The art of the possible...

- **Podium:** Prost 1h 18m 30.999s, Boutsen at 39.092, Senna at 43.088.
- **Fastest lap:** Mansell 1:11.291.
- **Senna:** 1:12.250.
- **Championship:** Prost 41, Senna 39, Berger 25.

Champagne cascade, Hungary. Senna sprays Boutsen – but Boutsen had won the race.

Germany, Hockenheim, 29 July 1990.
Qualifying: 1:40.198 (1); 1:46.843 (22). Pole.
Race weather: hot, humid.
Warm-up: 1:44.734 (1).
Result: First.

On the Friday Senna "made a small mistake on my second run when I hit the bump on the exit of the last chicane. That threw me across the kerb so I abandoned the effort. It was a shame because I felt I was quicker to that point on the circuit than I had been on my first run but I didn't want to go hard into the Stadium. I was worried there might be some damage to the underside of the car." He devoted the Saturday to work on the race set-up.

A tight start, Berger – sharing the front row – making a powerful bid to take the first corner. Even in these milliseconds you could see Senna dip his head towards the wing mirror to know Berger's positioning. "A combination of softer C compound tyres and a heavy fuel load made it hard to sustain the performance during the early stages when Gerhard was close behind so I came in for tyres at the end of lap 17. It proved to be the right choice." Nannini led. "I came out just behind Nannini who squeezed ahead into the first chicane. Then I lost power slightly and backed off but I realised he was running without a tyre change and as his grip gradually deteriorated I got closer and picked up a very

Done it. Senna wins Belgium from Prost.

good tow." Out in the country Senna feinted fractionally right, Nannini adjusted to block that and Senna drove round him.

- **Podium:** Senna 1h 20m 47.164s, Nannini at 6.520, Berger at 8.553.
- **Fastest lap:** Boutsen 1:45.602.
- **Senna:** 1:45.711.
- **Championship:** Senna 48, Prost 44, Berger 29.

Hungary, Hungaroring, 12 August 1990.
Qualifying: 1:20.389 (8); 1:18.162 (3). Row 2.
Pole: Boutsen 1:17.919.
Race weather: hot, sunny.
Warm-up: 1:22.618 (3).
Result: Second.

With grid positions so (theoretically) crucial, Senna endured a fraught Friday. "On my qualifying lap I came up behind [Gregor] Foitek [Monteverdi] whose tyres I could see were badly blistered and I naturally assumed he would move over but when he saw me he just accelerated hard, holding me up." On the Saturday "on the first lap of my second run I had a big moment at the bottom of the hill and decided to back off and try again. At the start of my second lap I just didn't have any grip from my tyres, then I locked the front wheels and slid over the kerb."

A curious race, as those at the Hungaroring often are. Boutsen made a big start, Berger round the outside of Patrese into second, Senna sixth. "I lost a few places and decided to sit back, knowing that all the leaders were bunched together at the front. I had a slight engine overheating problem and picked up a puncture." That was lap 22, Senna rejoining eleventh after the stop. He was tenth when "I saw Prost spin" – Prost, seventh, thought his transmission had failed. "I decided it was important to finish in the top three." Senna moved towards Nannini and, Berger pitting for tyres, they ran fourth and fifth, Boutsen repeating lap after lap in the lead. In a sharp moment Mansell challenged Patrese for second place on the start-finish straight, backed off and into turn one Nannini dived inside – and so did Senna. Patrese pitted for tyres: Nannini second, Senna third. Would Senna accept third? The perennial question which always had the two answers, yes or no, and always depended – as it always seemed – on Senna's mood as well as his logic. On lap 64 Senna gave his answer. No. Rushing the 90 degree right at the back of the circuit Senna selected the inside. It was not, is not and likely never will be an overtaking place unless the driver in front agrees. The inescapable laws of geometry were as valid here as in Suzuka and everywhere else. Senna crudely punted Nannini into the air. "Nannini didn't see me and closed the door just too much." Hmmm. Nannini didn't see it like that, insisted he was guilty of no more than pursuing the racing line and Senna appeared from nowhere. Senna continued and drew up to Boutsen, crowded him but Boutsen sailed stately on to the end.

- **Podium:** Boutsen 1h 49m 30.597s, Senna at 0.288, Piquet at 27.893.
- **Fastest lap:** Patrese 1:22.058.
- **Senna:** 1:22.577.
- **Championship:** Senna 54, Prost 44, Berger 29.

RACE 179

Belgium, Spa, 26 August 1990.
Qualifying: 1:52.278 (3); 1:50.365 (1). Pole.
Race weather: overcast, humid.
Warm-up: 1:56.401 (3).
Result: First.

Senna survived a freak accident on the Friday. Martin Donnelly (Lotus) went into the barrier and his right rear wheel was flung back at Senna who was arriving quickly. It beat against the McLaren's bodywork. That apart "the front tyres went off before the end of my quickest lap and I had a bit of understeer on the downhill left-hander just before the new circuit rejoins the old." He liked the Saturday lap and, it done, tried to explain the majestic mysteries of Spa and the margins there. "It is always possible to go a bit quicker through the corners but *you cannot be sure until you have gone through them.*"

The race was restarted after the customary bumpety-bump at La Source but this time a crash out in the country produced a second restart. Thus Senna led for the third time and initially

couldn't shed Berger. Mist hung like a late autumnal day partially masking the trees. Prost ran third until Berger's tyres wore, ran second facing a five-second gap to Senna and attacked.

	Senna	**Prost**
Lap 14	1:58.497	1:59.572
Lap 15	1:58.165	1:57.953
Lap 16	1:57.968	1:57.623

They both pitted on lap 22 for tyres but Prost was stationary four seconds longer. Senna emerged just in front of Nannini, who leant on him. Senna resisted. Traffic slowed Prost and he needed more than four laps to deal with Nannini, which ultimately persuaded him that second was no bad place after all.

- **Podium:** Senna 1h 26m 31.997s, Prost at 3.550, Berger at 28.462.
- **Fastest lap:** Prost 1:55.087.
- **Senna:** 1:55.132.
- **Championship:** Senna 63, Prost 50, Berger 33.

RACE 180

Italy, Monza, 9 September 1990.
Qualifying: 1:22.972 (1); 1:22.533 (1). Pole.
Race weather: hot, sunny.
Warm-up: 1:27.396 (2).
Result: First.

The championship tightened like a tourniquet. On the Friday "my left front tyre was absolutely on the limit going through Parabolica and I had to back off slightly on the exit at a point where you should be hard on the throttle." Senna adjusted the chassis twice on the Saturday and set the pole time. "There are lots of emotions, even too much for me. It is so pleasant to get it right under circumstances with so many problems, with no real opportunity to work on the car...to have to go much more on your instinct than anything else, on the feeling for the car...and for one single lap with qualifying tyres you don't know what the car is going to do, not being sure. In a place like this, not knowing exactly what the handling of your car will be where you have corners like the two Lesmos and Parabolica is very difficult. To be able to do it right is really a very, very special feeling."

Warwick crashed massively, forcing a restart. Senna led that from Berger and Prost, who stalked Berger for 20 laps before overtaking him – Senna 3.5 seconds up the road. In five laps Senna pressed it out to 7.8. These sort of decimals interested Prost and he went to work on them. They exchanged fastest laps. "It was a question of keeping the right pace lap after lap, corner after corner, using to the maximum the brakes, tyres and engine and also being careful with back-markers. I had some difficulty with them but that's normal. You cannot expect anything different." At the Press Conference Senna and Prost publicly healed their wounds from 1989. Hmmm.

- **Podium:** Senna 1h 17m 57.878s, Prost at 6.054, Berger at 7.404.
- **Fastest lap:** Senna 1:26.254.
- **Championship:** Senna 72, Prost 56, Berger 37.

RACE 181

Portugal, Estoril, 23 September 1990.
Qualifying: 1:14.246 (1); 1:13.601 (3). Row 2.
Pole: Mansell 1:13.557.
Race weather: warm, dry.
Warm-up: 1:19.306 (4)
Result: Second.

The Ferraris should have suited Estoril, tightening the tourniquet another notch. Moreover Senna judged his Friday lap "rough, not a quick one. The car was under-steering generally and this was a particular problem on the right-hander out onto the pit straight where I just had to let the car run wide up the kerb. If you lift at that point you've lost your chance of a really quick lap." On the Saturday he accepted, in qualifying anyway, that the Ferraris had more power.

Mansell slewed and almost sandwiched Prost against the pit lane wall at the green light leaving the left of the track open. Senna put the nose of the McLaren into that and Berger jinked in front of Mansell giving an order of Senna, Berger, Mansell, Piquet, Prost through turn one. The front trio ran in tandem until the tyre stops. Senna led from Mansell who inevitably attacked, paused to get his breath back, attacked again. On lap 50 Mansell nestled up for a 'tow' down the start-finish straight and classically went inside. "When Mansell slipstreamed me, fighting for the corner was too much of a risk with the championship outcome in mind. I couldn't really see where he was so I let him come by."

- **Podium:** Mansell 1h 22m 11.014s, Senna at 2.808, Prost at 4.189.
- **Fastest lap:** Patrese 1:18.306.
- **Senna:** 1:18.936.
- **Championship:** Senna 78, Prost 60, Berger 40.

A punctured radiator stopped him in Spain.

RACE 182

Spain, Jerez, 30 September 1990.
Qualifying: 1:18.900 (1); 1:18.387 (1). Pole.
Race weather: hot, sunny.
Warm-up: 1:24.713 (2).
Result: Retired after 53 laps, engine.

Donnelly crashed horrifically with eight minutes of the Friday qualifying remaining and lay unconscious on the track. "The accident was a very sad moment for all of us. I went to the place where he was on the ground and when I saw the consequences I thought about not running anymore." Senna then did "an amazing lap, unbelievable in the circumstances. I tried to put it [the accident] out of my mind as best I could but it was there." On the Saturday Senna reached for his Anglo-Saxon vocabulary to describe two back-markers occupying two- thirds of the track and having a slow-motion argument when he was on his flyer. "That was very dangerous. That behaviour is totally unacceptable in a qualifying session. We all saw yesterday what an accident can do. If I had hit one of them I would have taken off." Senna had his fiftieth pole.

He led to his pit stop on lap 27. "I thought I had a problem with my tyres which is why I made my stop but in fact it was water leaking from the right-hand radiator onto the right rear tyre." He pursued Prost but "when I saw the oil warning light come on as the temperature rose I decided to switch off and park it. This is the worst possible situation for the championship."

- **Podium:** Prost, Mansell, Nannini.
- **Fastest lap:** Patrese 1:24.513.
- **Senna:** 1:27.430.
- **Championship:** Senna 78, Prost 69, Berger 40.

RACE 183

Japan, Suzuka, 21 October 1990.
Qualifying: 1:38.828 (3); 1:36.996 (1). Pole.
Race weather: hot, sunny.
Warm-up: 1:43.353 (3).
Result: Retired no lap, accident.

Quietly we must approach it, the notorious race which remains notorious, and approach it at two levels. On the Friday morning Senna "made a mistake on the slippery track surface and spun off. This afternoon my car was OK but it bottomed out badly at one point just as I was changing from fourth to fifth and I got a little sideways – I was glancing at the rev counter at the time – but I feel quite satisfied with my performance as a whole." On the Saturday "the whole team really contributed: men and machine working extremely well." Senna had pole, on the right. At a private level Senna "had been asking the officials to move pole to the other side all weekend [where the track was cleaner] and their refusal to do so created so many problems." The refusal took Senna beyond reason.

Senna to the right, Prost to the left and both facing the headlong stretch to turn one, the right. Prost's Ferrari looked strong enough to be un-catchable if he led through that. Senna made a decision. He would allow Fate to decide. A quick change to green, Prost wringing speed, Senna folding in behind. Prost danced to mid-track and maybe that was the decisive instant, maybe not. Maybe Senna didn't care where Prost was, didn't care that for the instant a space seemed to have opened inside. Fate governed the pattern of movement, not he. Certainly a journalist at turn one heard the McLaren's Honda scream up and up, its scale never decreasing – as it would if Senna had lifted. Prost turned in, skimming across Senna and they touched, ploughed furrows into the gravel run-off area shrouded in dust. Prost was quoted as saying "in Islam for someone who is about to die death is a game. The problem today was we have seen Senna ready to take all the risks to win the championship." Senna responded: "He is always trying to destroy people. He tried to destroy me in the past on different occasions and he hasn't managed – and he will not manage because I know who I am and where I want to go." The healing at Monza had been six weeks before.

- **Podium:** Piquet, Roberto Moreno (Benetton), Aguri Suzuki (Lola).
- **Fastest lap:** Patrese 1:44.233.
- **Senna:** no lap.
- **Championship:** Senna 78, Prost 69, Berger 40.

Australia, Adelaide, 4 November 1990.
Qualifying: 1:15.671 (1); 1:15.693 (1). Pole.
Race weather: hot, sunny.
Warm-up: 1:19.516 (2).
Result: Retired after 61 laps, accident.

A tail-end of a season, anti-climactic, shrouded in the shadow of Suzuka. On the Friday Senna estimated the balance of the car improved, on the Saturday "I went out for my second run for the pure pleasure of driving even though my pole position was under no threat. I drive for pleasure and nothing else so this effort was to please the crowd at the track and those watching on television." Only Senna could have seriously suggested that he drove only for pleasure after Suzuka.

He led from Mansell and then Piquet until lap 62. "I had to be careful with the brakes from the start. I had too much brake balance on the rear to save the front brakes, which was a problem *so* I was on the absolute limit everywhere. Then I couldn't get second gear. I came to a left-hander stuck in neutral and I went straight into the tyre barrier."

- **Podium:** Piquet, Mansell, Prost.
- **Fastest lap:** Mansell 1:18.203.
- **Senna:** 1:19.302.
- **Championship:** Senna 78, Prost 73 (71 counting), Piquet 44 (43 counting) and Berger 43.

Above: The crash of '90 with Prost in Suzuka, Japan. Senna lets Fate decide whether there is a gap or not *Formula One Pictures*.
Below: The walk back.

1991

*B*erger stayed at McLaren, the friendship with Senna deepening. The other front-runners: Mansell and Patrese (Williams), Piquet and Michael Schumacher (Benetton), Prost and Alesi (Ferrari). A rule change opened up the season, 10 points for a win and all 16 races to count.

✳ ✳ ✳

RACE 185

USA, Phoenix 10 March 1991.
Qualifying: 1:23.530 (2); 1:21.434 (1). Pole.
Race weather: overcast.
Warm-up: 1:27.747 (1).
Result: First.

Berger spent the winter getting as fit as Senna and doing tracts of testing while Senna rested in Brazil. Berger reasoned he'd have a better chance to compete with Senna if he did that. Senna arrived and his qualifying times almost destroyed Berger.

Phoenix was a circuit existing entirely under the laws of geometry, of course, and it might have been built with a slide rule. Senna made a broad brush-stroke of a sweep into turn one, a right-hander. For the next two hours he turned left and right as the geometry demanded and at no stage lost the lead, even during his pit stop. "I had a minor problem with the gearbox and, because this was the first time we had run a full Grand Prix distance with the car, the balance was not quite right, making it very difficult to drive. I was able to maintain a good pace and get through the back-markers safely. I stopped for tyres at the right time."

- **Podium:** Senna 2h 00m 47.828s, Prost at 16.322, Piquet at 17.376.
- **Fastest lap:** Alesi 1:26.758.
- **Senna:** 1:27.153.

RACE 186

Brazil, Sao Paulo, 24 March 1991.
Qualifying: 1:18.711 (1); 1:16.392 (1). Pole.
Race weather: wet.
Warm-up: 1:21.000 (4).
Result: First.

Rain made it "very difficult to get it right" on the Friday. "The conditions were really dangerous this morning so it was just a question of staying out and accumulating experience in the wet." On the Saturday he spoke of the inspiration of driving in front of his own people. "At one point on my second run I went well over the limit, riding one of the kerbs" – for himself and for them, no doubt, a nice conjunction of interests.

The race pressed at the boundaries of the possible. Senna led from Mansell and deep into it Mansell stopped when the gearbox failed. On lap 60 of the 71 Senna led Patrese by 40 seconds. Rain spattered and spat and from around lap 50 Senna suffered "serious gearbox trouble. I lost third and fifth and one point just hooked it into sixth. I saw Patrese coming for me and I really didn't think I'd make it."

	Senna	Patrese
Lap 60	1:24.033	1:24.237
Lap 61	1:26.449	1:22.116
Lap 62	1:27.487	1:22.985

"Seven laps to go and the gearbox went completely crazy. I thought about it for one lap and I decided to leave it in sixth and drive around the circuit completely differently. In the high speed corners it was not so bad but in the medium and slow speed sections it was a disaster."

Senna in 1991.

Phoenix, the first race of 1991 – and a win from Prost.

	Senna	Patrese
Lap 63	1:26.143	1:23.891
Lap 64	1:24.887	1:22.174
Lap 65	1:28.305	1:21.990

"I was just trying to calculate how much I had to do to stay in front." On lap 67 the gap of 14.080 tumbled in a cascade. A lap later: 9.6. "I pushed the car regardless of the rain." On lap 68 Patrese loomed into view, the gap 5.4. "I was suffering from cramps and muscle spasms in my upper body, partly because the harness was so tight, partly through emotion." Two laps to go and Patrese enlarging, enlarging in the mirrors. On lap 70 – the gap 4.1 – the rain fell harder. Into the last lap – 3.6 Senna stabbed his arm upwards. Stop the race. He didn't need that. The rain slowed Patrese, washing out a decisive assault. "After the chequered flag I lost the engine completely. And then the pain was unbelievable. I tried to relax a bit. I had such a huge pain in my shoulders, in my side, and I didn't know whether to shout, to cry, or to smile. I didn't know what was going on. I just wanted to get back to the podium."

- **Podium:** Senna 1h 38m 28.128s, Patrese at 2.991, Berger at 5.416.
- **Fastest lap:** Mansell 1:20.436.
- **Senna:** 1:20.841.
- **Championship:** Senna 20, Prost 9, Patrese and Piquet 6.

RACE 187

San Marino, Imola, 28 April 1991.
Qualifying: 1:21.877 (1); 1:43.633 (9). Pole.
Race weather: wet, drying.
Warm-up: 1:27.115 (2).
Result: First.

On the Friday Senna "got a gear change slightly wrong on my first run so I knew it would not be quick enough. We made a few changes and I dipped below 1:22 on my second run." On the Saturday he had an engine problem in the morning and wanted the spare car – Berger's turn for that and he insisted on having it. Senna was angry, perhaps the first anger between them since Berger joined McLaren.

The weather was wet enough for Prost to pirouette on a rivulet during the parade lap and slither helplessly from the track. Patrese made a crackling start, Senna following, staying far enough behind to give him some vision through Patrese's spray. They were already clear of Berger. "When I was leading Senna in the first few laps," Patrese said, "I was smiling to myself all the time." Patrese pitted on lap 9, Senna slotting easily by as Patrese peeled into the pit lane. Patrese spent a long time talking to Patrick Head, something wrong with the engine. Berger cut the gap to Senna and they traded fastest laps. They pitted within a lap for dry tyres and when they'd reached racing speed Senna led by 1.4. On

Palm reading in Brazil? Nice palm-reader ...

lap 15 Senna set a new fastest time lap. Same lap, Berger beat that. Senna was assertive in traffic, expanding the gap and Berger had brake problems. Patrese emerged to give the car a run and by chance emerged as Senna was coming along. Senna went smoothly by and smoothly lapped de Cesaris, too. *Won't be seeing Patrese again, by the time he's overtaken de Cesaris I'll be long gone* Senna thought. He glanced in his mirrors and saw Patrese. Senna dissected the implications of this and asked himself what happens when the Williams becomes reliable? It darkened the victory which he described as "incredible given the dangerous conditions at the start. We had a compromise setting because we knew the track would dry. Halfway through my oil pressure dropped, the warning light came on and I thought I wouldn't finish so I slowed until Gerhard started to catch me."

- **Podium:** Senna 1h 35m 14.750s, Berger at 1.675, J.J. Lehto (Dallara) at one lap.
- **Fastest lap:** Berger 1:26.531.
- **Senna:** 1:27.168.
- **Championship:** Senna 30, Berger 10, Prost 9.

... and, anyway, Senna won.

RACE 188

Monaco, Monte Carlo, 12 May 1991.
Qualifying: 1:20.508 (1); 1:20.344 (1). Pole.
Race weather: warm, overcast.
Warm-up: 1:24.312 (2).
Result: First.

On the Thursday "I lost some time on the fast right-hander going into the tunnel *so* I waited until just before the end for my second try. I got a good clean lap." On the Saturday "the track conditions changed a lot but I managed to keep pole which is all that really matters. You have to find the right measure between the risk that everybody takes and what it takes to do it. On a circuit like Imola or Interlagos – a proper racing circuit – you have more margin for errors. That gives you the ability to push a little harder. Here you are running between the walls. Your apex points and braking points are solid things which you cannot touch. You have to be as precise as possible. That means throughout the lap in all the corners."

Stefano Modena (Tyrrell) shared the front row and if he led into Ste Devote who knew? He matched Senna from the green light but Senna maximised the advantage of the stagger. Modena tracked, Senna settling to his pace and rhythm untroubled by Modena's proximity. On lap 5 Modena made a mistake at Portier and that created the gap without Senna having to create it himself. Modena went to lap 43 (engine failure). The race as an unresolved competition ended then, Mansell too far back except that Senna saw "the big television screen showed Dernier Tour [last lap] and I couldn't understand that. As far as I knew from my pit board there were two. I kept going, got to the finish line again and Jacky Ickx gave me the chequered flag. I slowed down for about half a lap and then Ron Dennis called me on the radio, saying I should speed up because there was another lap to go! I'd already undone my belts but I did what he said because I didn't know what was going on."

- **Podium:** Senna 1h 53m 02.334s, Mansell at 18.348, Alesi at 47.455.
- **Fastest lap:** Prost 1:24.368.
- **Senna:** 1:25.250.
- **Championship:** Senna 40, Prost 11, Berger 10.

Canada, Montreal, 2 June 1991.
Qualifying: 1:35.843 (3); 1:20.318 (3). Row 2.
Pole: Patrese 1:19.837.
Race weather: hot, sunny.
Warm-up: 1:23.271 (3).
Result: Retired after 25 laps, alternator.

"Up until now people think we have had it easy with four pole positions and four wins but my performance today shows how competitive it really is out there." That was Senna on the Saturday. The glimpse of the future at Imola, he felt, was coming true: Patrese and Mansell on the front row and if their cars did prove reliable?

Mansell led from Patrese, Senna third, Prost hustling. Completing the opening lap the Williamses were already clear. Senna ran third to nearly half distance. "I stopped with an electrical problem but honestly I don't think I could have beaten the Williamses." The future was now.

- **Podium:** Piquet, Stefano Modena (Tyrrell), Patrese.
- **Fastest lap:** Mansell 1:22.385.
- **Senna:** 1:24.647.
- **Championship:** Senna 40, Piquet 16, Prost 11.

Mexico, Mexico City, 16 June 1991.
Qualifying: 1:17.264 (3); 1:18.711 (5). Row 2.
Pole: Patrese 1:16.696.
Race weather: overcast, then sunny.
Warm-up: 1:20.719 (3).
Result: Third.

"A big shunt" towards the end of Friday qualifying at Peraltada. "I went in too wide and too fast. The problem was that my fifth gear was too short and I was changing to sixth with one hand on the wheel when I hit a bump and lost control. I got onto the dusty part of the track and I couldn't control it. Once the car hit the tyre barrier backwards it tipped upside down and ended up in the sand." He'd recovered by the Saturday.

He ran second early on, then third to the end behind Patrese and Mansell. "The Williamses were very fast and it was difficult to get more power from our engine. I couldn't get too close to the cars in front because my temperatures were marginal. Nigel made it very hard for me but it was a great race and I think the result shows the championship is very open."

Qualifying at Imola, here behind Stefano Modena's Tyrrell *Braun*.

- **Podium:** Patrese 1h 29m 52.205s,
  Mansell at 1.336, Senna at 57.356.
- **Fastest lap:** Mansell 1:16.788.
- **Senna:** 1:18.570.
- **Championship:** Senna 44, Patrese 20,
  Piquet 16.

RACE 191

France, Magny-Cours, 7 July 1991.
Qualifying: 1:16.557 (1); 1:14.857 (3). Row 2.
Pole: Patrese 1:14.559.
Race weather: warm, overcast.
Warm-up: 1:21.170 (9).
Result: Third.

The pressure mounted on Senna as Senna tried to mount pressure on Mansell, Patrese and Prost. On the Friday "my qualifying lap was very hard work. I could not have kept up that level of performance for much longer." On the Saturday "I had a clear lap on both runs with just a little bit of oil which caused me to slide wide mid-way round the second lap. The most slippery place was right at the end of the lap where I spun, without damaging the car." That was into the start-finish straight and spectacular. He rounded the corner and at the lip of the outer kerbing the car pivoted. As it crossed the track – spinning – Senna dug smoke from the tyres under ferocious braking. The car kissed the barrier.

Senna made a self-confessed "poor start and knew I could not go with Prost or Mansell." Prost led from Mansell, Senna completing the opening lap off the pace. Apart from the tyre stops, Senna ran third the whole race. "We know we do not have the engine or chassis performance to match the Williamses and Ferraris at the moment but a third place adds to my points total." What else could he say? What else did he have to say to Honda?

- **Podium:** Mansell 1h 38m 00.056s, Prost at 5.003,
  Senna at 34.934.
- **Fastest lap:** Mansell 1:19.168.
- **Senna:** 1:20.570.
- **Championship:** Senna 48, Mansell 23,
  Patrese 22.

RACE 192

Britain, Silverstone, 14 July 1991.
Qualifying: 1:23.277 (3); 1:21.618 (2).
Front row.
Pole: Mansell 1:20.939.
Race weather: warm, sunny.
Warm-up: 1:29.281 (11).
Result: Ran out of fuel, classified fourth.

No holding Mansell by now, particularly here. On the Friday Senna complained that "the engine is not working well" and, on the Saturday, "I did my best, it was a good lap but Nigel deserves to be on pole. The Williams team is really strong at the moment." He understood the nuances of diplomacy: there is always a calculated understatement in your statement. *Autosport* reported Senna's quick lap: "This was going to be special. It was. Ayrton's lap was brilliant. There is no other word for it. Clearly the Williams-Renaults were about a second better than the McLaren-Hondas but Senna conveniently forgot this. It was neat and precise yet so close to the edge that you feared for the Brazilian. The commitment was startling. There was a collective intake of breath when he crossed the line." The McLaren was bottoming and, in the curves, molten flecks of sparks spat and flickered from both sides of the car.

Senna drew ahead into Copse. Mansell harried to Hangar Straight, got a 'tow', sprang out, led. He would not lose it. "I planned to run the whole race without a tyre stop and this plan was paying off. Towards the end my left front tyre blistered causing a slight vibration but it wasn't a problem. Then on the last lap the engine started to die as I went down the Hangar Straight. All I know is that it wasn't an electrical problem because my dash read-out was still working." Was this diplomatic-speak for a criticism of Honda? As Mansell came round on his slowing down lap he stopped and gave Senna a lift: one of the most evocative and telling images of the season.

- **Podium:** Mansell, Berger, Prost.
- **Fastest lap:** Mansell 1:26.379.
- **Senna:** 1:27.509.
- **Championship:** Senna 51, Mansell 33,
  Patrese 22.

Mastery, and victory, at Monaco.

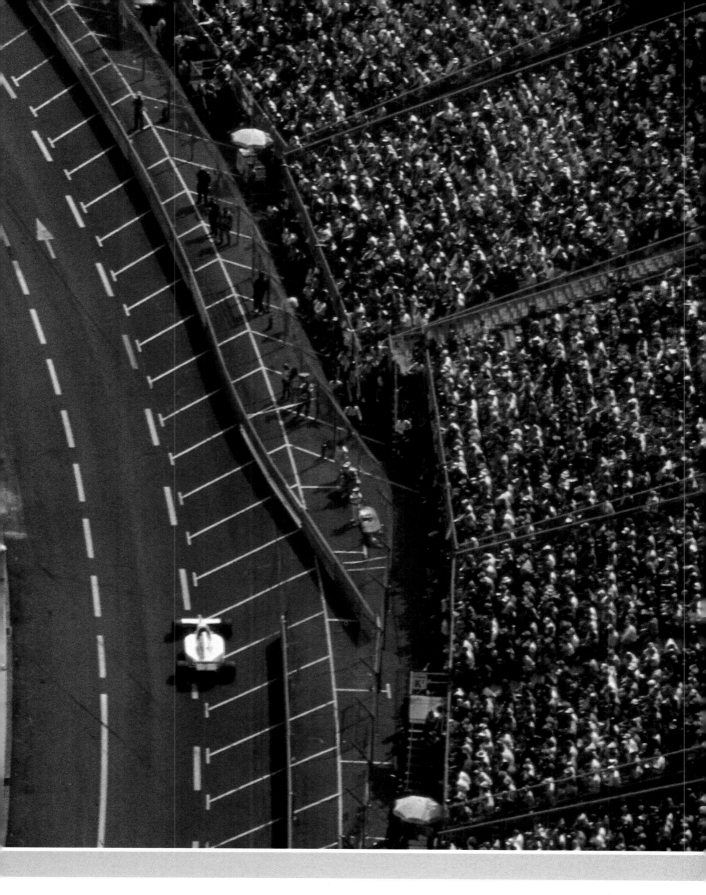

The fearsome (and feared) Peraltada corner in Mexico claims Senna during qualifying.

Germany, Hockenheim, 28 July 1991.
Qualifying: 1:38.208 (4); 1:37.274 (2).
Front row.
Pole: Mansell 1:37.087.
Race weather: warm, sunny.
Warm-up: 1:44.747 (3).
Result: Retired after 44 laps, out of fuel.

Senna insisted on honesty on the Friday. "We haven't had much progress since Imola. We have no real problems except, as at Silverstone, we are just not quick enough to compete with the Williamses." On the Saturday "I did my best. Maybe I could have gone one-tenth quicker but I was really on the limit."

Mansell off to a stormer, Berger past Senna, Prost fourth. Berger struggled to hold onto Mansell but more significantly Senna struggled to hold onto Berger. Prost observed. After the pit stops Mansell still led from Berger and Patrese, Senna fourth, Prost fifth – an arrangement conjuring lurid imagery. The combat endured from lap 22 to lap 38, reaching its full intensity around lap 35 when Prost drew up. Images at lap 38, the climax: Prost trying at the first chicane, Senna mid-track, Prost probe-right dance-left to the outside, Senna elbowing left, elbowing Prost to put two wheels on the rim and nearly over it. Prost's momentum pitched him up up the escape road, tyres wreathed in smoke. Prost would tick off his accusations: *don't understand the way Senna drives/unacceptable intimidation/moving over on me, pushing me towards the grass not once but "10, 15, 20 times."* Senna continued but on the final lap ran out of fuel. "I am too disappointed to make any comment." Whether that referred to Prost or the fuel (or both) was unclear. The diplomat, you know, and barely concealing it.

- **Podium:** Mansell, Patrese, Alesi.
- **Fastest lap:** Patrese 1:43.569.
- **Senna:** 1:44.213.
- **Championship:** Senna 51, Mansell 43, Patrese 28.

Just about to run out of fuel at Silverstone...

Hungary, Hungaroring, 11 August 1991.
Qualifying: 1:18.549 (2); 1:16.147 (1). Pole.
Race weather: hot, sunny.
Warm-up: 1:23.229 (6).
Result: First.

Senna played himself in with circumspection on the Friday – "it's very hot and my tyres were going off before the end of the lap so I had to be careful." On the Saturday he put together two runs in the 1:16s, both stunning: he radiated speed without rawness, drawing harmony from the car and himself and each curve and corner. He made the pastoral circuit a canvas and painted his brush strokes upon it, deft, exact and forming a picture you can never forget. "This has been longest time in the last few years that I have been off the pole position (smile) so today's result feels very good. When you experience something good you get used to it! This pole position is the result of our team's improvement and not because others have had problems."

Senna and Prost healed wounds again and (fortunately) that would not be tested in the race. At the green light Senna sweetly away but Patrese, inside, abreast into turn one. Senna outbraked him. "Riccardo made a good start and we were both on the limit but I had to go for it

because leading into the first corner is crucial here. My tyre choice was a calculated risk [Cs left, Ds right] and after two laps I thought I had a puncture. The team told me they were ready for me to come in but I tried one more lap and the problem disappeared. The car was very good out of the corner onto the main straight so I was able to control the race."

- **Podium:** Senna 1h 49m 12.796s, Mansell at 4.599, Patrese at 15.594.
- **Fastest lap:** Bertrand Gachot (Jordan) 1:21.547.
- **Senna:** 1:22.392.
- **Championship:** Senna 61, Mansell 49, Patrese 32.

Belgium, Spa, 25 August 1991.
Qualifying: 1:49.100 (1); 1:47.811 (1). Pole.
Race weather: hot, sunny.
Warm-up: 1:56.752 (3).
Result: First.

Without enough speed you're utterly vulnerable at Spa. On the Friday Senna had two "clean, good laps" but on the Saturday "I really had to push everything to the limit. On this circuit the balance of the car is of fundamental importance and changes significantly depending on the fuel load. I hadn't done Eau Rouge flat all weekend. I kept thinking *I CAN do it, I CAN do it* but every time I got there my foot came off. This time I was committed. If I'm honest I don't remember if I did it flat because there were two cars at the exit but I just managed to go between them, right on the limit. When I was coming to the quick corner before the Bus Stop somebody went off and put a big cloud of dust into the air. I couldn't see anything. You are in top gear and full throttle there. There is no way out. I could just see a car going through the dust. I didn't know what speed it was going so I was really scared. I hesitated a little bit and that cost me some time and after that the guy stayed in the way and it lost me time."

Senna alongside Prost on the front row. La Source? During the spurt to it they waved front wheels at each other then passed sensibly through, Senna leading and preparing The Tactic. Mansell overtook Prost for second place on lap 2. Senna had a slow pit stop "due to a problem refitting one of the rear tyres, I think." That made him third behind Mansell and Alesi. On lap 23 Mansell's electrics failed, Senna upon Alesi who resisted until lap 31 when Alesi's engine failed. Only Berger might now contest the lead and clearly he wouldn't for the sake of Senna's championship chance.

Podium: Senna 1h 27m 17.669, Berger at 1.901, Piquet at 32.176.
Fastest lap: Moreno 1:55.161.
Senna: 1:56.471.
Championship: Senna 71, Mansell 49, Patrese 34.

RACE 196

Italy, Monza, 8 September 1991.
Qualifying: 1:21.114 (1); 1:21.245 (1). Pole.
Race weather: warm, breezy.
Warm-up: 1:26.355 (4).
Result: Second.

Tight from Mansell on the Friday and Senna spoke of improving the chassis balance; tight on the Saturday too. "At the start of my second quick lap I heard over the radio about Mansell's best time so I knew it was just between me and Gerhard for the pole but I had to lift at the second Lesmo because Nigel was there and though he got off the racing line I didn't want to take the risk. That cost me two-tenths."

Mansell needed to win and did, following Senna from the start but never quite in an overtaking position. At one point Mansell let Patrese through – you have a tilt at him – while he took breath, not to mention that Italian Patrese at Italian Monza might do something total to overtake Senna. Patrese did overtake, spun. "My set up," Senna said, "was not good *so* I used up my tyres and lost grip. Then my left front began to vibrate and locked under braking. Soon after that [lap 14] Mansell passed me" – inside at the Ascari bend – "and I decided to stop for fresh rubber. If I had not I could not have finished second."

• **Podium:** Mansell 1h 17m 54.319s, Senna at 16.262, Prost at 16.829.
• **Fastest lap:** Senna 1:26.061.
• **Championship:** Senna 77, Mansell 59, Patrese 34.

... Mansell gave him a lift back on the slowing-down lap.

RACE 197

Portugal, Estoril, 22 September 1991.
Qualifying: 1:13.752 (2); 1:13.444 (3). Row 2.
Pole: Patrese 1:13.001.
Race weather: warm, sunny.
Warm-up: 1:19.798 (6).
Result: Second.

Berger took provisional pole. Senna felt it "a shame I could not get onto the front row with Gerhard" on the Saturday "but Riccardo deserved pole. His lap was smooth, tidy and he made no mistakes." Senna looked relaxed. "Williams are going for everything. They have nothing to lose and there are enough races left to make a radical difference to the championship."

From the second row Mansell hauled over in front of Senna to have turn one. "If I hadn't braked hard and pulled my car to the inside, Mansell and I would have had a big accident. OK he did have nothing to lose and he was going for it because of the championship but I think he went a bit too far. I made a big effort to avoid contact and even so I thought for a moment we were going to crash. We were that close. And immediately after the first corner he did the same with Gerhard. I think it's crazy to do that." Patrese led, Mansell second and Patrese ready to pass the lead to Mansell who accepted it gratefully enough on lap 18, Berger third, Senna fourth. When Mansell pitted the stop went wrong and as he accelerated a rear wheel unwound and spun off. Mansell would be disqualified because the wheel was refitted in the pit lane. Senna overtook Berger to be second. "Once I saw Patrese in the lead I pushed hard to see if he had any problems but I had to drive over the limits of myself and my car. In addition my right hand was hurting and I settled for second."

- **Podium:** Patrese 1h 35m 42.304s, Senna at 20.941, Alesi at 53.554.
- **Fastest lap:** Mansell 1:18.179.
- **Senna:** 1:18.929.
- **Championship:** Senna 83, Mansell 59, Patrese 44.

By Germany, the Championship was tightening. Senna, sombre, with Ron Dennis of McLaren.

RACE 198

Spain, Barcelona, 29 September 1991.
Qualifying: 1:19.474 (3); 1:19.064 (1). Row 2.
Pole: Berger 1:18.751.
Race weather: overcast, drizzle.
Warm-up: 1:46.561. (6).
Result: Fifth.

A new circuit which Senna described as "very smooth, very nice to drive on." On the Friday he felt "I could have done slightly better because when I changed cars I really wanted to use a mixed set of worn tyres but due to a slight misunderstanding they fitted my original set. I was a little bit tentative and cautious with the spare car and I lacked a little bit of commitment because I wasn't totally familiar with it." On the Saturday "when I started my second run the engine didn't feel quite right on the start-line straight and after a couple more corners it broke. The track marshals covered the oil with cement dust which slightly aggravated the problem when we resumed. The cars were carrying the cement dust on to the next corner."

After a trenchant drivers' briefing before the race – Mansell demanding of FISA's Jean-Marie Balestre why he was singled out for criticism the whole time but not Senna – Berger led from Senna, though Mansell overtook him on lap 3: a famous moment, the two cars snaking towards each other, wheels impossibly near. On lap 13 Senna spun and Mansell, rounding the corner, just missed him. "I feel I spun because the slicks we fitted to the left-hand wheels were too hard and I was fighting for grip in the wet. After the spin the left-hand tyres were blistered and I couldn't go any quicker."

- **Podium:** Mansell, Prost, Patrese.
- **Fastest lap:** Patrese 1:22.837.
- **Senna:** 1:24.771.
- **Championship:** Senna 85, Mansell 69, Patrese 48.

Senna in deep discussion with the crew.

Japan, Suzuka, 20 October 1991.
Qualifying: 1:36.490 (2); 1:34.898 (2). Front row.
Pole: Berger 1:34.700.
Race weather: warm, sunny.
Warm-up: 1:41.442 (1).
Result: Second.

Mansell needed to win and Senna finish third or lower for the championship to continue into Australia. After qualifying Senna said "as far as the World Championship is concerned I feel good but I am under no illusions. The race is going to be very tough but I think things are coming our way step by step."

Because the two McLarens had the front row, and Berger had pole, McLaren decided on an obvious ploy: Berger build a big lead while Senna restrained Mansell. It worked. On laps 1, 2, 3 and 5 Berger set fastest laps, pulling away – and Mansell must overtake Senna to catch and overtake Berger. Mansell tried on lap 10 into the first corner. Evidently he had a soft brake pedal because the Williams flowed over the kerbing and onto the run-off area never to return. Senna, seeing this, hardly felt sorry.

He and Berger raced and Senna led but the team instructed him to give it to Berger, who had yet to win for McLaren. Senna couldn't hear this radio message clearly and slowed to clarify the reception because he felt nobody would believe him if he said he hadn't heard it. He made a great demonstration of giving it to Berger just before the line (there are mixed reports about how Berger regarded this) and then launched an astonishing attack upon Balestre for what had happened the year before, four letter words and all. The eternal matter: self-control or the lack of it.

- **Podium:** Berger 1h 32m 10.695s, Senna at 0.344, Patrese at 56.731.
- **Fastest lap:** Senna 1:41.532.
- **Championship:** Senna 91, Mansell 69, Patrese 52.

Left: Hungary, and victory over Mansell.
Right: Spa, and holding the famous Red Five of Mansell at bay *Zooom.*

Victory at Spa by 1.901 seconds from Berger.

The third World Championship, Japan.

RACE 200

Australia, Adelaide, 3 November 1991.
Qualifying: 1:14.210 (1); 1:14.041 (1). Pole.
Race weather: wet.
Warm-up: 1:18.964 (3).
Result: First.

On the Saturday he took his sixtieth pole, "a target I set myself this season and we just made it at the last minute."

The race degenerated into a sodden shambles. "This place is terrible in the wet because the drainage is very bad and you get a lot of standing water. Really it is not suitable for racing in the rain. I only started because I felt a strong obligation to the team and with the Constructors' Championship in mind. It was agreed I'd see how things developed and would be free to stop if the conditions became impossible."

Senna led from Berger. On lap 3 Mansell overtook Berger but so many cars crashed that it was stopped at 14 laps.

- **Podium:** Senna 24m 34.899s, Mansell at 1.259, Berger at 5.120.
- **Fastest lap:** Berger 1:41.141.
- **Senna:** 1:42.545.
- **Championship:** Senna 96, Mansell 72, Patrese 53.

Keeping a steady eye on the immediate future.

Senna in 1992.

1992

*B*erger remained with Senna at Marlboro McLaren. The other front-runners: Mansell and Patrese (Williams), Schumacher and Brundle (Benetton), Alesi (Ferrari). A rule change banned qualifying tyres.

✳ ✳ ✳

RACE 201

South Africa, Kyalami, 1 March 1992.
Qualifying: 1:16.815 (3); 1:16.227 (2).
Front row.
Pole: Mansell 1:15.486.
Race weather: warm, overcast.
Warmup: 1:20.347 (4).
Result: Third.

The Williamses could not be resisted, here and virtually everywhere else. Senna described this rebuilt circuit as "interesting." On the Friday "without qualifying tyres it's impossible to really go for it on a single lap with maximum grip." On the Saturday he managed a clear lap.

Mansell led throughout, Patrese nestling between the McLarens from the green light. "I knew right from the start after such a good getaway from Riccardo it would be almost impossible to pass him. He went away a little bit and although I tried to keep the pressure on he was a little faster. I was able to maintain a short distance with him and periodically put in a spurt trying to get an opportunity in traffic or hope perhaps he would have a technical problem." It was the story of the whole season.

- **Podium:** Mansell 1h 36m 45.320s, Patrese at 24.360, Senna at 34.675.
- **Fastest lap:** Mansell 1:17.578.
- **Senna:** 1:18.140.

No holding Mansell in 1992. Senna finished a distant third in South Africa. Here he is in qualifying.

Mexico, Mexico City, 22 March 1992.
Qualifying: 1:23.063 (27); 1:18.791 (6). Row 3.
Pole: Mansell 1:16.346.
Race weather: hot, sunny.
Warm-up: 1:19.420 (5).
Result: Retired after 11 laps, transmission.

Drivers insisted the corrugation was worse and, of Peraltada, Senna said "in my opinion it is 10 times as bad as last year. It is very, very dangerous. An accident is inevitable. It is just a matter of time." By a paradox Senna crashed heavily 18 minutes into the Friday session but at the esses. The McLaren struck a large bump, bucked and twitched, travelled through 360 degrees and smote the wall. "I lost control completely. On a track like this, with no grip and so much dirt, when you hit a hump there is nothing really you can do. It was a very hard impact and the pain was unbearable. I hit both legs violently and I thought I had broken them." He had not yet qualified for the race. On the Saturday "sore and in pain" he couldn't hope to get near the Williamses.

He ran third to lap 12. "I had some sort of problem with the clutch or the transmission, not a problem I have had before. Until then it was a good race for me. I was prepared to wait and see how things developed." He could do little else. The art of the possible...

• **Podium:** Mansell, Patrese, Schumacher.
• **Fastest lap:** Berger 1:17.711.
• **Senna:** 1:20.721.
• **Championship:** Mansell 20, Patrese 12, Schumacher 7, Berger 5, Senna 4.

Brazil, Interlagos, 5 April 1992.
Qualifying: 1:19.358 (9); 1:17.902 (3). Row 2.
Pole: Mansell 1:15.703.
Race weather: hot, sunny.
Warm-up: 1:21.146 (9).
Result: Retired after 17 laps, electrics.

New McLaren cars but Senna felt it was "premature to make any comment" on the Friday. On the Saturday "we registered a significant improvement" – the favoured, understated phrase. "We tried some radical changes but it is still far from right. We are having difficulties getting the chassis to handle and the engine is not yet developed to its optimum so we are having to sacrifice down-force to make up for the lack of power."

He ran third, descending to sixth. "During the early stages my car suffered a serious and

The rain in Spain. *Zooom*

intermittent engine cut-out. The effect of this was totally unpredictable and could occur four or five times on one lap and not at all on the next. At times the cut-out was so bad that it felt as if I had applied the brakes. I continued, trying to cover this problem in the hope it would eventually go away while at the same time raising my arm to warn the drivers behind of my problem." The cut-out did not go away.

- **Podium:** Mansell, Patrese, Schumacher.
- **Fastest lap:** Patrese 1:19.490.
- **Senna:** 1:23.101.
- **Championship:** Mansell 30, Patrese 18, Schumacher 11, Berger 5, Senna 4.

RACE 204

Spain, Barcelona, 3 May 1992.
Qualifying: 1:21.209 (3); 1:46.581 (3). Row 2.
Pole: Mansell 1:20.190.
Race weather: cool, wet.
Warm-up: 1:44.964 (10).
Result: Retired after 62 laps, spin.

Senna estimated that "we have made some progress since Brazil, we have a better understanding of the car and how it works." On the Saturday it rained and "the car works better in the wet than it does in the dry partly because we are a little bit down on power and that matters less in the wet."

Mansell led throughout, Senna fifth to lap 8, fourth to lap 20 and third to lap 63. "At the start Alesi drove into me but it was wheel-to-wheel contact so we got away with it. When I spun the first time I was lucky to get back on the circuit but the car was aquaplaning everywhere and the second time I just couldn't hold it. Gerhard and I nearly had a coming together at one point early in the race when he overtook me. It didn't help matters that at some point in the race I pulled a muscle in my arm."

- **Podium:** Mansell, Schumacher, Alesi.
- **Fastest lap:** Mansell 1:42.503.
- **Senna:** 1:43.176.
- **Championship:** Mansell 40, Patrese 18, Schumacher 17, Berger 8, Alesi 7, Senna 4.

RACE 205

San Marino, Imola 17 May 1992.
Qualifying: 1:23.086 (2); 1:23.151 (3). Row 2.
Pole: Mansell 1:21.842.
Race weather: hot, sunny.
Warm-up: 1:26.665 (4).
Result: Third.

The search for the right chassis balance continued. "There is some improvement on the engine side but we could still do with more power." On the Saturday he felt "we have not made as much progress since yesterday as I would have hoped and the fact that the track conditions were slower didn't help."

Mansell led throughout, Senna third to lap 26 (his pit stop) then chasing and overtaking Alesi for third again on lap 40. Within the constrictions of what the car could do Senna demonstrated his timing and tactical skill. Coming down to the Rivazza he went round the outside of Alesi – smooth, smooth, smooth – which gave him the inside for the next left. A sort of inevitability hung over it.

- **Podium:** Mansell 1h 28m 40.927s, Patrese at 9.451, Senna at 48.984.
- **Fastest lap:** Patrese 1:26.100.
- **Senna:** 1:27.615.
- **Championship:** Mansell 50, Patrese 24, Schumacher 17, Senna and Berger 8.

RACE 206

Monaco, Monte Carlo, 31 May 1992.
Qualifying: 1:21.467 (2); 1:20.608 (3). Row 2.
Pole: Mansell 1:19.495.
Race weather: warm, overcast.
Warm-up: 1:25.116 (3).
Result: First.

"This is such a unique circuit that it doesn't accurately reflect the performance of the car. It's just a question of getting round the hairpins." On the Saturday "I spun my race car on my first quick lap. It was going to be a good one. I was driving over the limit trying to make up the time somehow." It was all he could do.

Mansell clean into Ste Devote, Senna going for it "at the last moment so as not to give

Riccardo [on the front row] any indication because otherwise he would have closed the door, of course. The problem was to stop the car before Mansell turned in. I was coming so quickly I thought he might not have seen me. After that I tried to keep the gap [to Mansell] as small as possible because there is always the possibility of the unexpected here." Senna circled in his patience and on lap 71 Mansell thought he had a puncture (a wheel nut was loose). He pitted for tyres, Senna leading. Mansell launched a major attempt, first catching Senna and then swarming him. "For the last five or six laps I had nothing left to give. My tyres were finished and I had no grip. I knew Nigel would catch me on fresh tyres – so I gave it everything. I knew *he* would try everything and all I could do was try and stay on the road and in the right place. On the straights it was like a drag race, you know, wheel-spin in third and fourth gear..."

- **Podium:** Senna 1h 50m 59.372s, Mansell at 0.215, Patrese at 31.843.
- **Fastest lap:** Mansell 1:21.598.
- **Senna:** 1:23.470.
- **Championship:** Mansell 56, Patrese 28, Schumacher 20, Senna 18.

Monaco, where Mansell pitted for a suspected puncture, opening the lead to Senna.

RACE 207

Canada, Montreal, 14 June 1992.
Qualifying: 1:19.775 (1); 1:20.590 (2). Pole.
Race weather: hot, sunny.
Warm-up: 1:23.964 (5).
Result: Retired after 37 laps, electrics.

"I am not really convinced about the Williams team's performance (Patrese second, Mansell fourth)," Senna said on the Friday. On the Saturday he quipped "it has been a long time since I can remember being on pole position! Conditions were more difficult and I was unable to improve but it is good to be fastest. I am under no illusions about the race."

Senna led, holding Mansell captive for 14 laps. Coming to the chicane on the fifteenth Mansell tried the inside, went broadside across the run-off area and ended on the start-finish straight pointing towards the oncoming traffic, the car savaged. "My opinion on Nigel's retirement is that he realised he couldn't brake in time for the corner so he lined the car up with the middle of the kerb and hoped to clear it – but he hit it with such force that he appeared to land on the car's nose." Mansell sat in the cockpit and as Senna passed next time round stuck an accusing finger towards him. Senna didn't let that disturb him but "eventually the engine just cut out."

- **Podium:** Berger, Schumacher, Alesi.
- **Fastest lap:** Berger 1:22.325.
- **Senna:** 1:23.728.
- **Championship:** Mansell 56, Patrese 28, Schumacher 26, Senna and Berger 18.

RACE 208

France, Magny-Cours, 5 July 1992.
Qualifying: 1:16.892 (3); 1:15.199 (3). Row 2.
Pole: Mansell 1:13.864.
Race weather: showers.
Warm-up: 1:32.516 (6).
Result: Retired no laps, accident.

Friday was difficult. "When the tyres were good, the engine wasn't – and when the engine was, the tyres weren't." On the Saturday "basically I did the best I could with the machinery."

Senna made "a bad start. Gerhard and I ended up side by side at the first corner. It was close but OK. I followed him down the straight, he braked very late so I was being careful and then Schumacher hit me from behind." It happened at the Adelaide hairpin. "I think he totally misjudged his speed and his braking point for that corner – considering it was the first lap – and he could not stop." Senna stood at the side of the track, head bowed, the championship fleeing from him every time Mansell passed by.

- **Podium:** Mansell, Patrese, Brundle.
- **Fastest lap:** Mansell 1:17.070.
- **Senna:** no lap.
- **Championship:** Mansell 66, Patrese 34, Schumacher 26, Senna and Berger 18.

RACE 209

Britain, Silverstone, 12 July 1992.
Qualifying: 1:21.706 (3); 1:41.912 (11). Row 2.
Pole: Mansell 1:18.965.
Race weather: warm.
Warm-up: 1:26.606 (5).
Result: Retired after 52 laps, gearbox.

Senna estimated "the gap between us and the Williamses is bigger here than normal, reflecting their strengths and our weaknesses." Drizzle fell on the Saturday.

Senna ran fourth behind Brundle. "I had a good clean fight with Martin. I was pushing like hell the whole race and it was really tiring. I was surprised that I could keep up such a performance under such pressure for so long. I never gave up because I knew the car would

Senna and Dennis after the Monaco victory.

perform better in the closing stages. On some corners I could catch him, on some he was going away. I tried many times. Sometimes the backmarkers helped, sometimes they didn't. I was also worried about my tyres. I had a lot of vibration and for the last 15 laps I could hardly see the track."

- **Podium:** Mansell, Patrese, Brundle.
- **Fastest lap:** Mansell 1:22.539.
- **Senna:** 1:25.825.
- **Championship:** Mansell 76, Patrese 40, Schumacher 29, Berger 20, Senna 18.

RACE 210

Germany, Hockenheim, 26 July 1992.
Qualifying: 1:40.331 (2); 1:39.106 (3). Row 2.
Pole: Mansell 1:37.960.
Race weather: hot, sunny.
Warm-up: 1:44.251 (4).
Result: Second.

No hiding at Hockenheim. On the Saturday "I was right over the limit and that was as fast as I could go."

The race settled Mansell, Patrese, Senna, each stretching from the other. During the pit stops a ploy revealed itself: Senna wouldn't be stopping. "The only way to get onto the podium was to go through and take a chance." Mansell came out behind Senna and attacked. Into a chicane Mansell level but Senna held that. At the next chicane Mansell went off the track, digging a dust cloud, rejoined. Gestures only by Senna, doing what you do which is all you can do. On a straight Mansell powered by. Now Patrese attacked. "I didn't know if I could cope with Riccardo. He had more top speed and his tyres seemed in better condition. The last 10 laps were very worrying because I had bad vibrations from my tyres." The Patrese attack/Senna defence evolved into a raw, manly, reflex thing: Patrese exploiting the width of the track to prod and probe, Senna exploiting the width of it to block. At the entrance to the Stadium Patrese tried a last time on the last lap and went onto the grass.

- **Podium:** Mansell 1h 18m 22.032s, Senna at 4.500, Schumacher at 34.462.
- **Fastest lap:** Patrese 1:41.591.
- **Senna:** 1:42.272.
- **Championship:** Mansell 86, Patrese 40, Schumacher 33, Senna 24.

Michael Schumacher gets the Adelaide hairpin wrong at Magny-Cours and takes Senna with him.

Hungary, Hungaroring, 16 August 1992.
Qualifying: 1:16.467 (3); 1:16.267 (3). Row 2.
Pole: Patrese 1:15.476.
Race weather: hot, sunny.
Warm-up: 1:19.408 (1).
Result: First.

On the Friday "it was very difficult to get a clear lap. There seemed to be cars going off everywhere. This is one of the problems of qualifying on race tyres. It's a good race tyre but it doesn't offer that extra margin when the car breaks away." On the Saturday everybody, it seemed, was spinning, including Senna. "My biggest achievement is that my mechanics won't have to spend time rebuilding my car." He could wield whimsical humour when he wanted as effectively as The Tactic.

The world watched Mansell prepare to win the championship. Senna locked into a bid to get a Williams drive for 1993 and before the race told former World Champion James Hunt, then of the BBC, that he'd drive for free – putting Mansell's position in jeopardy. Hunt would reveal this on air. Patrese led from Senna, who'd made an awesome getaway constructing a great arc round Mansell's outside into turn one. Senna circled second behind Patrese, Mansell fourth behind Berger. "I knew to have a chance I would have to get into the lead at the start. I made up one place and tried to stay with Riccardo for a single lap then I realised there was no way so I concentrated on running the race within my own limitations." The art of the possible. Patrese spun off on lap 39 and "I pressed harder," Mansell behind. "I wasn't sure if second position was good enough to win Nigel the title so I asked on the radio and they told me 'yes' I knew that even if he came close he wouldn't take any chances. I decided to try to open a gap because I was worried I would have no tyres by the end." A slow puncture made Mansell pit, leaving Senna isolated in the lead. Mansell clawed and cleaved to second place but distant enough for Senna to pit (on lap 67 of the 77) and retain the lead. Senna handled the final laps with imperious, seasoned, almost touching certainty.

- **Podium:** Senna 1h 46m 19.216s, Mansell at 40.139, Berger at 50.782.
- **Fastest lap:** Mansell 1:18.308.
- **Senna:** 1:19.588.
- **Championship:** Mansell 92, Patrese 40, Senna 34.

Problem-solving with Steve Hallam, an experienced race engineer, at Hockenheim.

RACE 212

Belgium, Spa, 30 August 1992.
Qualifying: 1:52.743 (2); 2:14.983 (14).
Front row.
Pole: Mansell 1:50.545.
Race weather: wet and dry.
Warm-up: 1:57.243 (4).
Result: Fifth.

A plea from the heart on the Friday. "The car seems to be the same as ever but I am still trying as hard as ever!" Saturday was typically wet and "I stayed on full tanks *because* there was no chance of improving. At least it gave me the feel of what conditions might be like if it rains for the race."

Conditions would resemble whole, shifting seasons of weather and that presented opportunities. Senna went outside Mansell into La Source. In the country Mansell crowded, stressing he had the Williams and Senna did not. Mansell overtook on lap 2; and drizzle dripped. At the Bus Stop Patrese overtook. The race reverted to type, vintage this 1992: Mansell and Patrese out of reach leaving a scrabble amongst the also-rans for whatever they could get, Schumacher bustling around Senna, Alesi bobbing around Schumacher. Mansell pitted on lap 3 for wet tyres, then Schumacher pitted, then Patrese pitted. The common judgement – the only sensible judgement – was for wet tyres, the pit lane a buzzing, busy corridor as the rush descended upon it for wets. Senna did not join this rush. He reasoned, examined and concluded *here is an advantage if I make my weather forecast right.* "Gambling on staying out was my only chance. The car was just on the edge of controllability. The others stopped early and I felt I had nothing to lose and if the drizzle stopped I would be in good shape." Picture it:

The beautiful drive in Hungary although Mansell took the championship.

the broad sweeps of Spa, the tarmac glistening and Senna in the mist man-handling a racing car in what was now heavy rain. The glistening tyres on the glistening tarmac offered virtually no grip. On lap 8 Senna covered 4.3 miles in two minutes 19.910 seconds. Arguably nobody else in the race could have done it. Certainly nobody else in the race thought of trying to do it. On their wet tyres Mansell and Patrese shredded Senna's lead but he offered a brave man's resistance as they went by. Token resistance, as they say, a matter of self-respect. "I hung on but the rain never stopped and eventually I had to come in for tyres." That was lap 14. Senna worked to sixth when "it dried so I picked a safe time to stop for slicks. I'd just learnt that the mechanics get a bonus for every point. I decided to give them two points instead of one." And did, overtaking Mika Hakkinen (Lotus) for fifth.

- **Podium:** Schumacher, Mansell, Patrese.
- **Fastest lap:** Schumacher 1:53.791.
- **Senna:** 1:54.088.
- **Championship:** Mansell 98, Patrese 44, Schumacher 43, Senna 36.

RACE 213

Italy, Monza, 13 September 1992.
Qualifying: 1:22.822 (2); 1:24.122 (6). Front row.
Pole: Mansell 1:22.221.
Race weather: hot, sunny.
Warm-up: 1:27.088 (4).
Result: First.

In the parkland Senna talked of this and that – "a bad failure with my race car, I'm not quite sure what it was" on the Saturday, but "it's difficult to say whether I could have matched Mansell."

Mansell made a big, big start but from the second row Alesi, cheeky and chancy, slotted his Ferrari between Senna and Mansell. Whadda you think about that? Senna thought he'd place the McLaren full left. Reaching towards the mouth of the funnelling first chicane Alesi had to be – and was – mid-track, Senna alongside and inside. The place to be. Senna braked so late he locked

wheels. Alesi backed off (a little) and, seeing that, Senna placed the McLaren mid-track to close the mouth of the chicane. To describe it like this is to slow it, rationalise it. It happened furious fast, flick-click-flick but it may well be that Senna didn't see it in those dimensions. He slowed it, saw it frame by frame. Whatever, "after the start I didn't think I could maintain my position but Nigel only pulled out a relatively small advantage and I was able to stay in touch. Then Riccardo caught me quite easily and made a very good overtaking manoeuvre." That was at this same chicane on lap 14, Patrese having dealt with Alesi. Patrese took a 'tow' along the wide start-finish straight and sprang out for the chicane, braked violently, smoke signals from screaming tyres. "Riccardo went onto the brakes really late and I thought he was going to go into the sand trap" [directly ahead]. Thereafter "I was always able to close the gap in traffic so I kept going at my own pace, sustaining the pressure in the hope that they might crack." Mansell retired after 46 laps, a hydraulic failure, and Patrese slowed, the active suspension playing tricks and the gearbox stuck in fourth. "I was happy to win because this was the best I could get out of the technical situation." The art of the possible...

- **Podium:** Senna 1h 18m 15.349s, Brundle at 17.050, Schumacher at 24.373.
- **Fastest lap:** Mansell 1:26.119.
- **Senna:** 1:27.190.
- **Championship:** Mansell 98, Schumacher 47, Patrese and Senna 46.

RACE 214

Portugal, Estoril, 27 September 1992.
Qualifying: 1:15.343 (4); 1:14.258 (2). Row 2.
Pole: Mansell 1:13.041.
Race weather: hot, sunny.
Warm-up: 1:20.531 (6).
Result: Third.

A 'moment' on the Friday. "The rear wing on the spare car broke just as I was down-changing for the first corner, about the only place on the circuit where this could have happened without damaging the car." On the Saturday "I ended with three or four really good laps."

Senna wins his third race of 1992, at Monza.

Mansell led throughout. Senna ran third behind, inevitably, Patrese. Senna pitted four times. "The circuit conditions were abnormal and therefore the tyre wear and the performance of the tyres was also abnormal. On my second set I started to think we would need a third. I was trying to do my best in second place (from laps 25 to 47 after Patrese pitted) when I was called in by the team for a precautionary change. On my third set the car felt really strange, as though it was running on three wheels. I've never experienced [a feeling like that] before. It was the same when I changed on to the fourth set, then it improved and finally the car went completely mad over the last few laps. At the finish I had a deflated tyre."

- **Podium:** Mansell 1h 34m 46.659, Berger at 37.533, Senna at one lap.
- **Fastest lap:** Senna 1:16.272.
- **Championship:** Mansell 108, Senna 50, Schumacher 47.

RACE 215

Japan, Suzuka, 25 October 1992.
Qualifying: 1:38.375 (3); did not run. Row 2.
Pole: Mansell 1:37.360.
Race weather: warm, sunny.
Warm-up: 1:44.520 (5).
Result: Retired after 2 laps, engine.

Senna hoped "that coming here we would have been able to close the gap to the Williamses but although the engines are running well they are not as quick as we expected." Torrential rain washed over the Saturday.

Senna ran third but "I felt the engine begin to fail and decided to park the car to avoid destroying the engine. It was extremely frustrating." The art of the understatement.

- **Podium:** Patrese, Berger, Brundle.
- **Fastest lap:** Mansell 1:40.646.
- **Senna:** 1:46.229.
- **Championship:** Mansell 108, Patrese 56, Senna 50.

After two laps of the Japanese Grand Prix, Senna's engine failed so he watched instead.

RACE 216

Australia, Adelaide, 8 November 1992.
Qualifying: 1:14.202 (2); 1:14.416 (1). Front row.
Pole: Mansell 1:13.732.
Race weather: cool, overcast.
Warm-up: 1:17.651 (3).
Result: Retired after 18 laps, accident.

The places don't really change. "As usual here, it's a tough one. You are always working hard. To get under the 1:15s takes tremendous effort and concentration." That was the Friday. "For a change we were able to be faster than the Williamses *so* it was a shame the circuit conditions were slower. The track was clear but the temperature just too high and the tyres were suffering more to sustain their high performance. Strategically I drove a little bit better but the circuit was certainly more than half a second slower." That was the Saturday.

Mansell led, Senna adopting mid-track to hem Patrese from the chicane. Patrese clambered around Senna out of the chicane, Senna clambered around Mansell. Along the back straight on the opening lap Senna ducked into the geometrical right-hander and, the McLaren heaving and hauling under braking, took the corner but the momentum pitched the car wide: the geometrical laws of the street circuit. Mansell, alert and sharp, cut back through on the inside. By lap 19 Senna pressed Mansell insistently, wanting it, wanting it. In the corner before the pit lane straight they collided nose to tail. "Nigel and I passed the car that had been holding us up then he braked earlier. He knew I was very close. I could not stop my car. There was a clear track ahead" [meaning Mansell did not have to brake early]. Mansell responded: "Senna has no business on the track. He has a screw loose in the head." Innocence and guilt. The old motor racing story. Who knows? Only they who enacted it and they tend to take opposite points of view. In a famous phrase, they would, wouldn't they?

- **Podium:** Berger, Schumacher, Brundle.
- **Fastest lap:** Schumacher 1:16.078.
- **Senna:** 1:17.818.
- **Championship:** Mansell 108, Patrese 56, Schumacher 53, Senna 50.

A study of speed at Adelaide, but he crashed with Mansell.

Senna in 1993.

1993

Honda withdrew from Grand Prix racing and McLaren had to reach for Ford engines. That seemed to condemn McLaren to a season of impotence against Williams and Renault, for whom Prost returned after a year off. Berger departed McLaren for Ferrari when he received an offer no man could refuse. It made him one of the highest paid people in the world. Michael Andretti crossed the Atlantic to partner Senna who, dubious about spending 16 Grands Prix of futility half a lap behind Prost, competed during the early part of the season on a race-by-race basis. Rule changes: No use of the spare car in qualifying and, from Brazil, a limit of 12 laps per driver in each qualifying session. The other front-runners: Damon Hill (Williams), Schumacher and Patrese (Benetton), Alesi (Ferrari).

* * *

RACE 217

South Africa, Kyalami, 14 March 1993.
Qualifying: 1:17.152 (2); 1:15.784 (2).
Front row.
Pole: Prost 1:15.696.
Race weather: hot, overcast.
Warm-up: 1:19.475 (2).
Result: Second.

Motoring News caught contradictory moods on the Friday. Senna "wasn't feeling particularly well and his mien reflected the rather tense, concentrated atmosphere that had surrounded McLaren since an ill-humoured Press Conference on Thursday. 'It was a good day without too many problems,' he said. 'In the second part of the session it became a little slippery as too many tried too hard but other than that I am delighted with how much the team has achieved in so little time.' What he omitted to mention was a fuel injector problem that lost him a good 20 minutes in the pits – thus making him the first real victim of the no spare car rule. Without that he would undoubtedly have gone quicker still." On the Saturday Senna went out early and pitched the McLaren to the edge, drawing dust as he rode over the kerbing. 1:16.683, and quicker than Prost's provisional pole. Prost, smooth, responded. 1:16.604. Senna responded to that. 1:15.784. Seven minutes remained when Prost settled it by an eye-blink.

Prost made a hesitant start and nearly stalled. Senna sprang on that and led Schumacher by 1.7 seconds on the opening lap. Soon enough Prost – reading the whole race distance and unhurried – overtook Schumacher and, after the pit stops, led, Senna literally powerless to do anything but follow. It wasn't quite that simple. On lap 40 Schumacher tried to go by. "He was quicker than me but not enough to overtake. I suppose he tried a little too hard. Eventually he realised that he couldn't stop the car and he couldn't get through either so he touched my rear wheel and I nearly spun. He damaged my rear wheel and for a bit I was worried my right rear tyre might be punctured."

- **Podium:** Prost 1h 38m 45.082s, Senna at 1m 19.824, Mark Blundell (Ligier) at one lap.
- **Fastest lap:** Prost 1:19.492.
- **Senna:** 1:20755

RACE 218

Brazil, Interlagos, 28 March 1993.
Qualifying: 1:18.639 (3); 1:17.697 (3). Row 2.
Pole: Prost 1:15.866.
Race weather: dry and wet.
Warm-up: 1:21.518 (3).
Result: First.

"We are in a closed circle whereby the power we have is obviously not great. To compensate you drop the wing level a lot but you are still slow on the straight, anyway, and you compromise the car a lot round the corners. It is such a difficult situation that there is no way out." Senna maximised what he had.

Prost led from Senna until, on lap 11, Hill overtook him at the *S do Senna* bend: a great moment in Hill's life. On lap 24 Senna was brought in for a 10 second stop-and-go penalty for overtaking Erik Comas (Larrousse) under a yellow flag. "I couldn't believe it. The guy lifted off to let me through. The people who make these decisions should have a different way of implementing them because I think it was a big mistake. I was really annoyed but I tried to cool down and keep myself under control." As Senna emerged a downpour fell. He pitted for wet tyres. Prost was en route to do the same when he ran over debris and was out. Hill led from Senna but the track dried. Senna pitted for slick tyres first, Hill a lap later and as Hill emerged

Senna cut by, not to be caught. "Above all, when God wants something to happen there is no technical disadvantage which can make a difference."

- **Podium:** Senna 1h 51m 15.485s, Hill at 16.625, Schumacher at 45.436.
- **Fastest lap:** Schumacher 1:20.024.
- **Senna:** 1:20.187.
- **Championship:** Senna 16, Prost 10, Hill and Blundell 6.

Europe, Donington Park, 11 April 1993.
Qualifying: 1:23.976 (1); 1:12.107 (4). Row 2.
Pole: Prost 1:10.458.
Race weather: damp, wet.
Warm-up: 1:30.206 (3).
Result: First.

England in spring? Unsurprisingly a wet Friday. Senna mastered the rain and was majestic, then mounted a late run but had a hydraulic failure – "I am glad it happened when it did and not earlier at full speed." Saturday was dry and he mounted another late run but a vast slide out of Goddard cost him too many fractions.

Senna needed a wet race to slow Prost and Hill. With hindsight it is easy to write such a short, simplistic and obvious sentence. From the green light Schumacher bustled across Senna and into the Redgate horseshoe he was fifth, cramped and hemmed and lost. Out of Redgate he overtook Schumacher. On the descending snake-snap Craner Curves he overtook Wendlinger on the outside – the art of the impossible. At the Coppice carving right he overtook Hill. At the noose of the Melbourne hairpin he out-braked Prost. He led the race, equally impossible. He drew massively from Prost and drove directly into mythology. He only lost the lead when he pitted for slick tyres, regained it a lap later when Prost pitted, and led by 5.141 at lap 20. The rain had stopped and now returned. Prost pitted for wets but Senna stayed out – an extraordinary and profound decision based squarely upon Senna's ability to control the car – and he didn't pit until lap 28. He retained the lead. The rain stopped and

His team-mate Michael Andretti who came from IndyCars, struggled to adapt, and went home *Formula One Pictures*.

Prost pitted for slick tyres on lap 33, Senna and Hill next lap. A problem with the left rear wheel kept Senna stationary for 20 seconds, passing a seven second lead to Prost. The rain returned and Prost pitted for wet tyres on lap 38, Hill on 41. Senna made another profound decision and stayed out. The track began to dry forcing Prost to the pits for slick tyres. Prost stalled and sank a whole lap, the whole 2.500 miles, down. At this point only Rubens Barrichello (Jordan) and Hill were on the same lap and when they pitted Senna was alone, quite alone, in that other dimension only he could reach. Bewildered team members, journalists and spectators would need long and quiet hours to unravel what he had created and how. In the intoxication of the aftermath it seemed inexplicable, almost mysterious, almost as if you'd been watching an illusion which actually happened. "If I don't race again I feel comfortable with this." If there has to be an epitaph to a racing career let these 10 words stand as it.

- **Podium:** Senna 1h 50m 46.570s, Hill at 1m 23.199, Prost at one lap.
- **Fastest lap:** Senna 1:18.029.
- **Championship:** Senna 26, Prost 14, Hill 12.

RACE 220

San Marino, Imola, 25 April 1993.
Qualifying: 1:24.042 (4); 1:24.007 (4). Row 2.
Pole: Prost 1:22.070.
Race weather: overcast, wet.
Warm-up: 1:26.752 (3).
Result: Retired after 42 laps, hydraulics.

Would he come, would he race? Because of the contractual uncertainty, mystery and rumour surrounded this. He arrived 15 minutes before the Friday un-timed session and spun off at Tosa; at the end of first qualifying he spun coming out of the Variante Bassa. "A pity. It was my best lap of the day. When I touched the kerb the car really twitched." Twenty two minutes into the Saturday session he spun into the wall at Acque Minerale.

Hill led, Senna holding Prost and, after the pit stops, he ran second to Prost. Approaching Tosa at more than 205 mph (330 kph) he felt the car losing its hydraulics. "It was close but I managed to stop in time. I lost all the hydraulics shortly after and that was it."

- **Podium:** Prost, Schumacher, Brundle.
- **Fastest lap:** Prost 1:26.128.
- **Senna:** 1:27.490.
- **Championship:** Senna 26, Prost 24, Hill 12.

Andretti was replaced by the fleet-footed Finn, Mika Hakkinen.

At home at Sao Paulo and victory over Damon Hill by 16.625 seconds.

Spain, Barcelona, 9 May 1993.
Qualifying: 1:20.221 (2); 1:19.722 (3). Row 2.
Pole: Prost 1:17.809.
Race weather: hot, sunny.
Warm-up: 1:24.066 (3).
Result: Second.

Unusually, perhaps uniquely, Senna insisted on the Friday that "there is nothing more to come out of me. Now we have to get more out of the car." He aborted his first serious Saturday attempt. "The sensor on the right front wheel was disconnected during lunch time when we made some changes. It was left disconnected. As I went out the car was pulling badly to the right."

Hill made the better start. Senna tucked to the inside of Prost into turn one, seeking to gain a place by nerve and reflex. What else could he do? Nothing from there on except keep Schumacher fourth. After 41 laps Hill's engine let go, Senna second and facing a long passage home. "The back-markers were really terrible and it was hard to maintain the pace. [Aguri] Suzuki [Footwork]...I nearly hit him when he braked in the middle of a corner you normally take almost flat. I don't know how I stayed on the road. There were a lot of blown engines or I was behind all of them when they blew! It happened four or five times and on each occasion my visor was coated with oil. I ran out of rip-offs. It's completely crazy the way some drivers blow up and stay on the track – on the line – for four or five corners more. It's time the stewards started penalising people who do that."

- **Podium:** Prost 1h 32m 27.685s, Senna at 16.873, Schumacher at 27.125.
- **Fastest lap:** Schumacher 1:20.989.
- **Senna:** 1:21.717.
- **Championship:** Prost 34, Senna 32, Schumacher 14.

Monaco, Monte Carlo, 23 May 1993.
Qualifying: 1:42.127 (5); 1:21.552 (3). Row 2.
Pole: Prost 1:20.557.
Race weather: hot, sunny.
Warm-up: 1:24.283 (3).
Result: First.

Was he having to push too hard? Moments at Monaco made you wonder. On the Thursday morning he moved into his seventh lap. He'd just done 1:25.205 on his sixth, fastest time. At Ste Devote at 160 mph the McLaren was pitched hard left by a bump and hit the barrier virtually head on, rebounded and hit the barrier at the other side. He jarred a thumb. "The rear got away. I was lucky because the impacts were terrible." On the Saturday he reached the harbour chicane and slithered down the escape road, battering the barrier there. "When you come to the braking point there is a crest on the downhill. It's quite bumpy and our car does not behave very well over bumps. The car bottomed out and turned to the outside. I couldn't handle it."

He employed his reasoning as he contemplated the race. "After my accident on Thursday I knew I had lost the edge, because the difference between going flat out here and going 99% is big. And in that shunt I lost the 100% possibility. I was thinking hard before going to bed on Saturday and when I got up on race morning I was thinking positively. When I couldn't make the front row [Prost and Schumacher] I knew I couldn't take the lead. I had to cope with their speeds and hope that their tyre wear would be worse than mine." Prost crept before the green light. "Prost jumped the start, perhaps in desperation to get to the first corner, a result of the pressure I exerted even though I was behind him." Mental pressure, Prost making bad start after bad start during the season, Senna leonine. Prost was given a stop-go penalty and Schumacher led from Senna until Schumacher's active hydraulics failed on lap 33, Senna leading. He pitted for tyres on lap 51 but "only because I knew we would be marginal by the end. I'd been trying to build a lead over Hill so that I'd have enough time for the stop. There was a problem with the front jack and they had to change it. I didn't lose too much time." He emerged still leading. "All I thought about was keeping my concentration. I know how you can lose it here." This victory, Senna's sixth at Monte Carlo, beat Graham (father of Damon) Hill's record of five.

- **Podium:** Senna 1h 52m 10.947s, Hill at 52.118, Alesi at 1m 03.362.
- **Fastest lap:** Prost 1:23.604.
- **Senna:** 1:23.737.
- **Championship:** Senna 42, Prost 37, Hill 18.

RACE 223

Canada, Montreal, 13 June 1993.
Qualifying: 1:21.706 (8); 1:21.891 (7). Row 4.
Pole: Prost 1:18.987.
Race weather: hot, sunny.
Warm-up: 1:24.170 (5).
Result: Retired after 62 laps, alternator.

"I will race defensively, waiting for the length of the race and the peculiarities of the circuit to take their toll. That is the best I can do." Thus Senna on the art of the possible on the Saturday.

He ran third behind Prost and Hill although somehow he managed to pressure Hill briefly, a gesture really before he submitted to waiting. Schumacher advanced on him. Hill had a chaotic pit stop – the team readied tyres for Prost – and Senna inherited second place, something he consolidated with a superb McLaren stop, 4.7 seconds stationary.

Schumacher advanced again and "the car suddenly started cutting out and I was so concerned about it that I did not see Schumacher coming on the outside. I am sorry that we touched." Schumacher offered the opinion that it had been close but they hadn't actually touched.

- **Podium:** Prost, Schumacher, Hill.
- **Fastest lap:** Schumacher 1:21.500.
- **Senna:** 1:22.015.
- **Championship:** Prost 47, Senna 42, Hill 22.

RACE 224

France, Magny-Cours, 4 July 1993.
Qualifying: 1:16.782 (4); 1:16.264 (5). Row 3.
Pole: Hill 1:14.382.
Race weather: hot, sunny.
Warm-up: 1:19.819 (3).
Result: Fourth.

Qualifying had become a prison cell. Senna had problems with the car's balance on the Friday and although it was "much better" on the Saturday he couldn't force it to the front of the grid. "When I did my laps I had no traffic and I

The European Grand Prix where only Hill could finish on the same lap *Formula One Pictures*.

was only hindered on my fast lap by some dust which another car had thrown up."

He ran fifth, Hill and Prost already gone and Schumacher behind him. Schumacher made two pit stops, Senna only one. "I didn't change for the second time because we felt it was best to wait and see what kind of stop Schumacher might have. Had it been a slow one I would have come in but my lack of power did not allow me to, then be overtaken, then try to get back in front of Schumacher."

- **Podium:** Prost, Hill, Schumacher.
- **Fastest lap:** Schumacher 1:19.256.
- **Senna:** 1:20.521.
- **Championship:** Prost 57, Senna 45, Hill 28.

RACE 225

Britain, Silverstone, 11 July 1993.
Qualifying: 1:37.050 (3); 1:21.986 (4). Row 2.
Pole: Prost 1:19.006.
Race weather: cool, overcast.
Warm-up: 1:28.468 (17).
Result: Fifth.

No concealing any power difference around Silverstone's broad, unyielding acres. On the Friday "it was hard to get a clear lap" and on the Saturday "the car is undoubtedly better but we still seem to have some trouble in balancing it. The [new specification] engine did help. Without it we would have been further behind."

At the green light Senna exploited his power. He pitched the car level with Prost who'd made another stutter-stammer start and he shifted Prost virtually onto the grass as he protected Copse corner. For six laps they grappled. This was frankly alarming, frankly dangerous, Senna blocking impossibly late at the speeds they were doing. It was so dangerous that Prost, normally talkative, wouldn't discuss it afterwards. Eventually Prost did get by and Schumacher overtook Senna too. On the last lap Senna stopped, fuel all gone. "The computer told us we had fuel when in reality we were running out. Apart from that we've had stability problems all weekend. To get over them we raced with a lot of wing but, of course, it slowed us down the straights – that's *why* Schumacher's Benetton could run away from me the way he did."

Monaco, and you know the story: mastery.

- **Podium:** Prost, Schumacher, Patrese.
- **Fastest lap:** Hill 1:22.515.
- **Senna:** 1:24.886.
- **Championship:** Prost 67, Senna 47, Schumacher 30.

RACE 226

Germany, Hockenheim, 25 July 1993.
Qualifying: 1:40.642 (5); 1:39.616 (4). Row 2.
Pole: Prost 1:38.748.
Race weather: warm, sunny.
Warm-up: 1:58.997 (2).
Result: Fourth.

In the Friday morning session "I went in too long at the first chicane, spun and then stalled the engine, so in the afternoon we had to start from scratch. We modified it for the second one and it was better but still not quite right." He judged the car "improved" on the Saturday; he could "drive it more."

Hill led from Schumacher, Senna and Prost contesting third. They weaved together – another alarming instant. At the first chicane Prost had the inside line and held it, Senna – turning in – realised Prost wouldn't give way. Senna skittered around the rim of the gravel run-off area and spun onto the track as the crocodile of cars weaved by. "Alain and I both braked very late. I don't know if we touched but

Tranquillity in Canada? No. The alternator failed.

we were both beyond our limit. I lost control. After that I had nothing to lose." He was twenty-fourth. "I started overtaking everyone" – three of them on the next lap. By lap 8 he was tenth, by lap 28 in the points; and, a mere five laps remaining, he pitted. "The car felt funny and the last thing I wanted was to risk a blow-out at 300 kph." When Hill's tyre let go with two laps remaining Senna rose to fourth.

- **Podium:** Prost, Schumacher, Blundell.
- **Fastest lap:** Schumacher 1:41.859.
- **Senna:** 1:42.162.
- **Championship:** Prost 77, Senna 50, Schumacher 36.

RACE 227

Hungary, Hungaroring, 15 August 1993.
Qualifying: 1:18.260 (5); 1:16.451 (4). Row 2.
Pole: Prost 1:14.631.
Race weather: hot, sunny.
Warm-up: 1:20.208 (4).
Result: Retired after 17 laps, throttle.

"On my first set of tyres we tried to find a little more speed by reducing the size of the rear wing. That did not work *so* we opted back to the larger wing but we still had problems of grip and balance" on the Friday. On the Saturday he talked of "significant improvements." You know the phrase.

Prost stalled on the parade lap, and had to start from the back of the grid. With pole vacant Senna made a hesitant start, Schumacher past him, Berger alongside on the outside. Senna twisted right searching for clear space but into turn one Berger – who always seemed to adore the possibilities of turn one – went between them. Berger's impetus carried him wide on the exit and Senna was through. "I could have taken Hill on the second corner but I opted for a more cautious approach because the car felt near the limit. Quite soon I started to experience problems with the throttle. This affected my control of the car and on some bends I felt like a passenger. I tried to re-set the electronics from the car but that caused the engine to misfire and the throttle to behave worse. Soon after, the car stopped completely."

- **Podium:** Hill, Patrese, Berger.
- **Fastest lap:** Prost 1:19.633.
- **Senna:** 1:22.838.
- **Championship:** Prost 77, Senna 50, Hill 38.

RACE 228

Belgium, Spa, 29 August 1993.
Qualifying: 1:51.385 (4); 1:49.934 (5). Row 3.
Pole: Prost 1: 47.571.
Race weather: hot, sunny.
Warm-up: 1:54.802 (4).
Result: Fourth.

Friday? "The car is not very good." Saturday? "We have improved the car from yesterday but unfortunately it wasn't good enough to maintain our position." The language of captivity – nearly diplomacy – again. However on the Friday morning Alessandro Zanardi's Lotus crashed and thrashed at some 150mph at Eau Rouge. Senna came upon the scene at speed and somehow avoided everything, including a marshal.

Senna declined to take part in the drivers' parade and the race organisers issued a statement apologising for his absence. Always, always he surprised by how gracious or ungracious he could be – like the control and lack of it. Grid:

	Prost
Hill	
	Schumacher
Alesi	
	Senna

Schumacher stalled, Senna instantly to midtrack to go round him. At that instant: Prost clear on the right, Hill on the left, Alesi in midtrack, Senna behind Alesi. Massive, compressed movement: Alesi darting right, Senna darting left, Prost at La Source, Hill turning in behind, Senna far left. Alesi tried a punt inside. Senna braked hard. Alesi baulked on the inside, Senna coming round the outside and level with Hill. On the sweeping descent to Eau Rouge Senna held left and overtook Hill. It all lasted 11 seconds. "The first few laps were fun but then I could not keep up the pace." Hill stalked him and on lap 2 simply employed the Renault's power. "I stopped early for tyres (lap 13) *because* I felt that would give me the best chance to fight with Schumacher. Ten laps from the end the car started to vibrate. It felt as if it was coming from the gearbox or the engine."

The alarming breath-taking duel with Prost at Silverstone which got a lot too close for anybody's comfort.

- **Podium:** Hill, Schumacher, Prost.
- **Fastest lap:** Prost 1:51.095.
- **Senna:** 1:54.185.
- **Championship:** Prost 81, Senna 53, Hill 48.

RACE 229

Italy, Monza, 12 September 1993.
Qualifying: 1:23.310 (4); 1:22.633 (4). Row 2.
Pole: Prost 1:21.179.
Race weather: warm, sunny.
Warm-up: 1:26.533 (5).
Result: Retired after 8 laps, accident.

Senna was quite pleased on the Friday, and on Saturday preferred to talk about the race and the "many unknown factors" that would involve; nothing else to say.

At the start "I followed Jean Alesi and we both took Damon Hill but Damon insisted on trying to stay on the outside and we touched". That was into the first chicane. "It was quite a hit but I landed more or less in the right direction and could carry on." Senna completed the opening lap tenth and rose to eighth when he came upon Martin Brundle and ran into the back of him. "The accident happened as we both late-braked. The rear of the car had been feeling light under braking for a while and when

I came up to Martin I just could not hold it. I was very close to him and without down-force the car lacked grip in the rear."

- **Podium:** Hill, Alesi, Andretti.
- **Fastest lap:** Hill 1:23.575.
- **Senna:** 1:27.939.
- **Championship:** Prost 81, Hill 58, Senna 53.

RACE 230

Portugal, Estoril, 26 September 1993.
Qualifying: 1:12.954 (3); 1:12.491 (3). Row 2.
Pole: Hill 1:11.494.
Race weather: warm, sunny.
Warm-up: 1:16.493 (3).
Result: Retired after 19 laps, engine.

Hakkinen joined Senna at McLaren, Andretti retreating to the United States after a highly unimpressive introduction to Grand Prix racing. Hakkinen astonished everyone by out-qualifying Senna, who complained of over-steer on the Friday. On the Saturday he had traffic on his fast laps but "it is just a question of luck;" nothing else to say.

Alesi led, Senna chasing but "the engine blew suddenly, with a big bang. I feared it might catch fire. Until then I had followed Alesi, which

That's what you call riding the kerbs. Senna at Spa, where he'd finish fourth.

was frustrating because he pulled away from me on the straights each time I caught him on the bends. I just couldn't overtake him." Championship, Prost.

- **Podium:** Schumacher, Prost, Hill.
- **Fastest lap:** Hill 1:14.859.
- **Senna:** 1:18.365.
- **Championship:** Prost 87, Hill 62, Senna 53.

RACE 231

Japan, Suzuka, 24 October 1993.
Qualifying: 1:38.942 (4); 1:37.284 (2).
Front row.
Pole: Prost 1:37.154.
Race weather: changeable.
Warm-up: 1:43.694 (4).
Result: First.

After his first flying lap on the Friday Senna felt "I had a lot more to come" but when he went out on his second set of tyres "the engine broke." On the Saturday "we decided that although I had five laps left I would only carry enough fuel for two fast ones. Unfortunately the tyres were not quite right on what should have been the first fast lap so I only had one lap to set my time. Had we decided on a different strategy we might have finished on pole. I'm starting once more from the inside position. I know it well and it makes life very difficult..."

"In the warm-up I deliberately drove down that side a few times to clean it up." Senna won turn one, no drama, Prost following. Senna pitted on lap 13. "Maybe I pushed too hard in the early stages because my tyres were losing grip. Also I could see the change in the weather. It wasn't raining but it looked to be on the way. In any case, now I would have to stop twice. I hadn't planned it but with heavy tyre wear I knew I wouldn't be able to hold Prost in the later stages." On lap 21 Senna had to stop for wets. He led, Prost chasing. He came up to lap Hill and Eddie Irvine (Jordan). Irvine – racing and sod it – retook Senna. It was a move capable of several interpretations, not least that this is what Irvine believed he had flown to Japan for, to race. But it was also a breach of etiquette and convention (whatever that really means). After the final stops for slick tyres Senna went comfy to the end, then marched to the Jordan team and explained the facts of life to Irvine – and cuffed him. "Irvine," Senna said publicly, "drove like a great idiot today. He was quick, sure, but this is Formula 1 not go-karts."

The first chicane at Monza and in the scrum there isn't room for both Senna and Hill.

- **Podium:** Senna 1h 40m 27.912s, Prost at 11.435, Hakkinen at 26.129.
- **Fastest lap:** Prost 1:41.176.
- **Senna:** 1:43.217.
- **Championship:** Prost 93, Hill 65, Senna 63.

RACE 232

Australia, Adelaide, 7 November 1993.
Qualifying: 1:13.371 (1); 1:14.779 (5). Pole.
Race weather: cool, overcast.
Warm-up: 1:16.642 (1).
Result: First.

"It was a tremendous lap, a pretty special one" on the Friday. "Had there been no traffic I could have done better. We also had a problem with the radio. I was wondering whether I should come in because of low fuel and since I wasn't getting a reply I was shouting, especially as I neared the pit entrance. Later I discovered my radio button was stuck so the pits couldn't talk back to me. The result was that I could not concentrate in the usual way and I couldn't improve my time."

Warmer Saturday weather made improvements rare, giving Senna pole. "It took a long time for this, my single pole of this year."

The last race for McLaren before he joined Williams. Senna was barely able to look at his old friend Jo Ramirez, the McLaren team co-ordinator. "The time before the race was incredibly tough. I had to keep my feelings very much under control because in those moments emotions were taking over. The last half hour before the race was very hard on me: these emotions kept coming back to me making me feel very uneasy." He led from start to finish (except briefly during the pit stops). Maybe it was meant to be. "I wanted to do my best for the team and for myself. I had to win this race. This is why I had to keep my emotions under control."

- **Podium:** Senna 1h 43m 27.476s, Prost at 9.259, Hill at 33.902.
- **Fastest lap:** Hill 1:15.381.
- **Senna:** 1:16.128.
- **Championship:** Prost 99, Senna 73, Hill 69.

Adelaide and Senna's final race for McLaren. Prost, who finished second to him, seems keen to make peace again. Senna incidentally, was very close to tears.

Chapter 8

Williams 1994

*I*t seemed the logical move to a proven, winning car and a proven, winning engine; and it seemed like Senna's fourth championship won before he'd turned a wheel. He'd partner Hill. The other front-runners: Schumacher (Benetton), Berger and Alesi (Ferrari): not many. Rule changes banned many electronic driver aids.

* * *

Senna in 1994, testing at Imola *Zooom*.

His team-mate, Damon Hill *ICN Bureau*.

RACE 233

Brazil, Interlagos, 27 March 1994.
Qualifying: 1:16.386 (1); 1:15.962 (1). Pole.
Race weather: warm, overcast.
Warm-up: 1:18.667 (1).
Result: Retired after 55 laps, spin.

Senna was immediately quickest on the Friday morning but Schumacher closed in the afternoon. A downpour dampened a Senna-Schumacher shoot-out for pole on the Saturday. "Certainly the new regulations make it harder. The electronic suspension was easier, more comfortable, except when it didn't work! Now the cars are harder to drive and set up. It is more of a challenge to get it right and it will be much more difficult in the rain. Traction control and active [suspensions] were a great help: now you are stuck with what you have got. You can no longer lift the car to avoid the puddles or use the traction control on the throttle."

Senna led, Alesi past Schumacher. On the opening lap Senna used The Tactic and the race seemed decided within the first few corners. On lap 2 Schumacher crowded Alesi and went by. By lap 17 Schumacher was within a second of Senna. They both pitted on lap 21 – Schumacher getting a quicker stop to lead. Decisively Schumacher wielded The Tactic against Senna, constructing a gap of almost five seconds; by the second pit stops (Senna lap 44, Schumacher 45) Senna could only hope that Schumacher's pit stop went wrong. It didn't. Senna pressed but "Michael was a little bit quicker and only towards the end was I able to push a little bit more and go with him." Then "I was driving right on my limit and I was caught out at the exit of the third gear corner onto the main straight." Senna went off. "There was nothing wrong with the car but when I tried to restart I stalled the engine."

- **Podium:** Schumacher, Hill, Alesi.
- **Fastest lap:** Schumacher 1:18.455.
- **Senna:** 1:18.764.

Adulation at Sao Paulo.

Even the adulation didn't help. He spun off.

RACE 234

Pacific, Aida, Japan, 17 April 1994.
Qualifying: 1:10.218 (1); 1:19.304 (24). Pole.
Race weather: warm, sunny.
Warm-up: 1:12.872 (1).
Result: Retired no laps, accident.

Two 45 minute sessions on the Thursday for everyone to learn this new circuit and Schumacher finished a second quicker than Senna. "Yes, I'm on the limit." On the Friday "here the problem is very low speed in several corners. We have to deal with it. Everybody uses a lot of wing, which compensates a little bit. The surface is smooth, too, which helps." Saturday was slower, Senna and Hill spinning out at a corner called Revolver. "It's odd it happened the same for both of us. I don't really understand because the car was nice. I had a good direction into the corner with one of the best positions I'd had there all weekend so it should have been no trouble at all."

The Pacific Grand Prix at Aida, Japan, and Senna contemplates having been rammed off at the start.

Senna spent 30 minutes before the race lying motionless on the floor of the Williams paddock cabin, concentrating. At the green light Schumacher made the better start and moved right-left hogging the circuit to turn one, a right hander. Senna might have tried inside him but "in an 83 lap race with three potential pit stops there was no point." Hakkinen prodded into him and spun the Williams. As it rotated onto the run-off area Nicola Larini's Ferrari rammed it.

• **Podium:** Schumacher, Berger, Rubens Barrichello (Jordan).
• **Fastest lap:** Schumacher 1:14.023.
• **Senna:** no lap.
• **Championship:** Schumacher 20, Barrichello 7, Hill and Berger 6 (Senna 0).

RACE 235

San Marino, Imola, 1 May 1994.
Qualifying: 1:21.548 (1); did not run. Pole.
Race weather: hot, dry.
Warm-up: 1:22.597 (1).
Result: Retired after 6 laps, accident.

As long as anyone cares about racing motor cars, and the consequences of racing motor cars, the three days of Imola will remain static in time. The sequence of consequences is so stark it will always sustain that. On the Friday Barrichello, Senna's protege, crashed and went to hospital. Senna somehow put together a lap good enough for provisional pole after that, although he couldn't concentrate. On the Saturday a relative newcomer, Roland Ratzenberger in a Simtek, crashed fatally. Senna, disturbed – perhaps distraught – contemplated not racing.

Imola, 1 May 1994.

The final green.

The racers circle behind the pace car: Senna, Schumacher, Berger, Hill.

He raced. From the conflicts and confusions of his emotions he drew a beautiful beginning from himself. He balanced power, acceleration and movement at the green light and reached for The Tactic. On the opening lap he tried to break Schumacher but a startline crash produced the safety car which they all followed until the debris had been cleared. At the end of 'lap 5' the signal was given to race again and Senna reached for The Tactic a last time, onto the power instantly, digging it, drawing it from the engine: Senna against Schumacher, skill against skill, man against man, the eternal combat bearing eternal consequences. Through the corner called Tamburello – a left of utter speed – Schumacher noticed the Williams 'bottoming.' Through Tamburello next time round the Williams went straight off and pounded a concrete wall. In the final 1.8 seconds of his life Ayrton Senna was able to reduce the speed of the car from 192 to 136 miles an hour. It was not enough.

Once upon a time someone asked Senna if he understood how dangerous motor racing was. He seemed bemused by such a question. Only idiots could fail to understand the danger, he said, and do you think I am an idiot?

He knew, and accepted.

Did Senna know and accept on 1 March 1981 when Dave Coyne (regarded as the coming man) led into Paddock Hill Bend and he – Senna – began his exploration of the possible, fifth? An unfair question. Did he foresee? Another unfair question. Let's leave it at that.

I do not propose to give the podium at Imola and I do not propose to give who set fastest lap or their time. I offer you one statistic and no more. It is Ayrton Senna's best lap – 1:44.068.

Moving away from us.

Chapter 9

Statistics

Ayrton Senna da Silva. Born 21 March 1960, Sao Paulo, Brazil.
Died at the Maggiore Hospital, Bologna, Italy, 1 May 1994.

First kart race, Interlagos 1973, won
1974: Sao Paulo junior champion
1976: Sao Paulo champion
1977: South American champion
1978: World Championship, Le Mans, 6
1979: World Championship, Estoril, 2
1980: World Championship, Nivelles, 2
1981: World Championship, Parma, 4
1982 World Championship, Kalmar, 14

First car race FF1600, Brands Hatch 1 March 1981
First win, Brands Hatch, 15 March 1981
First pole, Mallory Park, 22 March 1981
First fastest lap, Oulton Park, 24 May 1981

1981: Townsend Thoresen and RAC champion
1982: Pace British and EFDA European champion
1983: Marlboro British F3 Champion

First Grand Prix, Brazil, 1984
First fastest lap, Monaco 1984
First pole, win, Portugal, 1985
First World Championship, McLaren 1988
World Champion 1990, 1991

The all-time records, as at 1 May 1994

Total points per driver:
Prost – 798.5
Senna – 614
Piquet – 485.5
Mansell – 469
Lauda – 420.5

Most poles:
Senna – 65
Clark – 33
Prost – 33
Mansell – 31
Fangio – 29

Most poles in a season:
14 – Mansell 1992
13 – Senna 1988, 1989
13 – Prost 1993
10 – Senna 1990
9 – Lauda 1974, 1975
9 – Peterson 1973
9 – Piquet 1984

Most successive poles:
8 – Senna 1988/89
7 – Senna 1990/91
7 – Prost 1993

Most wins:
Prost – 51
Senna – 41
Mansell – 30
Stewart – 27
Clark – 25
Lauda – 25

Most wins in a season:
9 – Mansell 1992
8 – Senna 1988
7 – Prost 1984, 1988, 1993
7 – Clark 1963
7 – Senna 1991

Most fastest laps:
Prost – 41
Mansell – 30
Clark – 28
Lauda – 24
Fangio – 23
Piquet – 23
Moss – 19
Senna – 19